CAYCE / W COLUMBIA

P9-DGU-052

BIO
BROWN
TER

Terrible swift sword

WITHDRAWN

Terrible Swift Sword

Recommended Source

WCC __Supplementary__ 11/16 DC

OBCB _____

OTHER _____

CAYCE-WEST COLUMBIA
BRANCH LIBRARY
1500 AUGUSTA ROAD
WEST COLUMBIA, S. C. 29169

Terrible Swift Sword

THE LEGACY OF
JOHN BROWN

Edited by Peggy A. Russo and Paul Finkelman

Ohio University Press
Athens

Ohio University Press, Athens, Ohio 45701
www.ohio.edu/oupress
© 2005 by Ohio University Press
Printed in the United States of America
All rights reserved
Ohio University Press books are printed on acid-free paper ⊗ ™
12 11 10 09 08 07 06 05   5 4 3 2 1

Library of Congress Cataloging-in-Publication Data

Terrible swift sword : the legacy of John Brown / edited by Peggy A. Russo and
Paul Finkelman.
    p. cm.
  Includes bibliographical references and index.
  ISBN 0-8214-1630-8 (cloth : alk. paper) — ISBN 0-8214-1631-6 (pbk. : alk. paper)
  1. Brown, John, 1800–1859. 2. Brown, John, 1800–1859—Influence. 3. Abolitionists—
United States—Biography. 4. Antislavery movements—United States—History—
19th century. I. Russo, Peggy A. II. Finkelman, Paul, 1949–
  E451.T37 2005
  973.7'114—dc22

                                                                    2005002786

For Chris and Dan
For Abby, Isaac, and Kaysi

He hath loosed the fateful lightning of His terrible
   swift sword:
His truth is marching on.

—*Julia Ward Howe, "The Battle Hymn of the Republic"*

Mighty with the sword of steel, he was mightier
with the sword of the truth, and with this sword
he literally swept the horizon.

—*Frederick Douglass, "John Brown," address at the
fourteenth anniversary of Storer College,
Harpers Ferry, May 30, 1881*

Contents

ONE
Contemporaries and Supporters of John Brown

TWO
John Brown Defined

THREE
Behavioral Analyses of John Brown

FOUR
Literary Representations of John Brown

FIVE
John Brown and Cultural Iconography

Plates

Preface

Thirteen Ways of Looking at John Brown

The time seems especially ripe for renewed interest in John Brown. Americans have traditionally viewed terrorism as a problem endemic to Europe and the Middle East. But as the attack on the World Trade Center and the Pentagon as well as the earlier World Trade Center and Oklahoma City bombings have demonstrated, terrorism is not foreign to us and, in fact, never has been. While most Americans would condemn the IRA for bombing a pub in London or an American Jew for bombing a mosque in Israel, some Americans have given money to the IRA, and many Americans, during the late sixties and early seventies, admired or even supported the anti–Vietnam War Weathermen, who were in the business of bombing civilian establishments.

John Brown's attack on Harpers Ferry as a means to end slavery provides but one example of such acts from our past that fit the definition of terrorism—the use of force, threats, or intimidation as a political weapon. The question of whether it is necessary to use force as a means to a good end is always controversial. Thus, Brown remains one of the most controversial figures in American culture—his ends deemed laudable by most, his means highly questionable by many. He floats in the eye of a storm—calm in the certainty of his right to act—on the cusp of a moment in history when the past was soon to be swept away in mass destruction. He bore the seeds of that destruction and the destruction of himself—empathy for those who suffered from the evils of slavery and antipathy for those who caused it. And the question keeps being asked: Was John Brown a terrorist? The answer will always be problematic because of the Pottawatomie massacre. In my mind, he is no Nat Turner, but neither is he a Martin Luther King. Perhaps he is more like Nelson Mandela, who seemed to embrace terrorism (reluctantly) in 1963 and later eschewed it. Brown certainly looks like a terrorist at Pottawatomie, but the man who ordered his men to avoid shedding blood at Harpers Ferry is not the same man who ordered and helped to carry out that massacre. It appears that Brown learned from Pottawatomie. He was only fifty-six at the time—not too old to learn from his mistakes. And during his trial, he learned to use the power of the word rather than the sword. With the whole world watching, he used his testimony as a means to put slavery on trial. The words of his last prophecy reveal his disappointment that slavery could not be ended peacefully. His actions in Bleeding Kansas represent his attempt to end it with the shedding of blood. His actions at Harpers Ferry reveal his attempt to do so "without *very much* bloodshed" (John Brown, "A prophetic note written by Brown on the day of his execution predicting the establishment of abolition through bloodshed," John Brown papers, Chicago Historical Society).

Because of his acts at Harpers Ferry and in Kansas, Brown has become a major American icon, evoking emotions either strongly negative or strongly positive. This legacy of controversy is readily apparent in images that depict Brown as an iconographic figure. Biographers Richard J. Hinton and John Redpath both remark that they first saw Brown with his long beard on June 25, 1858, in Lawrence, Kansas; he had grown it to disguise himself since he had a price on his head (see plate 3). Thus, for almost fifty-eight of his fifty-nine years, John Brown was clean-shaven (plate 2), and when he arrived in Harpers Ferry on July 3, 1859, he had changed his disguise again, shortening the beard to an inch and a half. Yet in most pictures after the raid, Brown sports that long, flowing beard—obviously the preferred iconographic image, which could be used for either positive or negative propaganda. In a Currier and Ives print published in 1863, for example, Brown becomes a compassionate martyr on the way to his execution who pauses on the steps of the Charles Town, Virginia, jail before kissing a black child held by a Madonna-like slave woman. The guards who surround him are sinister and the flag of the state of Virginia flies overhead, symbolically ironic, since it bears the motto *Sic semper tyrannis* (plate 7). Brown appears in a less heroic artistic image circa 1859, holding a copy of the *New York Tribune* and resembling a slightly superior, smug publicity hound (plate 4). In two even more negative pieces of art, *Harper's Weekly,* on November 19, 1859, depicts the "effect of [the] raid at the South," showing slaves determined to fight against Brown and his followers (plate 5) and on November 26, a cartoon shows a slave refusing to accept a pike from Brown (plate 6). These images effectively undercut the heroic aspects of Brown's efforts by making fun of his methods. The controversial legacy continues into the twentieth century as revealed in three murals with differing viewpoints. In John Steuart Curry's Kansas statehouse mural, a fanatical

Brown (with beard) brings the apocalypse to Kansas and to the country (plate 13). Mexican muralist Diego Rivera, on the other hand, depicts Brown as a positive and heroic catalyst of the Civil War (plate 14), and Arthur S. Covey paints Brown as a heroic liberator (plate 12). Obviously, artists create iconographic images reflecting their own attitudes and rhetorical purposes. No one, it seems can be neutral about John Brown;, not even his own descendants agree about whether to view him as a saint or as a fanatic. Brown's controversial character makes him a fascinating subject for study, and he is not merely of interest to artists and to American and Civil War historians; rather, he provides a nexus where many different disciplines converge. Scholars of literature, psychology, sociology, popular culture, journalism, law, African American studies, political science, military history, speech, theater, philosophy, and religious studies share with historians a compulsion to interpret Brown's acts.

In July 1996 the Mont Alto campus of the Pennsylvania State University hosted a conference that proved to be unique. Not only was it the first such conference devoted exclusively to John Brown, but it was not exclusively for historians. Promoted in the call for papers as a multidisciplinary symposium entitled John Brown: The Man, the Legend, the Legacy, it attracted sixty participants from all over the United States and one from Israel, representing many of the academic disciplines mentioned above. In our final roundtable discussion, participants agreed that because of the conference's multidisciplinary approach, there had been new light shed not only on the troublesome nature of John Brown's character and motives but also on the nature of a troubled society before, during, and after the Civil War. The proposals submitted; the twenty-five papers delivered; and the queries, before, during, and long after the conference was over, attest to the large number of people from varied disciplines who are interested in Brown, and that interest provided the impetus for this volume.

While one of the plenary speakers was a historian—Paul Finkelman, editor of *His Soul Goes Marching On* (1995)—the other was a novelist—Bruce Olds, author of *Raising Holy Hell* (1995). The disciplines of film and theater were represented by a screening of the 1940 Michael Curtiz film *Santa Fe Trail,* starring Raymond Massey as John Brown, and a production of Stephen Vincent Benét's *John Brown's Body.* Moreover, as a constant reminder of the multidisciplinary nature of the conference, conferees were seated in a large rectangular space so that participants faced the center and each other. We were to visualize John Brown in that center space—in the eye of the storm—while each of us viewed him through the prism of our own perspectives and disciplines.

We intended to use the multidisciplinary approach to foster interdisciplinary harmony and understanding. But initially, some folks found it difficult to look at John Brown in new ways. Many discussions grew into heated debates; some descended to angry diatribe. Nevertheless, during the final roundtable discussion everyone agreed that sharing our multiple and often differing points of view had altered our own views of John Brown. We each saw a three-dimensional image and had come to the realization that neither one person nor one discipline can claim ownership of John Brown's legacy.

In the decade leading up to the bicentennial of his birth, we saw evidence of renewed interest in that legacy; we also see evidence of a growth in multidisciplinary approaches to Brown, as demonstrated by the following list (no doubt incomplete) of publications in fiction and nonfiction, conference activities, and television and theatrical productions:

Gwen Everett, *John Brown: One Man against Slavery* (1993)
"John Brown's War," *Civil War Journal,* a History Channel Presentation hosted by Danny Glover (1993)
George MacDonald Fraser, *Flashman and the Angel of the Lord* (1994)
Robert R. Potter, *John Brown: Militant Abolitionist* (1994)
Paul Finkelman, ed., *His Soul Goes Marching On: Responses to John Brown and the Harpers Ferry Raid* (1995)
Bruce Olds, *Raising Holy Hell* (1995)
Edward J. Renehan, Jr., *The Secret Six: The True Tale of the Men Who Conspired with John Brown* (1995)
"John Brown: The Man, the Legend, the Legacy," a multidisciplinary symposium, Penn State–Mont Alto, July 24–27, 1996
W. E. B. Du Bois, *John Brown: A Biography,* ed. John David Smith (1997)
Russell Banks, *Cloudsplitter: A Novel* (1998)
"John Brown at Harpers Ferry," a roundtable discussion at the conference of the Society for Historians of the Early American Republic (SHEAR), Harpers Ferry, WV, July 1998
Stan Cohen, *The Thundering Voice of Jehovah* (1999)
Jean Libby et al., *John Brown Mysteries* (1999)
"John Brown's Perpetual Resurrection," special session at the Modern Language Association (MLA) Convention, Chicago, December 28, 1999

Thomas Streissguth, *John Brown* (1999)

Greg Artzner, Terry Leonina, and Richard Henzel, "Sword of the Spirit," a play based on the life and letters of John and Mary Brown (2000)

John Brown's Holy War, PBS television production directed by Robert Kenner (2000)

"John Brown, 2000," bicentennial conference, Harpers Ferry National Historical Park, May 15–17, 2000

Louis A. DeCaro Jr., *"Fire from the Midst of You": A Religious Life of John Brown* (2002)

John Stauffer, *The Black Hearts of Men: Radical Abolitionists and the Transformation of Race* (2002)

Franny Nudelman, *John Brown's Body: Slavery, Violence, and the Culture of War* (2005)

Merrill D. Peterson, *John Brown: The Legend Revisited* (2005)

David S. Reynolds, *John Brown, Abolitionist: The Man Who Killed Slavery, Sparked the Civil War, and Seeded Civil Rights* (2005)

A picaresque adventure story, several novels, two TV productions, children's literature, conference sessions at the MLA? Obviously, John Brown has become more than a subject fit only for historians, but is this a good thing? Could the "real thing," the *real* John Brown, be lost in this multidisciplinary shuffle?

When he first brought the dilemma surrounding the "Two Cultures" to world attention in 1959, C. P. Snow clearly hoped that the separation between the major disciplines of science and humanities would narrow and perhaps even end. More than forty years later, however, the situation remains little changed; too often, scientists and humanists look on each other with disdain. Beyond that, within these two major cultures, there exist smaller subcultures (history and literature, for example); and beyond even that, there exist sub-subcultures (Marxist, feminist, new historicist, old historicist, postcolonial, cultural, new critical, postcritical, humanist, and possibly antihumanist studies), all of which owe their existence to academic specialization and the members of which avoid as much as possible even a nodding acquaintance with colleagues who do not share their enlightened and sometimes narrow points of view—even though such isolation hinders the search for truth.

Attempts to solve the mystery of El Niño provide an example of the evils of specialization. Until the mid-1970s atmospheric and oceanographic meteorologists belonged to separate academic sub-subcultures. Compelled to cooperate, in an attempt to learn the truth about El Niño, they discovered that they could barely understand each other because they did not use the same language even in describing similar phenomena. After sharing their expertise and methodologies, however, meteorologists in both disciplines have become better able to understand and predict weather patterns. In other words, multidisciplinary cooperation led to interdisciplinary study which, in turn, is leading to greater knowledge of El Niño—which is, no doubt, a good thing for us all.

In similar fashion, in this volume scholars from many different disciplines attempt to foster greater knowledge of the legacy of John Brown. In part 1 contributors discuss *contemporaries of Brown:* Dean Grodzins (history and literature) reveals why a white Northerner, Theodore Parker, chose to support Brown; Hannah Geffert (oral history) reveals that, despite former scholarly views, many blacks in the Harpers Ferry area supported Brown; Jean Libby (African American studies) reveals that a black minister, Thomas Henry, long suspected of being a collaborator with Brown, did not, in fact, take part in events leading up to the raid. In part 2 authors *define Brown* using different criteria: Scott Hammond (political science) defines Brown as a "founder" based on definitions ascribed to Machiavelli and Rousseau; Eyal Naveh (history) discusses why Brown ultimately failed to fit America's criteria to be defined as an American martyr; Charles Holden (history) describes Brown as a "lawless fanatic," as defined by postbellum Southern writers. In part 3 scholars analyze *Brown's behavior:* James Gilbert (criminal justice) examines Brown's terrorist activities and psychopathic personality but determines that he is viewed positively in American history; Kenneth Carroll (psychology) analyzes Brown's actions and personality according to psychodiagnostic procedures and concludes that he had bipolar disorder. In part 4 contributors examine the ways in which *Brown is depicted in literature:* William Keeney (literature) shows that, immediately after the raid on Harpers Ferry, all American poets (with the exception of William Dean Howells) misrepresented Brown because of Brown's "troublesome" aspects; Bruce Olds (journalism and creative writing) argues that both historians and writers of fiction always distort historical facts about Brown for their own narrative purposes. Olds discusses his own writing process to back up what he says. In part 5 writers discuss the iconography of Brown: Paul Shackel (archeology) traces the cultural history of the John Brown Fort; Peggy Russo (literature and theater history) traces the changing iconographic image of John Brown's body in popular culture through the examination of two films.

Despite the often positive results of interdisciplinary study, most academics cling to our habit of specialization. Most of us belong to our own specialized academic organizations, read and publish in our own specialized journals, attend and present papers at our own specialized conferences, and spend most of our working hours associating with other academics in our own departments. Indeed, we are almost xenophobic about sharing ideas on *the same subject* with colleagues from disciplines foreign to us. The 1996 multidisciplinary symposium on John Brown offered such an opportunity. Viewing the complex subject of John Brown from many perspectives proved exhilarating, enlightening, and enriching; above all, it was an *educational* experience.

In his poem "Thirteen Ways of Looking at a Blackbird," poet Wallace Stevens offers a seemingly arbitrary combination of thirteen different points of view on the same subject, yet the poem's separate parts function as a whole and serve to delight and stimulate the imaginations of his readers. It is our hope that the combination of thirteen different points of view on John Brown, represented by the volume's introduction and its twelve chapters, will prove similarly holistic, delightful, and stimulating and will foster further experiments in multi- and interdisciplinary study.

Acknowledgments

This collection includes papers originally presented during the multidisciplinary symposium entitled John Brown: The Man, the Legend, the Legacy, held July 24–27, 1996, on the Mont Alto campus of the Pennsylvania State University. Those who contributed financial support for the symposium include Penn State's Institute for the Arts and Humanistic Studies, Office of Commonwealth Education System, Department of History, Department of English, and the Mont Alto campus. We are also indebted to Bruce Noble, then chief of interpretation and cultural resources management at Harpers Ferry National Historical Park, and to members of the park staff. Also supplying encouragement and support were Corinne Caldwell, then campus executive officer of the Mont Alto campus; William Curley, then director of business services and continuing education at the Mont Alto campus; and Johanna Ezell, who directed a production of Stephen Vincent Benét's *John Brown's Body* especially for the symposium.

But the symposium would not have come about without the hard work and dedication of four Mont Alto students: Troy Cool, Linda Kelly, Mike Moreland, and Valerie Hovetter. These students constituted Peggy Russo's entire staff and helped with all phases of the symposium: initial planning, the call for papers, mailings, manuscript reading, session planning, organization of side trips to Harpers Ferry and Gettysburg, menu selection, and running the symposium itself. Mont Alto students Linda Kelly, Mike Moreland, and Brian Dondero also contributed to this publication in its early stages.

In addition, we are grateful to the Pennsylvania State University for granting Peggy Russo a sabbatical leave in the fall of 1998 to begin work on this collection.

We are also indebted to those who helped us in our search for illustrations: members of the staff at Harpers Ferry National Historical Park, including Dave Gilbert, Nancy Hatcher, Richard Raymond, and Wade Myers; Gail Kruppa of the Torrington Historical Society; Craig Cooper and Nancy Sherbert of the Kansas State Historical Society; Jeffrey T. Hermann, Director of

Penn State University Publications; Jean Libby, one of the contributors to this volume; and staff members at the Library of Congress.

We owe special thanks to the late George Payette and to the anonymous reader at Ohio University Press, both of whom performed careful reviews of early versions of the manuscript. And finally, we are grateful to the many people at Ohio University Press for their help in preparing this edition, particularly Nancy Basmajian, Gillian Berchowitz, Bob Furnish, Richard Gilbert, Carolyn King, and Sharon Rose.

Introduction

Paul Finkelman

Madman, monster, murderer, terrorist, fanatic! Humanitarian, civil rights hero, rescuer of slaves, martyr to human freedom! Over two centuries after John Brown's birth and almost a century and a half after his death, his legend and legacy go marching on. His memory haunts us, troubles us, and always fascinates us. Was he a martyr or a madman, a monster or a humanitarian? Was a he liberator of slaves or a terrorist murdering innocent civilians? However we think of him, John Brown remains one of the most controversial and complex figures in America's history. He is iconic and powerful.

Brown is most remembered for his actions at Harpers Ferry, Virginia, and for his execution in December 1859. In Kansas he participated in the mini–civil war known as Bleeding Kansas and directed his men as they killed a group of Southern settlers and proslavery sympathizers at Pottawatomie Creek. At Harpers Ferry he seized a federal armory and fought a day-and-a-half battle with local militia and U.S. Marines, before finally being captured. He was then tried for treason against Virginia—a crime he surely had never committed. Since he was never a citizen of Virginia, he could hardly have committed treason against the state. But he was nevertheless convicted and hanged. His hanging secured his martyrdom in the North. Moreover, his stoic and brave demeanor, throughout the last month of his life, including the day of his death, impressed even his enemies. Virginia's governor, Henry Wise, found Brown "cool, collected and indomitable."[1] He was, said Wise, "the gamest man [I] ever saw."[2]

Brave, committed, and unalterably opposed to slavery. But also violent. He killed men—or ordered them killed—in Kansas. His actions in Harpers Ferry led to the deaths of others. He stoically faced pain and death and expected others to do the same. While his son lay dying in the engine house at Harpers Ferry, Brown urged him to act, and die, like a man.

How then do we understand Brown? At one level, his life is one of total failure. Everything he did seems to have been a failure. Until Kansas he was an unknown, small-time abolitionist. He was a failure in business. He had visions of commercial success, which always ended in failure. No one, not even his enemies, thought he was dishonest, but his incompetence and his lack of discipline meant that he often abused the trust others placed in him. His early legacy was bankruptcy and financial chaos. Before Kansas he lived his life in obscurity, preaching against slavery and in favor of racial justice, often only a step ahead of his creditors and just as often on the verge of economic catastrophe. His move to Kansas did not change his fortunes but did give him fame. The events at Pottawatomie thrust him into the limelight, even as he denied any part in the killings. His warfare in Kansas may have helped keep that place a free territory, but it is unlikely that Congress would have allowed Kansas to enter the Union as a slave state in any event.

His raid at Harpers Ferry was also a failure. He did not start a slave rebellion; most of his "soldiers" were killed or captured, and he too was wounded and captured. His raid probably had little effect on the presidential election of 1860. All the candidates denounced his violence and illegal actions. He may have helped Lincoln a little by making the Republicans look more moderate on the slavery issue, but he also surely scared some moderate slaveholders into voting for the Southern Democrat John C. Breckinridge and some moderate Northerners into supporting the Democratic candidate from their region, Stephen A. Douglas, or even the Constitutional Union ticket of Senator John Bell and Edward Everett. He is remembered as a major catalyst for the American Civil War, although surely the war would have come whether he raided Harpers Ferry or not.

Yet for all his failures, he is remembered—and remembered correctly—as an icon of the antebellum crisis and a harbinger of the violence and death that was soon to sweep over the nation. He accomplished nothing and caused nothing, and yet, in some way, he accomplished a great deal and moved the nation dramatically closer to civil war. Indeed, it was in his death and his martyrdom that he accomplished so much and gave his life meaning. But what do we make of this meaning? How do we understand and evaluate his life?

His actions are seldom viewed neutrally; they either evoke commendation or provoke condemnation. Because of such ongoing controversy, scholars in various disciplines share a desire to analyze and interpret Brown's legacy. His legacy is even more compelling in our own age, because some people see Brown as a prototype of a modern terrorist, striking fear and hoping to achieve political change through violence. But Brown is an odd model for the modern terrorist. Brown's violence was never random—he was not like Timothy McVeigh or the Muslim fanatics who demolished the World Trade Center. His violence was always focused. Those killed at Pottawatomie were, for the most part, combatants in a ruthless civil war. One of the men killed had threatened to kill Brown and his sons and other Free State settlers. All those killed were allied with slavery in the fight over the status of freedom in Kansas. Similarly, at Harpers Ferry, Brown's goal was not death or mayhem; it was to lead slaves to freedom. Brown's final statement in his life, given to his jailer just before he was led away to die, reveals his goals: "I John Brown am now quite *certain* that the crimes of this *guilty land: will* never be purged *away*; but with Blood. I had as *I now think; vainly* flattered myself that without *very much* bloodshed: it might be done" (emphasis Brown's).[3] Had Brown wanted destruction, he could certainly have accomplished it. He controlled an armory full of weapons and powder. He might easily have blown up much of the town or slaughtered civilians in their sleep. He did not, because it was freedom for slaves, and not the death of slave owners, that he sought.

If not a terrorist specializing in random terror, was Brown the precursor of the antichoice fanatic who bombs women's health clinics? Some of those who have murdered in the name of saving the lives of the "unborn" have invoked Brown's memory. They argue that just as Brown killed proslavery men in Kansas who threatened Free Staters, so the antichoice avenging angels plant bombs at women's clinics or kill doctors and others who work there. But this analogy quickly falls apart.

Brown lived at a time when the political process and democratic values had been undermined, or destroyed, by slavery. In Kansas the sword and the gun, not the ballot and the printing press, had become the method of determining what kind of government the territory and future state would have. Violence and fraudulent elections were the rule. A war was in progress, and one can view Pottawatomie as a tragic event in a tragic war. But even here Brown is clearly not a terrorist; he killed only soldiers or potential soldiers for the enemy at Pottawatomie, and he did not kill children or women, nor did he destroy buildings or other property. He killed those who threatened to kill him. This after all, is what warfare is about.

The modern analogy to antichoice terrorists or the Timothy McVeighs of the world falls apart on another level. In the modern United States, the freedoms of speech, press, and assembly allow for peaceful discussion of all public issues and provide forums to persuade voters and legislators. The political process is open, and change through democratic means is possible. But by the 1850s democracy in America was in crisis. In the South there was no discourse on slavery. No debate was tolerated, and agitation against slavery was illegal. Thus there was no possibility for internal change in the South. The Constitution did not allow the national government to interfere with slavery in the states. Thus there was no political process that could end slavery or even challenge it where it existed. In Kansas there was an open political process, but violence, intimidation, and vote fraud undermined the legitimacy of any elections. For Brown, revolution was the only way to significantly challenge slavery. Thus some modern Americans see Brown as a hero of civil rights, challenging slavery in a nation where a proslavery constitution made political change impossible.

Brown continues to fascinate us. We have paintings of him as a heroic figure and a gentle saint. One of the early likenesses of Brown shows him on the way to the gallows, gently and lovingly kissing a black child (see plate 7 for a similar image). In the 1940 film *Santa Fe Trail,* Brown appears as an Old Testament prophet, even as the film tries to turn him into a bloodthirsty villain. In the end, the power of Brown's legacy overcame the screenplay. Similarly, while remembered in Kansas for the killings at Pottawatomie, Brown is portrayed in heroic style on the walls of the state capitol (plate 13). Brown attacked a federal armory, destroyed federal property, and was captured by federal troops. But a heroic Brown leads slaves to freedom in the John Brown mural in the U.S. post office in Torrington, Connecticut (plate 12). In 2000 the National Park Service held a two-day symposium to study—and honor—the legacy of John Brown at Harpers Ferry National Historical Park.

In this volume twelve scholars—representing history, literature, creative writing, psychology, criminal justice, oral history, African American studies, political science, film studies, and anthropology—offer insights through the prisms of their own disciplines to give new interpretations and understandings of Brown's life and the personal, psychological, and social forces driving him. These scholars also place Brown, as both an individual and an "icon," in the context of the collapse of the American Union in 1861. The essays include discussions of Brown's contemporaries and their reasons for supporting him, attempts to define Brown using different criteria, analyses of Brown's behavior and psychology, literary portrayals of Brown, and examinations of the iconography surrounding Brown. None of us agree wholly on how to interpret Brown or how to evaluate him.

When all is said and done, I side with those who see him as a hero of civil rights and a tireless advocate of racial equality. At a time when many whites, even some abolitionists, were uncomfortable in the presence of blacks, John Brown shared his meals with them and recruited them as soldiers in his army of liberation. While many antebellum whites doubted the equality of blacks or their innate abilities, Brown was willing to stake his life on the abilities of his black recruits to take orders, execute commands, and fight bravely. As the American nation spiraled toward civil war, Brown helped prepare the North for the coming conflict. He understood that in times of crisis, self-sacrifice is essential. While other opponents of slavery talked about how bad the system was, Brown ventured into Missouri and helped a score of slaves escape to Canada.

Brown as a hero also underscores the limits of heroism. He was not a saint. He was not a dishonest businessman but was so negligent and sloppy that his economic ventures failed, and his behavior was almost criminal. He lied about his business affairs and about his political and revolutionary intentions. He kept records of correspondence with his backers that, for their safety and his, he should have destroyed. He was charismatic and mesmerizing but was also hard and almost cruel to his children and to those who disappointed him. He was a hero of civil rights and freedom but was perhaps not someone to trust or even someone who was very likeable. One might love or admire Brown, but one would not want him as a role model.

He was in the end an enormously passionate, complex, and compelling figure. He was larger than life while alive, and larger still when dead. He saw himself as a Christlike martyr and fully understood the value of both his life and his death. Before he was sentenced, he told the Virginia court: "Now, if it is deemed necessary that I should forfeit my life for the furtherance of the ends of justice, and mingle my blood further with the blood of my children and with the blood of millions in this slave country whose rights are disregarded by wicked, cruel, and unjust enactments, —I submit; so let it be done!"[4] While in jail, Brown wrote hundreds of letters, building an image of martyrdom. His friends wanted to rescue him from jail or try to get him released on an insanity defense, but he would have none of it. He assured his brother, "I am worth inconceivably more to *hang* than for any other purpose."[5] And so he was.

Had he died in jail or been placed in an institution, he would be but a footnote to the struggle against slavery and the collapse of the United States on the eve of the Civil War. But dead on the gallows, surrounded by hundreds of Virginia soldiers protecting his execution from an abolitionist rescue, he was a martyr to freedom and the embodiment of all that the powers that upheld slavery feared. As poet Stephen Vincent Benét put it:

> He had no gift for life, no gift to bring
> Life but his body and a cutting edge,
> But he knew how to die.[6]

From his death came his martyrdom and our endless fascination with his life.

NOTES

1. Quoted in Henry David Thoreau, "A Plea for Captain John Brown," in *Civil Disobedience and Other Essays* (New York: Dover Publications, Inc., 1993), 42.

2. Ibid., 36.

3. John Brown, "A prophetic note written by Brown on the day of his execution predicting the establishment of abolition through bloodshed," John Brown Papers, Chicago Historical Society.

4. John Brown, *Life and Letters of John Brown, Liberator of Kansas, and Martyr of Virginia,* ed. F. B. Sanborn (1885; repr., New York: Negro Universities Press, 1969), 585.

5. Quoted in Stephen B. Oates, *To Purge This Land with Blood: A Biography of John Brown,* 2nd ed. (Amherst: University of Massachusetts Press, 1984), 335.

6. Stephen Vincent Benét, *John Brown's Body* (1928; repr., New York: Holt, Rinehart and Winston, 1965), 48.

John Brown Chronology

1857	In Boston, New York, and throughout New England, Brown gains financial backers, including Secret Six; orders one thousand pikes in Connecticut, then travels to Tabor, Iowa, to continue guerrilla activities
1858	Attends Chatham Convention in Ontario, May 8–10; in December leads raid into Missouri, frees eleven slaves
1859	Escorts freed slaves to Canada, January 20–March 12; arrives in Chambersburg, Pennsylvania, June 30; travels to Harpers Ferry, July 3, rents Kennedy farm; begins raid on Harpers Ferry armory and arsenal, Sunday, October 16; captured, October 18; convicted of murder, treason, and inciting a slave insurrection, November 2 at Charles Town; hanged, December 2; buried at North Elba, December 8

PART ONE

Contemporaries and

Supporters of John Brown

one

WHY THEODORE PARKER
BACKED JOHN BROWN

The Political and Social Roots of
Support for Abolitionist Violence

DEAN GRODZINS

John Brown envisioned his assault on the federal arsenal at Harpers Ferry as the opening of a guerrilla war against slavery. Marshaled behind him were not only his tiny Provisional Army but also an extensive network of supporters across the North. His most famous and influential backer was the Reverend Theodore Parker of Boston.

Parker, with Ralph Waldo Emerson, was one of the two principal figures of the Transcendentalist movement. While Emerson took Transcendentalism into literature, Parker led it into religious and social reform, and his ideas found a wide audience. His sermons drew three thousand listeners a week; his lectures filled halls from Maine to Illinois; his writings sold well on both sides of the Atlantic.

THE WARRIOR AND THE INTELLECTUAL

Parker and Brown met in January 1857; the famous intellectual and the hard-scrabble warrior formed an instant rapport. The following year, Parker was one of the handful of leading white abolitionists to whom Brown revealed parts of his plan for a Southern war. Parker gave the plan, as he understood it, his full support. He helped form a secret committee to furnish Brown with money, supplies, and weapons and was a key figure in its deliberations. He also served as a Brown propagandist. Before Harpers Ferry, Parker tried to prepare public opinion for what he believed was about to happen, warning in speeches and sermons that slavery "must fall . . . in violence and blood."[1] Later, after Brown's failure at the ferry, when the old man's reputation hung in the balance, Parker wrote a widely circulated public letter defending the raid.[2] Parker and Brown could work together because each believed in using violence (some today would say terrorism) to achieve abolitionist ends. But the two men took very different paths to this common ground. Brown's route was direct. He thought that the Bible gave divine sanction for a war against American slavery and that God had given him a commission to wage it. These views apparently came to him in a kind of spiritual revelation early in his career, and he held to them tenaciously thereafter. Parker's path to violence was far more circuitous. He came to support Brown's war in part as a result of a long argument with other abolitionists over the means appropriate to fight slavery, and in part as a consequence of a bitter feud with the conservative elite of Boston. A study of why Parker backed Brown, in other words, reveals much about both the internal dynamics of the abolitionist movement and the relationship of social conflict within the North to sectional conflict between North and South.

THE ABOLITIONIST DEBATES OVER VIOLENCE AND POLITICS

The day Parker and Brown first met, Sunday, January 4, 1857, at the Music Hall in Boston, where Parker had just finished leading a morning religious service, Parker took part in a debate over the appropriate means to fight slavery.[3] Brown had arrived in the motherland of abolitionism from the West a day or two earlier for what turned out to be a four-month stay. At that time, the bloody, bushwhack war between proslave and Free-Soil militia was in progress for control of the Kansas Territory, and Brown, a prominent Kansas Free State fighter, was looking to raise money for his cause. Parker apparently invited Brown to a reception at his townhouse that evening. He hosted receptions every Sunday evening, as part of his ongoing campaign to break up the dour monotony of the old Puritan Sabbath.[4]

Reformers of all sorts frequented these gatherings. One regular attendee, who also came the day Brown dropped by, was William Lloyd Garrison, the famous abolitionist and "non-resistant."[5] Inevitably, he and Brown got into an argument over whether Garrison's strict interpretation of the injunction to "resist not evil with evil" was religiously justified. Parker joined in, taking the side of Brown, his new acquaintance, against Garrison, his old friend.[6]

The moment is telling: Parker, while debating Garrison, supported Brown. Not that Parker became an advocate of antislavery violence as a result of this particular Sunday night conversation. He was already a leading backer of the Free Kansas Fighters and for nearly a year had been raising money to supply them with Sharps rifles. Yet Parker had been debating abolitionist strategy and tactics with Garrison and others for years, and his support of Brown was in part a product of these debates.

Parker started down the road to Harpers Ferry when he began to extol violence for personal self-defense. This step he took as a result of an argument with nonresistant abolitionists like Garrison. The argument began in 1850. In the 1840s, although Parker was not a nonresistant, he had often sounded like one due to his strong opposition to the Mexican War (1846–48) and to capital punishment. Then, in 1850, Congress passed a new Fugitive Slave Act. It empowered commissioners of the federal courts (until this time minor functionaries) to issue warrants for the arrest of fugitive slaves and to try accused fugitives. Besides establishing this national slave-catching bureaucracy, the act obligated all citizens to support the rendition of fugitives.

Abolitionists were unanimous in asserting that they should oppose the law, but they disagreed over how to do so. Garrison held that even the fugitives themselves should use only peaceful means. As he told one mass meeting in 1850, he hoped fugitives would be "more indebted to the moral power of public sentiment than to any display of physical resistance."[7] Parker disagreed. He thought effective self-defense for fugitives required that they at least be able to threaten violence.

To counter support for nonviolence, especially among the many fugitives who admired Garrison, Parker took a strong proviolence stand. He insisted that, in the fugitives' case, killing was both just and necessary. In a widely noticed sermon, "The Function and Place of Conscience," preached days after the Fugitive Slave Act became law, Parker declared that "the man who attacks me to reduce me to slavery in that moment of attack alienates his right to life, and if I were the fugitive, and could escape in no other way, I would kill him with as little compunction as I would drive a mosquito from my face."[8]

In a discourse from 1852, Parker contrasted the fate of two Boston fugitives, William Craft and Thomas Sims. Craft had stood off the "kidnappers" (as Parker called anyone involved in executing the Fugitive Slave Act) and successfully escaped to Canada with his wife; Sims had been arrested and taken back to South Carolina. A major reason for the different fates of the two men, according to Parker, was that Craft had armed himself "pretty well," while Sims had been a "heedless young fellow" who had gone about "very imperfectly armed." Sims had carried only an "unlucky knife," which "knocked at a kidnapper's bosom, but could not open the door."[9] Craft, by contrast, had both knife and guns. Parker reported inspecting them himself, and he described the weapons admiringly: "His powder had a good kernel, and he kept it dry; his pistols were of excellent proof, the barrels true and clean; the trigger went easy; the caps would not hang fire at the snap. I tested his poniard; the blade had a good temper, stiff enough, yet springy withal; the point was sharp." So equipped, Craft walked the streets boldly, "but the kidnappers did not dare touch him."[10] Parker had to lay such stress on being ready to kill because he knew Garrison and others would be vigorously promoting pacifist views.[11]

During the 1850s, Parker's advocacy of violence moved beyond personal self-defense, and his language grew increasingly bellicose, especially during the Kansas War. At times he sounded downright bloodthirsty; he urged slaves to "hew down" their masters by the thousands and "walk blood red from Texas to Canada" if necessary to achieve freedom.[12] Using such rhetoric helped prepare Parker psychologically to become a supporter of Brown's Virginia plan, which, had it been fully implemented, would have done much to redden Southern soil. But Parker made every such statement with one eye on Garrison. Most of Parker's more grossly gory utterances were made at abolitionist gatherings with Garrison present.

Parker's position in the intra-abolitionist debate over nonresistance accounts for some of his intensity in supporting violence. His role in another debate, over whether to work within the American political system, helps explain why he was so open to using violence in the first place. Those abolitionists who voted and held political office Parker called the "political antislavery party"; those who refused to do so, he referred to as the "moral antislavery party," or sometimes the "antislavery party proper." Between these two par-

DEAN GRODZINS

ties, Parker self-consciously sought to be a mediator.[13] As such, he developed a version of antislavery ideology that made him especially open to supporting political violence and therefore John Brown.

Parker became a mediator between political and moral agitators because he thought both were necessary to free the slaves. The moral agitators were needed to develop the idea of abolitionism and spread it in its purest form. The political agitators, by contrast, were needed to organize the abolitionist idea into laws and institutions. In Parker's view, neither group could succeed without the other. The political abolitionists would turn the antislavery ideal into fact, but if the moral abolitionists did not place the ideal before them and rouse public opinion behind them, the politicians would be able to do nothing.

Parker understood that conflict between the moral and political factions was inevitable because the former would always see the latter as falling short of its standards, and the latter would always see the former as self-righteous and impractical. But Parker thought the chronic and bitter controversies that occurred between them were counterproductive and unnecessary. He tried, on a personal level, to mediate particular disputes between individual political and moral abolitionists, and he kept channels open to both sides by taking a middle ground on the most contentious issue between them: the nature of the U.S. Constitution.

The moral faction, the most prominent member of which was Garrison, held that the Constitution recognized and protected slavery and was therefore a "covenant with death and an agreement with Hell."[14] This faction insisted that no true abolitionist could serve, with good conscience, in a government position that required an oath to uphold the Constitution; they refused to vote, at least in national elections, and they called on the Northern states to renounce the Constitution by seceding from the Union. Some in the moral party, Garrison among them, went even further and rejected all governments except the Government of God. The political faction, meanwhile, among whom could be classed organizers of the Liberty, Free-Soil, and Republican Parties, held the Constitution to be at least neutral on the slavery issue. Some went further and argued that it was an antislavery document.

These contrasting views of the Constitution would seem to be irreconcilable, but Parker set out to reconcile them.[15] He developed a conception of the Constitution that seemed to validate both sides of the argument. This view was closely related to his Transcendentalist understanding of the Bible.[16]

That Parker should use the same interpretive approach to the Bible and the Constitution, the two master texts of American life, is not surprising. He was hardly the only person to do so. Some people gave both texts literal or narrow constructions, and some gave each a "liberal" construction by going "behind the text." Among the latter group were New Englanders who were both Unitarian in theology and Federalist or, later, Whig in politics.[17] Parker himself belonged to this group as a young man, having begun his career as a Unitarian minister with Whiggish leanings.

As he matured, however, he rejected the authority of both the Bible and the Constitution. Solving the problem of biblical authority was the central intellectual struggle of his twenties, when he first became exposed to German higher criticism of the Bible. He emerged from this struggle a member of the New England Transcendentalist circle and an ally of Ralph Waldo Emerson.[18]

Parker came to believe the Bible was full of myths and mistakes and so could in no sense be considered, as he himself had once considered it, a miraculous, infallible revelation. He in fact denied that such a revelation was possible. According to Parker, the authors of the Bible were inspired no differently from people today: insofar as they were good and pious, just so far were their writings true. The Bible was only an approximation of what he liked to call *absolute religion*. As such, he considered it valuable, even precious. Yet, he also believed the Bible could be—had to be—transcended. Parker argued that if we are more good and pious than biblical writers are, then we must be free to practice a higher religion than the one they enjoin.

Parker's Transcendentalist interpretation of the Bible affected him as an abolitionist because it left him largely uninterested in a project that obsessed many of his colleagues in the abolitionist movement: to prove that scripture was against slavery. This project was vital for those who still regarded the Bible as having miraculous authority. For Parker, by contrast, all that mattered was that religion, that is, absolute goodness and piety, was against slavery. Therefore, the Bible, insofar as it was religious, was against slavery. If some passages of the Bible seem to condone slavery, they are evidence only that their authors had not risen above the barbarous times in which they lived. As he once remarked, if Paul was in favor of slavery (e.g., in the Epistle to Philemon), so much the worse for Paul.

Parker's interpretation of the Constitution was similarly Transcendentalist. Just as the Bible was only an approximation of absolute religion, so the Constitution for him was only an approximation of what he liked to call *the*

American idea—that is, of freedom. Just as the Bible was valuable, so was the Constitution—Parker frequently praised the American system of government for achieving the difficult balance between "National Unity of Action" and "Individual Variety of Action." Just as the Bible should be transcended, as people understood better absolute religion, so the Constitution should be transcended, as people understood better the American idea. Moreover, just as Parker was uninterested in proving the Bible to be antislavery, so he was uninterested in proving the Constitution antislavery. According to Parker, all that ultimately mattered was that absolute religion and the American idea were against slavery.

His attitude meant that unlike others in the antislavery movement, he felt no need to accept or reject the Constitution in toto. This made him one of the few neutrals on the question of whether the Constitution was a proslavery document. He summed up his position neatly in a speech from 1848: "Some men will try political action. The action of the people, of the nation, must be political action. It may be constitutional, it may be unconstitutional. I see not why men need to quarrel about that."[19] Parker himself acted like both a political abolitionist and a moral abolitionist. Between 1855 and 1857, for example, he proposed a program of political agitation, argued that slavery should be regarded as unconstitutional (because the states were required under the Constitution to have republican forms of government whereas the form of government in slave states was obviously despotic), and provisionally endorsed disunionism as a basis for moral agitation.[20]

Parker saw no contradiction in his positions because he viewed his activities as part of a process. He believed that absolute religion and the American idea were the twin goals of history and that all his actions contributed to the achievement of those goals. Every great historical change, he observed, required a great variety of means to produce it.

Parker's teleological, process-oriented outlook made him particularly susceptible to using violence. He lacked the checks to violence that inhered in both the political and the moral abolitionist positions. The political abolitionists tended to reject violence, or at least attempted to limit their use of it, due to their commitment to remain within the law and to support constitutional institutions. Parker had no such commitment. Moral abolitionists, meanwhile, tended to link rejection of the Constitution with rejection of all other forms of what they perceived as oppression, including violence.[21] That Garrison was the leading abolitionist opponent of both violence and political

Why Theodore Parker Backed John Brown

action is no accident. Parker, although he admired Garrison's moral absolutism, viewed politics as a necessary part of the historical process that would lead eventually to a society without oppression.

He thought the same of violence. A revolution, he believed, was not baptized in rosewater, and the achievements of the great historical revolutions were worth all the blood they cost. The great constitutions had been created through violence. Parker made this point in a speech from March 1858, delivered to an antislavery audience on the very day he secretly met with Brown and first discussed with him his Virginia plan: "No doubt the civilized world is ruled partly by constitutions, written on parchment; but the only parchment which kings and people respect very much, is the parchment of the drum-head. The great charters of human freedom have been writ in an ink very costly, very precious,—it is the ink a man carries in his heart. . . . I believe there is no other ink which will secure the freedom of the African people."[22]

THE CIVIL WAR CLOSE AT HAND

Debate among abolitionists was not the only controversy to shape Parker's response to Brown. Just as important were Parker's fierce fights with the conservative elite of Boston. These conflicts convinced Parker that liberty in America was under dire threat and that a civil war over slavery was imminent.

His growing sense of a coming civil war can be tracked through the imagery he used regarding the American idea. Before 1850 he had said without qualification that this idea, which lay "at the basis of all our truly original, distinctive and American institutions," was that of freedom. Parker saw freedom as a great onrushing force. Slavery was merely an obstacle in its path, and one that would soon be overcome.[23]

Abruptly, in the spring of 1850, as Congress debated the Fugitive Slave Bill, Parker stopped talking about a unitary American idea. Instead, he began speaking of two ideas, locked in a battle for the national soul: freedom and despotism.[24] Parker was quite self-conscious of this change. "I used to call [freedom] 'the American Idea,'" he said in 1854; "it was when I was younger than I am to-day."[25] Between 1850 and 1856, Parker returned again and again in his speeches and sermons to the image of this epochal struggle. Each time, the position of freedom looked weaker and weaker. By the spring of 1856 he was predicting that if the Republicans lost the presidential election that year,

DEAN GRODZINS

and a new proslavery administration took office, there would be civil war. Just in case, he began drastically cutting back his expenses.[26]

The Republicans did lose; the victor, Democrat James Buchanan, was notoriously proslavery. In the weeks following, Parker told anyone who would listen that the choice now was between "slavery, or battle." In his journal, he grimly weighed the chances that his property would be confiscated and he himself hanged as a traitor. He took measures so that his wife would be provided for in case of such emergencies.[27] This was Parker's apocalyptic mood in January 1857 when he and John Brown first met; it was one reason for his positive reaction to Brown, a man who lived perpetually on the brink of apocalypse.

Why was Parker so certain civil war was impending? Sectional conflict was intense in this period, but the civil war Parker envisioned was not strictly a sectional one—between North and South. Rather, it also would be fought within the North. He imagined he would be hanged not by some invading Southern army, but by proslavery neighbors. The nearness of his enemies gave his fears their special intensity. The enemies that most preoccupied him were among the elite of Boston.[28]

This elite was among the most clearly defined and powerful of any in antebellum America.[29] It was a network of about forty mercantile, banking, and manufacturing families, closely intermarried, who had risen to unprecedented wealth and power in the early nineteenth century by establishing and controlling the first great textile mills. They were united not only by marriage, but by worldview: their politics was Whig and their religion Unitarian.[30] These Boston Brahmins, as they were to be called later in the century, had enormous influence over the politics of Massachusetts and dominated its leading cultural institutions—Harvard University, the Boston Athenaeum, the oldest and most prestigious churches, the major newspapers and journals.

Yet this elite never quite achieved hegemony. In the late 1840s and 1850s, especially, its authority came under repeated challenge.[31] These challenges generally were led by middle-class reformers, Parker foremost among them. Parker's own conflict with the Boston patriciate was rooted in personal resentment. He had been born an outsider, had struggled mightily to become an insider, but had been turned away.

His father had been a pump maker; his mother a goodwife; his brothers had become farmers, artisans, and factory hands who married goodwives; and his sisters had become goodwives who married farmers, artisans, and factory

Why Theodore Parker Backed John Brown

hands.[32] But Parker, the last of eleven children, early set his sights on bigger things. He wanted to join the Boston elite. This ambition was reasonable since the elite was, in the years of Parker's youth, fairly open. All a poor boy needed to do was work hard, find patrons, get an education, enter an acceptable profession, join the Whig Party and a Unitarian Church, and, most important, marry well.

Parker made all the right moves: he became a Unitarian minister,[33] voted Whig,[34] and married Lydia Cabot, a member of perhaps the most eminent family of the Boston bourgeois aristocracy (as the old saw goes, Boston is where "the Lowells talk to the Cabots, and the Cabots talk only to God"). He pursued his education with a terrifying intensity—and largely on his own, because his family had been unable to afford to send him to college. Despite this handicap, by the age of twenty-five he had completed the course of study at Harvard Divinity School (which he had entered with the help of a patron) and learned to read twenty languages (among them: Greek, Hebrew, German, Icelandic).

By some measures, Parker's efforts to get ahead were successful. His father was worth only fifteen hundred dollars when he died, in 1836; when Parker himself died, in 1860, he and his wife together were worth at least fifty thousand dollars, placing them among the wealthiest one percent of Massachusetts residents.[35] Nevertheless, despite his prosperity and his connections, Parker had not succeeded in joining the Boston aristocracy. His youthful dream had failed him. First, it dried up like a raisin in the sun. Then it exploded.

The drying up occurred for personal reasons. He and his wife turned out not to be well matched, intellectually or temperamentally, and he came to regard her family as so many insufferable philistines.[36] Through personal acquaintance, he came to realize that aristocrats of Boston were not his kind of people. The scorn he developed for them was considerable. Throughout his career, he was to devote much of his social criticism and many of his most barbed comments against these "snobs" and their institutions, such as Harvard. He famously remarked that while the Egyptian embalmers had taken seventy days to mummify a dead man, Harvard Divinity School took three years to mummify a live one.[37]

Parker's dream exploded due to theological and political controversy. The Boston elite defined itself as conservative in theology and politics; Parker, largely through his association with New England Transcendentalism, came to define himself as a radical.[38] Consequently, he was shut out of elite soci-

DEAN GRODZINS

ety. He became persona non grata at Harvard; he was barred from preaching in the foremost Boston churches; the leading newspapers and journals denounced and ridiculed him. Parker's contempt for the Boston elite was mixed with anger toward them for trying to keep him down. It was the rage of a self-made man. "*Why* have I been opposed," he asked in an autobiographical note from 1846, "not because [I] said what was not true, . . . not *honest,* not friendly to the *interests of Man.* . . . With what intention have I been opposed? To ruin me, to give me no chance."[39]

Ironically, the more he was denounced and renounced by the establishment, the more popular he seemed to become. As he often said, when he spoke to the people, they heard his words gladly. He had tapped into what turned out to be a widespread popular resentment against the pretensions of the Boston elite. In particular, he drew a following from people like himself—those who were middle class or who had middle-class aspirations. The membership of Parker's own "free church" in Boston appears to have been disproportionately middle class when compared to the general population, but less oriented toward the elite than the conservative Unitarian churches of the city, which had shut Parker out.[40]

Middle-class people were in Parker's day coming to be aware of themselves as a distinct social group, defined by a way of life and a cultural style. He was one of their champions and, as such, was one of the thinkers who helped define what the middle class was for his time and place.[41] Although Parker rarely used the term *middle class* and did not consistently use the word *class* in its modern sense, he generally did conceive of society as having three horizontal layers, each with a distinct character, and with the middle one being the most important for social progress.

In the bottom layer of society, said Parker, were the "laboring classes," the "perishing classes" (that is, the abjectly poor) and most of the "dangerous classes" (that is, the criminals). People at this social level generally were degraded, because they had been unable to develop their spiritual natures. They therefore needed to be aided and elevated. He constantly praised the dignity of manual work and attacked the social prejudices against it, and he supported a wide variety of reforms he believed would alleviate poverty and degradation, from better public schools to temperance to a shorter workday.[42]

At the top of society, according to Parker, was a group he clearly modeled on the Boston elite. He usually called this the controlling class (because it controlled the state, the press, and church); its members he called the capitalists

Why Theodore Parker Backed John Brown

(because they influenced the world by means of their capital), or even the snobs. Parker portrayed the snobs as neither terribly moral nor terribly religious. They thought religion to be vulgar and decidedly low—good for ordinary people but not for them. They used their vast influence to oppose any reform of church, state, or society. As such, Parker saw the elite as a far greater threat to religious, political, and social progress than the degraded but largely powerless lower class.[43]

Parker put his hopes for progress in neither the laboring nor controlling classes, but in the middle group, which he believed constituted the large majority of society. Members of this group, he said in a sermon from 1846, were characterized by seriousness and earnestness of purpose, for they had made their own way in the world. They had "mingle[d] more with all sorts of men" than had members of the other two classes and so had learned to feel the common nature of humanity, to ignore the accidents of situation, and to appreciate the spiritual value of "man as man." Among these people, religious ideas had always found a home. The mission of this middle group was to help the class below them and to challenge the class above them.[44]

By the mid-1840s, then, Parker had declared opposition to the Boston elite to be a religious duty for the middle class. But opposition became for him imperative during the controversy over the Fugitive Slave Law of 1850, when he began talking about the death struggle between freedom and despotism. Specifically, what prompted such talk was not the passage of the law by Congress, in September 1850, but the endorsement of it the previous spring by the Boston elite.

The elite seem to have shared with their fellow Northerners a general dislike of slavery in the abstract.[45] Yet they profoundly distrusted abolitionism, which they thought threatened the social order. Considerable evidence supports the claim, widely asserted at the time, that the antislavery movement drew "a line of cleavage through all Boston society, leaving most of the more powerful and wealthy families on the conservative side."[46] These families used their influence to keep the slavery issue off the political agenda or sought to quell agitation with rhetoric and symbolic gestures. In the late 1840s, however, those tactics failed them. The issue of whether slavery should spread to the Western territories was too pressing; abolitionist ideas were becoming, in their view, dangerously popular. The Free-Soil Party arose in Massachusetts, and for the first time Whig Party control over the state, and therefore elite control, was threatened.

The Fugitive Slave Law had the potential to make the antislavery movement even more popular because it turned slavery, hitherto a somewhat abstract question for Northerners, into an immediate one. As Parker's friend Ralph Waldo Emerson wrote, before 1850 he had never suffered "any known inconvenience from American slavery." Having not seen Southern slavery nor "heard the whip," it "was like slavery in Africa or in Japan for me." The new law, however, changed everything, because it "required me to hunt slaves."[47]

Emerson here was expressing a common sentiment, but the Boston elite saw things differently. The Fugitive Slave Bill was proposed as part of the Compromise of 1850, which was supposed to settle the slavery issue forever; the compromise would therefore render agitation against slavery moot, and the reformist threat to elite control would be removed. When on March 7, 1850, Senator Daniel Webster, the reigning monarch of Massachusetts Whiggery, gave a dramatic speech in Congress endorsing the compromise and the bill, the Boston elite seized the moment. They had celebratory cannons fired on Boston Common; they presented Webster with a petition of thanks signed by nearly a thousand leading citizens; they organized rallies in his support. Meanwhile, the leading newspapers and the ministers of the most prominent city churches urged Massachusetts to obey the law.

All this appalled Parker. He saw the controlling class as having rejected the American idea and flouted the higher law of God. He began identifying as the opponents of freedom and friends of despotism not only the slaveholders of the South but the "greater portion" of the "wealthy and educated men" in the large Northern towns.[48]

His confrontation with the Boston elite grew especially intense owing to the Anthony Burns fugitive slave case and the events surrounding it. Burns, a Baptist preacher who had escaped from Virginia, was arrested on May 24, 1854. In response, Parker organized a mass protest rally for the evening of May 26, at which he was one of the principal speakers. While he was delivering a rousing speech to the excited crowd, a band of abolitionists stormed the nearby jail where Burns was being held.[49] They failed to liberate him, but during the ensuing riot, in which members of the protest meeting took part, a volunteer policeman was killed. The next morning, Burns's hearings before the fugitive-slave commissioner, Edward G. Loring, began. After a week, during which the streets of Boston were filled with police, state militia, and federal troops, Loring ruled that the fugitive should be sent back South. Tens of thousands of protesters lined the route as Burns was marched to his ship, escorted by soldiers.[50]

The riot and the rendition of Burns became subjects of bitter, personal controversy between Parker and the Boston elite—in particular between him and the family of Commissioner Loring. Loring was related to the Curtis clan of merchants and lawyers, who were dominant figures in the local elite. "It has been thought," Parker remarked in 1854, "that Boston belonged to the Curtises."[51] They were also all conspicuous supporters of the Fugitive Slave Law.

Parker used public anger over the Burns case to try to destroy Curtis influence. He publicly blamed the policeman's murder on Commissioner Loring and helped launch the campaign, which became a cause célèbre in Massachusetts politics over the next few years, to get Loring fired from his position as probate judge. He also repeatedly denounced the "Curtii" as conspirators against freedom.

Meanwhile, the Curtises tried to harass and imprison Parker. Charles P. Curtis (Loring's stepbrother), a lawyer who was on the board of the corporation that owned the hall where Parker's church gathered, attempted unsuccessfully to get its lease revoked on the grounds that the property was being misused to disseminate both sentiments subversive of law and order and slanders against his kinsman.[52] Benjamin Curtis (Charles P. Curtis's cousin and son-in-law), a U.S. Supreme Court justice and federal circuit judge, charged a grand jury to indict Parker for his actions during the riot, which were construed as obstructing a federal official (the marshal of Boston) in the conduct of his duties. A grand jury with another Curtis relative on it issued the indictment. Parker was arrested in November 1854 and released on bail.

The trial, which Parker publicly attacked as a blatant, politically driven attempt to silence him, did not open until May 1855. It was anticlimactic. After a week of hearings, the case was thrown out of court on a technicality. Parker believed that the Curtises had let him go because public outrage had made their position politically untenable. Trying him, much less jailing him, would have caused them only embarrassment, and so they had beaten a tactical retreat.[53] He remained convinced, however, that they and the class they symbolized still wanted to impose despotism on America.

Parker made this belief clear in May 1856, when his friend, the antislavery senator from Massachusetts, Charles Sumner, was beaten insensible on the Senate floor by a South Carolina congressman. In a celebrated sermon, Parker argued that the assault was part of a wide-ranging, long-term effort to "spread bondage over the whole country" and "'crush out' freedom of speech." Parker laid blame for the attack only partly on the "ferocity" of Southern slaveholders, although a Southern slaveholder had done the deed. Just as responsible, said Parker, were the "allies of that ferocity," the "corrupt men in the midst of us" who had "betrayed the people" and "promoted this wickedness."[54] In particular, he identified about a hundred Bostonians "of property and standing" and their two to three thousand "flunkies." This group was considered the "respectable" class of the city, yet according to Parker, it had encouraged and abetted Southern aggression at every stage.[55] The South knew this class hated Sumner and would be pleased to see someone shut him up. Parker might have added that this class thought the same way about him.

With the 1855 trial fresh in his mind and his friend Sumner an invalid, no wonder Parker worried at the end of 1856 that he would be arrested and possibly hanged. Little wonder, too, he gave John Brown such a warm reception. They agreed that violence against supporters of slavery was under the circumstances justified and necessary. Besides, Parker's enemies were wealthy, sophisticated, urbane, and Unitarian, while Brown was poor, rough, plain, and Calvinist. Brown, then, must have been especially appealing to Parker because he was the antithesis of a Brahmin.

NOTES

The following abbreviations are used in the notes:

ASAOS   Theodore Parker, *Additional Speeches, Addresses, and Occasional Sermons*, 2 vols. (Boston: Little, Brown, 1855)
SAOS   Theodore Parker, *Speeches, Addresses, and Occasional Sermons*, 2 vols. (Boston: Crosby and Nichols, 1852)
TP   Theodore Parker
WTP   Theodore Parker, *The Works of Theodore Parker*, centenary ed., 15 vols. (Boston: American Unitarian Association, 1907–11)

1. TP, "The Effect of Slavery on the American People" (sermon 911, July 4, 1858), *WTP*, 14:34–45. See also the speech by TP, May 26, 1858, at the New England Anti-Slavery Convention: "The time, I think, has passed by when the great American question of the 19th century could have been settled without bloodshed." TP, *The Relation of Slavery to a Republican Form of Government* (Boston: William L. Kent, 1858), 20.

2. See TP to Francis Jackson, November 24, 1859, *WTP*, 14:420–37.

3. John Brown, *The Life and Letters of John Brown, Liberator of Kansas and Martyr of Virginia*, ed. Franklin B. Sanborn (1885; repr., New York: Negro Universities Press, 1969), 511.

Why Theodore Parker Backed John Brown

4. See James Freeman Clarke, "Theodore Parker," in *Memorial and Biographical Sketches* (Cambridge, MA: Houghton, Osgood, 1878), 120; John White Chadwick, *Theodore Parker, Preacher and Reformer* (Boston: Houghton, Mifflin, 1900), 295. For TP's liberal views on Sunday observance, see TP, "Some Thoughts on the Most Christian Use of Sunday" (sermon 492, January 30, 1848), in *SAOS*, 2:337–71.

5. For a description of one of these gatherings with Garrison present, see Julia Ward Howe, *Reminiscences* (Boston: Houghton, Mifflin, 1899), 152–53.

6. Wendell Phillips Garrison and Francis Jackson Garrison, *William Lloyd Garrison*, 4 vols. (Boston, 1889; repr., New York: Negro Universities Press, 1969), 3:487–88. The Garrison-Brown debate is referred to in many books; I am able to date it. Many historians have assumed that TP held a special reception for Brown in order to introduce him to prominent abolitionists. Based on this assumption, certain historians have held that Samuel Gridley Howe and Wendell Phillips probably were present. As I point out, however, Brown was invited to a regular Sunday reception. No evidence exists that any prominent abolitionist other than Garrison came that night or that even he came specially to meet Brown. Henry Mayer questions whether anything like a formal debate took place or that Garrison recognized Brown as his opposite. Mayer, *All on Fire: William Lloyd Garrison and the Abolition of Slavery* (New York: St. Martins, 1998), 475. I am inclined to think that the Garrison brothers would not have related the story unless their father had told them (probably years later) that something of the sort had occurred. The incident must only have seemed memorable, however, in retrospect, because no observer recorded it at the time. For example, Louisa May Alcott, who probably was present at the reception, does not mention Brown in her journal; see Alcott, *The Journals of Louisa May Alcott*, ed. Joel Myerson, Daniel Shealy, and Madelaine Stern (Boston: Little, Brown, 1989), 84.

7. Mayer, *All on Fire*, 410. Note that some abolitionists, such as Richard Henry Dana, held that the means should be both legal and nonviolent; Garrison, with his anarchistic tendencies, was less concerned about legality than violence.

8. TP, "The Function and Place of Conscience" (sermon 598, September 22, 1850), *SAOS*, 2:258.

9. TP, "The Boston Kidnapping" (discourse before the Committee of Vigilance, April 12, 1852), *ASAOS*, 1:65.

10. Ibid., 1:55. TP used similar language in 1856 after the assault of his friend, Senator Charles Sumner, by a Southern congressman; Parker explained why the other senator from Massachusetts, Charles Wilson, had been left alone: "Mr. Wilson has not the reputation of a non-resistant. . . . He carried his pistols to Washington, and caused it to be distinctly understood that he had not the common New England prejudice against shooting a scoundrel. He has not been insulted, and he will not be." See TP, "A New Lesson for the Day" (sermon, May 25, 1856), *WTP*, 14:265.

11. Note that Garrison did shift his ground somewhat under the pressure of debate and events. He began to argue that if, as most white Americans professed to believe, rebellion against tyrants were obedience to God, then white Americans must admit that slaves had as much right to kill their oppressors as had the English colonists during the Revolution, and had much more cause to do so. Garrison is

quoted in Jane H. Pease and William H. Pease, *The Fugitive Slave Law and Anthony Burns: A Problem in Law Enforcement* (Philadelphia: Lippincott, 1975), 21; see also Garrison's address at the Crispus Attucks celebration, March 5, 1858, in the *Liberator,* March 12, 1858. Scholars have noted Garrison making a similar argument in 1859, in response to Harpers Ferry, and assume he shifted his ground only at that point; in fact, this had been his publicly declared position for many years. On the other hand, he continued to call himself an "ultra" peace man, to criticize efforts to fight slavery with "carnal" weapons, and to encourage his followers not to use such weapons. In April 1856, when TP used a church service to raise money to buy rifles for the Kansas Free State Company, Garrison strongly criticized him in a newspaper editorial: "It gives us unfeigned sorrow to find . . . Mr. Parker . . . vindicating the rightfulness of defensive war. . . . Defensive war is no better than defensive lying, or holding men in bondage for their good." "We incomparably prefer the tocsin sounded by an Apostle eighteen centuries ago:—Put on the whole armor of God, that ye may be able to stand against the wiles of the devil. For *we wrestle not against flesh and blood,* but against principalities, against powers, against the rulers of the darkness of this world; against wickedness in high places." Garrison probably made similar points in his argument with Brown at TP's house nine months later. Garrison, "Is It Right to Kill Our Enemies?" *Liberator,* April 4, 1856; emphasis original. See also Mayer, *All on Fire,* 410, 479–80, 502–4.

12. See TP, "The Present Aspect of the Anti-Slavery Enterprise" (speech before the Anti-Slavery Convention, January 30, 1857), *Liberator,* February 27, 1857.

13. TP made many of his mediating statements in speeches to antislavery conventions and celebrations. See for example, "Doings of the Abolitionists" (speech before the New England Anti-Slavery Convention, May 31, 1848), in *SAOS,* 2:107–18, esp. 113–17; "The Aspect of Freedom in America" (speech before the Mass Anti-Slavery Celebration of Independence, July 5, 1852), in *ASAOS,* 1:107–29, esp. 123–28; "Speech at the West India Emancipation Celebration" (August 3, 1852), *Liberator,* August 27, 1852; "Present Aspect of the Anti-Slavery Enterprise" (speech before the American Anti-Slavery Society, May 7, 1856), *WTP,* 12:397–429, esp. 404–9, 425–28.

14. Mayer, *All on Fire,* 313.

15. Note, too, that when TP edited the *Massachusetts Quarterly Review* (1847–50), he allowed supporters of both sides of the argument to publish lengthy articles explaining their respective positions. For the argument that slavery was unconstitutional, see [Richard E. Hildreth], "Has Slavery in the United States a Legal Basis?" vol. 1 (March 1848): 145–67, and "Has Slavery in the United States a Legal Basis?" (contd.), vol. 1 (June 1848): 273–93; for a reply that slavery was constitutional, see [Henry I. Bowditch], "Constitutionality of Slavery," vol. 1 (September 1848): 463–508; for Hildreth's response, see "The Legality of American Slavery," vol. 2 (December 1848): 33–39.

16. For an interesting study of the formal parallels between biblical and constitutional interpretation, see Jaroslav Pelikan, *Interpreting the Bible and the Constitution* (New Haven: Yale University Press, 2004).

17. For example, William Ellery Channing, the great Unitarian preacher who was a hero to the young TP, declared that Unitarians "reason about the Bible precisely as

Why Theodore Parker Backed John Brown

civilians do about the constitution under which we live; who, you know, are accustomed to limit one provision of that venerable instrument by others, to fix the precise import of its parts, by inquiring into its general spirit, into the intention of its authors, and into the prevalent feelings, impressions, and circumstances of the time in which it was framed." Channing, "Unitarian Christianity," in *The Works of William Ellery Channing* (Boston: American Unitarian Association, 1901), 369.

18. Dean Grodzins, *American Heretic: Theodore Parker and Transcendentalism* (Chapel Hill: University of North Carolina Press, 2002), chs. 2–4.

19. TP, "Doings of the Abolitionists," *SAOS,* 2:116.

20. For TP's program of agitation, see the summary of his speech to the American Anti-Slavery Society (May 9, 1855) in the *Liberator,* May 18, 1855; for TP's provisional endorsement of disunionism, see TP to Thomas Wentworth Higginson, January 18, 1857, in the *Liberator,* January 23, 1857; this letter also contains a statement of TP's theory about the slave states defying the possibility of a republican form of government. Note that TP frequently had repudiated disunionism; see Garrison's criticism of TP on this point in the *Liberator,* April 11, 1856.

21. This link is examined in Lewis Perry, *Radical Abolitionism: Anarchy and the Government of God in Antislavery Thought* (Ithaca, NY: Cornell University Press, 1974).

22. TP, "Remarks of Rev. Theodore Parker" (Boston Massacre Commemorative Festival, March 5, 1858), *Liberator,* March 12, 1858.

23. See especially "The Political Destination of America" (1848), in *SAOS,* 2:1–39. The quotation comes from TP, "Slave Power in America" (speech at the New England Anti-Slavery Convention, May 29, 1850), in *SAOS,* 2:176.

24. TP first worked out this dichotomy, which he used many times thereafter, in "The State of the Nation" (Thanksgiving sermon, November 28, 1850), in *SAOS,* 2:287–96.

25. TP, "The Dangers Which Threaten the Rights of Man in America" (sermon, July 2, 1854), in *ASAOS,* 2:251.

26. See TP to Edouard Desor, August 9, 1856, in John Weiss, *The Life and Correspondence of Theodore Parker* (Boston: D. Appleton, 1864), 2:188–89; TP to John P. Hale, October 21, 1856, in Weiss, *Life and Correspondence,* 2:87.

27. See TP to Sarah Hunt, November 4, 1856, in Octavius Brooks Frothingham, *Theodore Parker: A Biography* (Boston: James R. Osgood, 1874), 439. See also TP's journal, vol. P, p. 2 (November 4, 1856), quoted in Weiss, *Life and Correspondence,* 2:190.

28. Some of the paragraphs that follow also appear, in slightly altered form, in Dean Grodzins, "Theodore Parker and the Twenty-Eighth Congregational Society: The Reform Church and the Spirituality of Reformers in Boston, 1845–1859," in *Transient and Permanent: The Transcendentalist Movement and Its Contexts,* ed. Charles Capper and Conrad E. Wright (Boston: Massachusetts Historical Society, 1999), 96–100.

29. For three different portrayals of this elite, each valuable, see Ronald Story, *The Forging of an Aristocracy: Harvard and the Boston Upper Class, 1800–1870* (Middle-

town, CT: Wesleyan University Press, 1980); Robert Dalzell, *Enterprising Elite: The Boston Associates and the World They Made* (Cambridge, MA: Harvard University Press, 1987); Betty G. Farrell, *Elite Families: Class and Power in Nineteenth-Century Boston* (Albany: State University of New York Press, 1993).

30. Jane H. Pease and William H. Pease, "Whose Right Hand of Fellowship? Pew and Pulpit in Shaping Church Practice," in *American Unitarianism, 1805–1865,* ed. Conrad E. Wright (Boston: Massachusetts Historical Society), 181–206. For a generally sympathetic view of the elite's religious and political outlooks, see Daniel Walker Howe, *The Unitarian Conscience: Harvard Moral Philosophy, 1805–1861* (1970; Middletown, CT: Wesleyan University Press, 1988) and *The Political Culture of the American Whigs* (Chicago: University of Chicago Press, 1979), 96–108, 210–37; also, Dalzell, *Enterprising Elite,* 164–90.

31. See Story, *Forging of an Aristocracy,* 135–59; Dalzell, *Enterprising Elite,* 198–224. John R. Mulkern, *The Know-Nothing Party in Massachusetts: The Rise and Fall of a People's Movement* (Boston: Northeastern University Press, 1990), is useful for emphasizing the class dimensions of Massachusetts politics in the 1840s and 1850s; he errs, however, in denying the significance of slavery to the controversy and in insisting that the fulcrum of conflict was between the working class and the elite, rather than between the middle class and the elite. His analysis of the Know-Nothing movement has been partly superseded by Tyler Anbinder, *Nativism and Slavery: The Northern Know Nothings and the Politics of the 1850s* (New York: Oxford University Press, 1992).

32. New England women of ordinary status were traditionally called *goodwives.* See Laurel Thatcher Ulrich, *Good Wives: Image and Reality in the Lives of Women in Northern New England, 1650–1750* (New York: Vintage, 1980, 1982).

33. TP considered becoming an Evangelical in 1831 but decided against it, perhaps because the Evangelicals were predominantly lower class, representing what he wanted to leave, while the Unitarians represented the class he wanted to join. See Grodzins, *American Heretic,* 12, 18, 25–26.

34. TP consistently voted Whig through 1844, with the exception of 1840, when the Log Cabin and Hard Cider campaign so disgusted him that he elected not to vote at all. After 1844, TP voted for antislavery candidates and parties. See Grodzins, *American Heretic,* 208, 471–72.

35. The estate records for TP's father, John Parker, are in the Middlesex County Records at the Massachusetts State Archives. The estate records for TP and his wife, Lydia Dodge Cabot Parker, are also in the archives, in the Suffolk County Records. See also report on the Parker household in the Massachusetts census of 1860.

36. Grodzins, *American Heretic,* 96–100, 326–28, 496–98.

37. See TP to Samuel Joseph May, October 24, 1853, Autograph File, Houghton Library, Harvard University. TP adds: "I think at Meadville they do it in less."

38. Grodzins, *American Heretic,* chs. 4–7.

39. Note to "Farewell Sermon to West Roxbury" (sermon 413, February 6, 1846), MS in Theodore Parker Papers, Boston Public Library; emphasis original.

40. See Grodzins, "Twenty-Eighth Congregational Society," 99–100, 104–7.

41. On the formation of the middle class, the literature is extensive. One book I have found especially useful, because of the subtlety and flexibility of its interpretation, is Stuart Blumin, *The Emergence of the Middle Class: Social Experience in the American City, 1760–1900* (Cambridge: Cambridge University Press, 1989).

42. See TP, "Thoughts on Labor" (1841), in *The Critical and Miscellaneous Writings of Theodore Parker* (Boston: James Munroe, 1843), 109–35; "The Education of the Laboring Classes" (1842), in *Critical and Miscellaneous Writings*, 192–219; "The Perishing Classes of Boston" (sermon 435, August 30, 1846), in *SAOS*, 1:133–62; "The Dangerous Classes of Society" (sermon 454, January 31, 1847), in *SAOS*, 1:201–38; "Poverty" (sermon 532, January 14, 1849), in *SAOS*, 1:239–60.

43. TP discusses the particular failures of this group especially in his antislavery writings, as will be seen below, but see also "Merchants" (sermon 445, November 22, 1846), in *SAOS*, 1:163–200; "The Obstacles Practically in the Way of Christianity" (sermon 426, May 10, 1846), MS in Theodore Parker Papers, Andover-Harvard Library.

44. See TP, "Obstacles."

45. See, e.g., Howe, *Unitarian Conscience*, 270–94.

46. Thomas Wentworth Higginson, *Cheerful Yesterdays* (Boston: Houghton, Mifflin, 1898), 125–26.

47. Ralph Waldo Emerson, "The Fugitive Slave Law," in *Emerson's Antislavery Writings*, ed. Len Gougeon and Joel Myerson (New Haven: Yale University Press, 1995), 74, 80.

48. TP, "The State of the Nation," *SAOS*, 2:292. TP was hardly the only one to make this kind of connection; linking the "lords of the lash and the lords of the loom," to use Charles Sumner's phrase, was a staple of Free Soil rhetoric.

49. They were led by Thomas Wentworth Higginson, a Transcendentalist minister and TP protégé (Higginson's Worcester church was modeled on Parker's Boston society), who would later join him on the secret committee that financed John Brown.

50. See Albert J. Von Frank, *The Trials of Anthony Burns: Freedom and Slavery in Emerson's Boston* (Cambridge, MA: Harvard University Press, 1998); Pease and Pease, *Fugitive Slave Law*.

51. TP to Samuel Gridley Howe, September 26, 1854, Theodore Parker Papers, Moorland-Spingarn Research Center.

52. TP, *The Trial of Theodore Parker* (Boston, 1855; repr., New York, Negro University Press, 1970), 206. For more details, see TP's Anthony Burns Scrapbook, Theodore Parker Papers, Boston Public Library, part 2.

53. TP, *Trial*, vi, 9, 17.

54. TP, "A New Lesson for the Day," *WTP*, 14:257, 267.

55. Ibid., 14:248, 260.

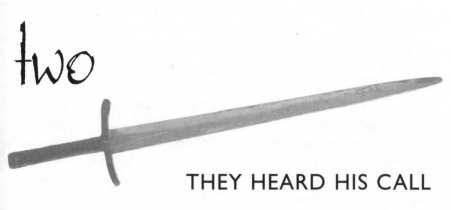

THEY HEARD HIS CALL

The Local Black Community's
Involvement in the Raid on Harpers Ferry

HANNAH GEFFERT

Conventional wisdom presumes that when John Brown moved on Harpers Ferry in October 1859 the local slave and free black community ignored his call and—with the exception of those slaves who were "threatened" by Brown's men—did not actively participate in the raid. However, a careful examination of why Brown chose Harpers Ferry and of what happened during and after the raid demonstrates that the local black community did, in fact, take an active part and was central to John Brown's actions.

EVENTS LEADING UP TO THE RAID

Following the *Dred Scott* decision in 1857, when it became obvious to Brown that slavery would not be ended by legislative or court action, he began seeking a new way to weaken slavery and to keep antislavery agitation vigorous.[1] He reasoned that if slavery could be driven out of a single county in one state, the whole system would be weakened in that state and in the country as a whole.[2] But which county and which state would offer Brown the best opportunity for success?

Brown studied census returns and the distribution of the black population. He made maps of fugitive slave routes. He knew about Denmark Vesey; insurrections in South Carolina, Virginia, and Tennessee; and about Nat Turner.[3] He studied the history of Haiti and Jamaica, reading everything he could on Toussaint L'Ouverture.[4] He knew about the activities of the Underground Railroad and of organized resistance in Pennsylvania and Maryland to the Fugitive Slave Act.[5] For many years, the mountains of Virginia had provided a comparatively safe route to freedom. Harriet Tubman, who participated in planning the raid, often used the Appalachian route, known as the Great Black Way, in her efforts to aid escaping slaves.[6] John Brown knew this. Decisive for Brown was the knowledge that the safest natural entrance to the Great Black Way was Harpers Ferry, Jefferson County, Virginia (plate 1).

Jefferson County was an unusual place in the South because of its high percentage of free blacks and nonslaveholding whites. It contained large and small farms, mills, and factories; people who made their living with and without the use of slave labor; and free blacks as well as slaves. The county had been settled by two distinct waves of immigration—one from the tidewater region of Virginia, the other from Pennsylvania. Virginians began sending overseers and slaves to the west side of the Shenandoah River as early as 1738.[7] And before 1738 free blacks and whites from Pennsylvania crossed the Potomac into western Virginia. The first settlers arrived in the county in the fall of 1731. They were Joist Hite, a German Quaker, and his family, accompanied by a free black family, the Johnsons, who in the 1720s had been purchased in eastern Virginia and "given immediate freedom."[8] Starting in the 1730s and 1740s, Pennsylvania Quakers began to make their way into the Shenandoah Valley.[9] Because both Southerners and Northerners had settled the area, political sentiment in Jefferson County reflected the full range of political alignment seen in the nation. From 1830 through 1860, the ratio of whites to blacks in the county remained constant at about two to one. There were about 540 free blacks, but slaves made up the vast majority of blacks.[10] Most slaves were scattered throughout the rural sections of the county, although some were in the towns, while the free black population was concentrated in small self-contained black communities or in towns. By the 1840s the free black population of Harpers Ferry, Bolivar, and Virginius Island was equal to that of the slave population.[11]

The U.S. armory supported an economy that attracted free blacks to Harpers Ferry. Free black women worked as cooks, laundresses, and housekeepers. While most men worked as laborers and harvesters, a few were businessmen who acquired some property. Additionally, contractors brought a number of free blacks to Harpers Ferry to construct buildings for the armory.[12] During the 1840s and 1850s the census shows that there were many white armorers in Harpers Ferry who had adult free blacks living with them, and in almost every house in Bolivar there were whites and blacks—either slave or free—living together.[13]

Free blacks also congregated in Johnsontown, five miles northwest of Charles Town in the Leetown-Bardane area. Johnsontown was a community of free blacks surrounded by white Quakers and Free Will Baptists who provided a buffer between the black community and the predominantly white county.[14] Within the protective walls of Johnsontown, a united and autonomous black community grew.

In Jefferson County, Quakers, as well as free blacks and slaves who operated the ferries in Harpers Ferry and in nearby Shepherdstown, aided fugitive slaves along the Great Black Way.[15] Loss of slave property was so prevalent in the area that a petition was sent to the Virginia state legislature requesting that a company be incorporated in Jefferson County to insure against such losses and urging that Pennsylvania be encouraged to pass laws that would make it possible to recapture slaves within its borders.[16] Brown was convinced that slavery could be most effectively attacked in Jefferson County. Harpers Ferry would be seized but not held. After the first blow, blacks from the North and from Canada would join Brown and in turn inspire support among the slaves. Slaves would be funneled North, along the Great Black Way, to freedom; a small cadre would stay with Brown. The fight would be carried on in the mountains of Virginia, North Carolina, and Tennessee, and then in the swamps of South Carolina.[17] Virginia's mountains would be an opportune place to begin a guerrilla war.

But before Brown could put his plan into action he wanted a "general convention or council" to "aid and countenance" his activities. He did not look to his white financial backers for this; seeking black support, he traveled to Chatham, Ontario, to meet with Martin Delany, who, Brown believed, would be able to orchestrate such an effort.[18]

It was not an accident that Brown sought out Delany, a native of Jefferson County, who was born in 1812 in Charles Town, only a few blocks from where

Local Involvement in the Raid on Harpers Ferry

Brown would be tried for treason. In 1822 the Delany family had been forced to leave Charles Town after Martin's mother, Pati Delany, was accused of violating the 1804 Virginia statute that prohibited teaching black children to read. The family was also in jeopardy because the eldest Delany son, Samuel Jr., was in the habit of forging passes for other family members. Eventually, the family moved to Chambersburg, Pennsylvania, which would later be used as the staging area for the raid on Harpers Ferry.[19] In Canada, Delany told Brown about his family, the environs of Harpers Ferry, and the attitudes of the local black population. Delany's stories and Brown's knowledge of the black network of independent churches, organizations, and the Underground Railroad assured him that in the region of Harpers Ferry he would find hundreds of blacks ready to fight for liberty. Many white abolitionists doubted that slaves would fight for their own liberty and accepted white preconceptions of the slave's character as being as "submissive as Uncle Tom."[20] Brown, however, rejecting the all but universal belief in the submissiveness of blacks, repeatedly stressed his belief that it was necessary for slaves to fight for their freedom. Unlike most whites, Brown had confidence in their willingness to fight.[21]

Moreover, Brown was aware that Northern, free blacks, denied admission into state militias, had formed their own military organizations, including the Massasoit Guards of Massachusetts, Attucks Guards of New York, Attucks Blues of Cincinnati, Loguen Guards of Binghamton, and Henry Highland Garnet Guards of Harrisburg, Pennsylvania.[22] Through information supplied by George G. Gill, an ally of Brown's in Kansas, Brown also knew of such organizations "in existence among the colored people . . . through most, or nearly all, of the slave states."[23] After the Fugitive Slave Act became law, Brown had organized a self-defense group of forty-four black men known as the League of Gileadites.[24] He also had firsthand knowledge of other black self-help groups, such as the League of Freedom, the Liberty League, the American Mysteries, and in Canada, the True Bands, which had several hundred members each.[25]

From his many discussions with free blacks, Brown anticipated that there would be a positive slave response, but the initial phase of his plan never included the assistance of a sizeable number of armed blacks.[26] Because travel by both slaves and free blacks was restricted, it was impossible to transport any significant number of black men, especially armed black men, to Harpers Ferry.[27] Brown's strategy, therefore, was to encourage black leaders like Frederick Douglass and Martin Delany to join him first.[28] After gaining the confidence of the black community through an initial success at Harpers Ferry, more men would join him, and it was then that the black militia and secret societies would supply aid and recruits.[29]

Brown's attempt to win the support of black leadership culminated in the Chatham Convention, arranged by Martin Delany at Brown's request.[30] Forty-six people—thirty-four blacks and twelve whites—attended the convention, which began May 8, 1858.[31] Two men who would be with Brown at Harpers Ferry, John Henry Kagi and Osborn Perry Anderson, were secretaries.[32]

The main order of business was the adoption of Brown's "A Provisional Constitution and Ordinances for the People of the United States," to serve as a code of conduct for the men fighting with Brown, and his election as commander in chief. There was limited debate on ratifying the constitution, with the exception of Brown's demand that the flag of the provisional government be the same one used during the American Revolution, insisting that he was "defending the Union and the Government" which he felt was threatened "by the existence of chattel slavery."[33]

Although Brown's constitution had been written at the home of Frederick Douglass, Douglass did not attend the Chatham Convention. Brown believed that Douglass's support was the key to winning the assistance of large numbers of Northern blacks and would give "the venture the air of credibility."[34] If Douglass, "the first great national Negro leader," would go to Harpers Ferry with him, others would follow.[35] Brown had first disclosed his plan to Douglass in 1847, telling him that he was "looking for colored men to whom he could safely reveal his secret." The object of Brown's plan was to destroy all the money value of slave property by "rendering such property insecure."[36] Brown rationalized his intended actions, saying that "slaveholders had forfeited their right to live; that the slaves had the right to gain their liberty in any way they could; [and that he] did not believe that moral suasion would ever liberate the slave, or that political action would abolish the system."[37]

Although Douglass agreed with Brown's objective and rationale, he "could never quite believe that John Brown's tremendous plan was humanly possible." Douglass and other black leaders also knew that if the project failed, black men would pay the cost. Perhaps Underground Railroad methods could be enlarged and systematized, Douglass argued; however "only national force could dislodge national slavery."[38]

Local Involvement in the Raid on Harpers Ferry

In a final appeal for Douglass's support, a conference was scheduled in Chambersburg for August 19, 1859, in an abandoned stone quarry on Conococheague Creek. The meeting place was arranged by a free black man, Joseph Richard Winters, whose father had made bricks for the arsenal at Harpers Ferry.[39] Henry Watson, whose barbershop was the center of the Underground Railroad operation in Chambersburg, escorted Douglass to the quarry. In planning for the raid, Brown was particularly interested in "learning of the colored men who could be trusted." He found allies in the black infrastructure that existed among independent black churches, organizations such as the Prince Hall Masons, and supporters of the Underground Railroad. Among those whom Brown identified as "reliable friend[s]" were Watson and Rev. Thomas Henry of Chambersburg.[40] Watson helped in preparations for the assault on Harpers Ferry, serving as general agent to forward men, mail, and freight from Chambersburg to the Kennedy farm in Maryland.[41] While waiting to travel into Virginia, the black members of John Brown's army boarded with Watson and his wife, Eliza.[42] Martin Delany, Joe Winters, Henry Watson, and Rev. Thomas Henry were all members of the St. James AME Church of Chambersburg.

Douglass characterized the meeting as being "in some sense a council of war." The men spent Saturday and Sunday conferring on the question of whether or not "the desperate step should then be taken." Douglass disagreed with Brown's strategy of going into Harpers Ferry proper, wanting instead to move into the mountains and begin the guerrilla aspect of the plan. Finally, Douglass told Brown that it was impossible for him to join the action, saying that he "could see Harper's [sic] Ferry only as a trap of steel, and ourselves in the wrong side of it."[43]

Also at the quarry meeting with Brown and Douglass were John Henry Kagi and Shields Green, usually known as the Emperor. About twenty-four, Green had escaped slavery in South Carolina after his wife died but had left a son behind still enslaved.[44] Brown had asked Douglass to bring Green, having previously met him at Douglass's house in February 1858.[45] At the quarry, Green listened as Douglass and Brown argued. When the meeting was over and Douglass was leaving, he asked Green if he were going with him. But the Emperor decided to go "with the old man," John Brown.[46]

Four other blacks joined John Brown at Harpers Ferry.[47] Osborn Perry Anderson, twenty-four, was a freeborn Pennsylvanian. A printer by trade, he met Brown in Canada. John A. Copeland Jr., twenty-two, was born free in

HANNAH GEFFERT

Raleigh, North Carolina, reared in Oberlin, Ohio, and educated at Oberlin College.[48] Lewis S. Leary, Copeland's uncle, was born a slave in North Carolina, reared in Oberlin, and had become a harness maker.[49] Dangerfield Newby was a freeman from the Shenandoah Valley with ties to the Harpers Ferry region. His wife and six children lived in slavery about thirty miles south of Harpers Ferry, in Warrenton. Harriet Newby, a seamstress, was pregnant and about to be sold to a New Orleans trader.[50] Because of his familiarity with the area, Newby was able to live within the community until the night of the raid, supplying Brown with information.[51]

Two of the white men with Brown also developed or had ties to the region. John Edwin Cook, originally from Connecticut, arrived in Harpers Ferry in June 1858, moving there as Brown's advance man. In Jefferson County he worked as a writing teacher and a map and book agent.[52] On April 27, 1859, Cook's local ties became more firmly established when he married Mary Virginia Kennedy, daughter of the owner of his Harpers Ferry boardinghouse. Like Newby, Cook supplied Brown with intelligence.[53] John Henry Kagi also knew the area. His father was from the Shenandoah Valley, and as a boy Kagi had lived with an uncle in the area and had drawn attention to himself by helping a slave escape.[54]

Brown was expected to begin carrying out his plan shortly after the Chatham Convention adjourned. He originally scheduled the raid for the summer of 1858, with Harriet Tubman suggesting the Fourth of July because of its symbolic value.[55] However, Brown's financial backers postponed the raid when Hugh Forbes threatened to reveal the conspiracy to influential political leaders in Washington, D.C.[56] Brown rescheduled the raid for 1859, although the exact date of the attack remained undecided. Kagi said the assault "was to be in the spring, when the planters were busy, and the slaves most needed."[57]

Brown then indicated he would strike on Independence Day, 1859.[58] But the raid was delayed again because the men and materials needed could not be assembled until October. Franklin Sanborn said that Brown had originally planned to strike "about" October 25 and that the timing of the raid caught Harriet Tubman unaware, coming while she was engaged in recruiting followers for him.[59] Richard Hinton was still in Chambersburg "at a black-operated Underground Railroad post," awaiting word to join Brown. In addition, reports from Ontario revealed that at the time of the raid, three black companies from Buxton, Chatham, and Ingersoll were on their way via Detroit to join Brown.[60] Meanwhile at the Kennedy farm, the date for the raid was changed yet again. The move on Harpers Ferry was made eight days earlier than the October 24 date on which Brown had settled. A local woman had spotted a black man at the farm. Rumors circulated that officials and neighbors were suspicious of activities there and that it would soon be visited by the sheriff. While law enforcement officials never came to the farm, Brown was aware that his real intentions might soon be exposed.[61]

How much local blacks knew about the raid is uncertain. Benjamin A. Matthews, a Storer College student who lived a generation after the raid, claimed that the local population believed the raid was to be on October 24 but that the date had been changed after a "council by the raiders."[62] News stories from New York indicate that the same date had been rumored among free blacks to be the beginning of a "rising all over the States of Maryland and Virginia." Brown had given orders to his men "to trust no one with our secret and to hold no conversation with the slaves."[63] Martin Delany wrote that in Jefferson County, slaves around the depot and house servants were trained to be suspicious and mistrustful of strange blacks.[64] There may have been, however, some breach of Brown's instructions "to hold no conversation with the slaves." For example, Hinton reported that Cook claimed he met a party of two freemen and two slaves before the raid and asked them if they ever thought about their freedom. They replied that "they thought they ought to be free," but expressed doubts that they ever would be. Cook told them that the "time might come before many years, but for the present to keep dark and look for the good time coming."[65] Similarly, Osborn Anderson, in an 1870 conversation in Washington, D.C., with Richard Hinton, estimated that there were at least one hundred and fifty actively informed slaves and "Negroes who tilled small areas of land and worked around who could be depended upon."[66] Given the importance of maintaining secrecy and Brown's constant vacillation as to when the raid would take place, it is no wonder that local blacks were surprised when the attack came on October 16 rather than October 24.

THE RAID

On October 16, 1859, John Brown led twenty-one men to Harpers Ferry, where he attacked and held the federal arsenal until a company of marines commanded by Lt. Col. Robert E. Lee and Lt. J. E. B. Stuart dislodged them the next day. Brown's raiders armed twenty-five to fifty slaves during the initial phase of the raid.[67] Osborn Anderson distributed pikes—to slaves who came with Brown's men from the plantations and to others who came forward without having had communication with any of the raiders—leading to early reports that the commander of the raid was a "colored man named Anderson." Cook and Charles Plummer Tidd also armed slaves. Among those who eagerly accepted weapons were several farmhands who had come in on hearing of the raid from "underground wires."[68] Eyewitness accounts tell of considerable local black activity: of "Negroes," in the early hours of the fight, being in and around "John Brown's Fort" and of slaves, with spears in their hands, being near the engine house.[69] One hostage said Harpers Ferry "looked like war—negroes armed with pikes, and sentinels with muskets all around."[70]

At least fourteen black men transported arms from the Kennedy farm to the schoolhouse.[71] Other blacks assisted at the schoolhouse and protected the weapons; still others guarded prisoners and the engine house.[72] They acted as messengers between Brown's men and spread news of the raid to the local community.[73] The result was that many blacks "gathered to the scene of action."[74]

The hillsides became congested with frightened people seeking refuge, and for a time armed slaves were seen in some numbers: "Armed and unarmed black and white" came to see what was happening.[75] The engineer of the train that had been stopped by the raiders took particular notice of a crowd of at least three hundred people, among whom were black men shouting that they "longed for liberty, as they had been in bondage long enough."[76] Troops fired across the Potomac to the Maryland side at black men who had been armed the day before at the Kennedy farm.[77] Forced to retreat, the armed black men scattered as troops crossed the bridge in pursuit.[78] As late as 1887, Andrew Hunter, John Brown's prosecutor, asserted that the mountains and woods were full of John Brown's men.[79]

Among the hostages taken by the raiders were Col. Lewis Washington (great-grandnephew of George Washington) and John Allstadt. Washington's slaves—Jim, Sam, Mason, and Catesby—and Allstadt's slaves—Henry, Levi, Ben, Phil, George, and Bill—were also taken to Harpers Ferry.[80] Washington's coachman Jim willingly accepted a pistol and a supply of ball cartridges from Brown's men. Jim was said to be one of the boldest combatants, fighting "like a tiger." When the engine house fell, however, Jim fled. He succeeded in reaching the Shenandoah River, only to drown near Hall's Rifle Works. He had "joined the rebels with a good will," reported the Virginia

Committee of Claims in turning down Dr. Fuller's petition for compensation for his loss of property.[81] Mason, another Washington slave, loaded weapons all day. Later he convinced Virginia authorities that he and the group with him returned to their masters as soon as they could escape.[82] Other local blacks who fought with Brown also tried to slip back to their masters.[83] During the battle, Allstadt's slave, Phil Luckum, knocked holes in the engine house wall to shoot through until he was mortally wounded.[84] Phil's brother, Ben, helped guard the Rifle factory, was arrested, and died in jail.[85]

On hearing of the raid, some black men immediately agreed to join, saying that they "had been long waiting for an opportunity of this kind."[86] Others firmly refused to take part; a house slave of Washington's declined to accept a pike. When told he was free and should fight for his liberators, he replied that he "was free enough before you took me. I am not going to fight until I see Massa Lewis fighting, and then I fights for him."[87]

But most of the slaves greeted news of the raid with "joy and hilarity." One old slave mother, upon hearing of Brown's work, cried, "God bless you! God bless you!" She then asked all present to kneel and offered a prayer to God for His blessing on the enterprise and for its success. Another old slave woman said the liberation of the slaves was the very thing she had longed for, prayed for, and dreamed about, time and again; and her heart was full of rejoicing over the fulfillment of a prophecy that had been part of her faith for many years. At the slave quarters, there was apparently general jubilee, and the slaves "stepped forward manfully with out [*sic*] impressing or coaxing." Osborn Anderson recalled that in only one case was there any hesitation: "A dark-complexioned freeborn man refused to take up arms, showing the only want of confidence in the movement, and far less courage than any slave consulted about the plan."[88]

Black men participated in the killing and the dying at Harpers Ferry. In the early morning, William Leeman, one of Brown's raiders, gave a double-barreled shotgun to an elderly slave. When a white townsman ignored the slave's orders to halt, the slave discharged his weapon's "terrible load" into the townsman, who "fell, and expired with out a struggle." When Dangerfield Newby was shot in the head, his "death was promptly avenged by Shields Green."[89] The first person to die in the raid was Heyward Shepherd, a "slave counted as free," employed by the Baltimore and Ohio Railroad as a baggage master.[90] The term "slave counted as free" was used to circumvent a Virginia law that required freed blacks to leave the state. Shepherd's former owner, and possibly still legal master, was Fontaine Beckham, the mayor of Harpers Ferry, who also died during the raid.[91] To this day there is no firm agreement about how many men died fighting with Brown. Reports vary from seventeen to twenty-seven. Only ten were with Brown at the Kennedy farm. The others, between seven and seventeen, were local blacks who joined Brown.[92] Of the men shot on the rocks when Kagi's party retreated to the river, some were slaves.[93] Mill workers poured "several hundred rounds of ammunition into three of Brown's men and three local slaves at Hall's Rifle Works."[94]

Others fled. Five of Brown's men managed to escape—Owen Brown, Tidd, Barclay Coppoc, Francis Merriam, and Osborn Anderson. William C. Goodridge, a wealthy black man in York, Pennsylvania, gave Osborn Anderson shelter during his escape and also assisted Merriam, delivering him to William Still of Philadelphia.[95] Richard Hinton, who had been waiting in Pennsylvania to join the raiding party, escaped from Chambersburg with the help of local blacks.[96]

Several local blacks are known to have escaped slavery at the time of the raid. Reginald Ross's father escaped and then returned after the Civil War. Charles Williams, who worked at the hotel, was not seen after the raid and presumably escaped.[97] A slave, "direct from the Harper's [sic] Ferry—passed through Syracuse on the Underground Railroad"; others were expected to follow the same route.[98] A fugitive slave from Harpers Ferry came into Auburn, New York, on his way to Canada. Reportedly, he was "the slave who guided John Brown into the arsenal at Harpers Ferry."[99] Following the Chatham Convention, Mary Ellen Pleasant, masquerading as a jockey, disseminated information in the Roanoke River area and other parts of the South about Brown's approaching assault on Harpers Ferry. After the raid, she too was forced to flee Virginia.[100]

In a deluded attempt to dishonor the dead supporters of Brown, Virginians threw black and white bodies into communal graves. Oliver Brown was pitched into a shallow trench on his back with Dangerfield Newby in his arms.[101] William Henry Leeman, Jeremiah G. Anderson, and Stewart Taylor were tossed together into the same grave, where they remained until students from the medical school in Winchester exhumed their bodies. The medical students also unearthed John Henry Kagi and others from their resting places on the banks of the Shenandoah. The hostility toward the black raiders was further illustrated by Gov. Henry A. Wise's refusal to give up the dead bodies unless "white men came after them."[102]

After the first excitement about the raid ebbed, it was replaced by fear as to how far Brown's conspiracy extended among slaves and free blacks. The entire South was put into a state of panic. Citizens of Richmond, Baltimore, and Washington voiced concern. Guards were posted in Charleston and New Orleans.[103] Virginia counties organized and strengthened mounted patrols, with orders to arrest any outsider unable to produce a local person as a reference. Within a four-week period, Baltimore arms dealers sold over ten thousand pistols to Virginia buyers.[104]

The brunt of anti-Brown sentiment fell on the free blacks. Old restrictions on them were strictly enforced and new ones added.[105] After the raid, Charles Town enacted a new ordinance prohibiting more than two free blacks or slaves from gathering on the streets at any one time.[106] In Virginia and Maryland all slaves who were "suspects," unruly, or turbulent were sold South, causing prices for slaves to fall.

According to George Sennott, a lawyer for Brown, Charles Town was "in a state of excitement and suspicion resembling insanity."[107] Lewis Washington was said to be "plenty scared" and "unwilling to return home for several days in fear of his slaves."[108] James Moore, a Harpers Ferry farmer, mistook the cry of a whippoorwill for the screams of his neighbors being murdered by abolitionists and blacks and rode to town warning the townspeople to arm themselves.[109] Rev. Charles White, in a letter to relatives in Massachusetts, stated that several masters had been "beaten or attacked by their servants" following the raid.[110]

A. R. H. Ranson noticed the effect the raid had on his slaves:

> At the time of the Raid, I was living on a farm six miles southwest from Charlestown, and therefore fourteen miles from Harpers Ferry, on this turnpike road. On Monday morning of the 20th of October 1859, I was overlooking the work of the men, who were cutting off corn in a field near Ripon, our post office station. I noticed that the men often turned their eyes on me as I followed behind them in their work,—a thing I had never observed before. There [*sic*] glances made me feel uncomfortable and doubtful,—an entirely new sensation in my experience as a slave owner.[111]

Anyone who expressed support for Brown's actions was "run out of town and told never to return."[112] Betsey Peats, a black woman, was arrested in

Bolivar and questioned before a judge regarding "suspicion of having communication with the conspirators." Peats admitted that she knew Cook and told stories about him and others of Brown's men. The authorities concluded the stories were lies, and "she was let off easy."[113] A squad of cavalry was sent to arrest a white man living near Charles Town who had aroused suspicion because of his "manner with the slaves." The arrest was never made because "the bird had flown."[114]

The presence of Northern reporters undermined Virginia's attempts to conceal support for the raid. Southern officials were apprehensive about the content of Northern correspondents' reporting of the trials, and later the hangings, because many Northern reporters had been in Kansas and had supported Brown.[115] The South preferred the reporting of loyal Virginians, who tried to reassure whites that they had nothing to fear from their slaves. Southern reporters de-emphasized the loyalty of the slaves and told of how blacks had been terrified as Brown's men approached, hiding themselves in barns, stables, and haystacks.[116] The South wished to portray slaves as cowards who preferred Virginia masters and slavery to freedom.[117] Governor Wise and his confederates wanted the world to believe that the slaves refused to join the insurrection, that they had been forced to join Brown, and that as soon as possible they returned to their masters.[118] John Brown, however, never lost faith in the black community's ability to fight for its liberation: "I knew, of course, that the Negroes would rally to my standard. If I had only got the thing started, you Virginians would have opened your eyes; and I tell you if I were free this moment, and had five hundred Negroes around me, I would put these irons on Wise himself before Saturday night."[119]

From the time Brown and his men were arrested until their executions, undeclared martial law prevailed in Jefferson County. Among the troops enforcing this state of affairs were members of local militia, some of whom had engaged in fighting with Brown's men before Robert E. Lee and the marines arrived, such as the Jefferson County Guards of Charles Town and the Hamtramck Guard, from Shepherdstown.[120] Troops were present from Frederick, Baltimore, and Hagerstown, Maryland, and Winchester, Virginia.[121] Additionally, volunteer companies poured into the county until over a thousand troops were present.[122]

Despite the massive presence of military force, black guerrilla activity persisted. A series of fires swept the region. "[T]he heavens are illuminated by the lurid glare of burning property," reported a Richmond daily.[123] Crops, stockyards, stables, haystacks, agricultural implements, and barns of slave-holders in Jefferson and Berkeley Counties were set afire, presumably by local blacks. Farmers, fearing fires, threshed wheat earlier than usual, rather than letting it stand until the other fall work had been done.[124]

On October 31, 1859, the *Virginia Free Press* reported the burning of the barn and stable of George Fole of Berkeley County, near Swan Pond, as the "work of a Negro boy." On November 10, it was reported that "three large straw ricks belonging to John LeRue," of Jefferson County, and "the granary and carriage house of Dr. Stephenson," near Cattleman's Ferry in Jefferson County, were destroyed by fire. Wheatland, the farm of George Turner, a slave owner killed during the raid on Harpers Ferry, was reported burning in the *New York Times* of December 3, 1859.[125] His brother, William F. Turner, had several of his horses and sheep die suddenly, as if by poison.[126] Property of John Burns, Walter Shirley, and George H. Tate—all of whom served on juries that convicted John Brown's men—was destroyed within the same week.[127] A January 12, 1860, petition sent to the General Assembly of Virginia from the citizens of Jefferson County asked that Walter Shirley, the foreman of the jury that convicted Brown, be compensated for losses. The petition stated, "There is not the shadow of a doubt but that the fire grew out of his connection with the trials."[128] Additional attempts were made on the premises of John Burns. The impression was strong that the "Abolition confederates of Brown & Co." were setting the fires.[129]

A letter to Governor Wise from one of the victims said that the guerrillas' method "partly was to fire stockyards and destroy property—they are now carrying it out—three stockyards have been burnt in this county alone since their capture and since their trial—last night one of mine was burned destroying not less than $2000 worth of property . . . we can only account for it on the grounds that it is Cook's instructions to our negroes."[130]

The commander of the troops in Jefferson County, Col. J. Lucius Davis, wired Governor Wise on November 19 that Negroes were setting the fires.[131] Colonel Davis asked Governor Wise for reinforcements. The governor sent five hundred more troops to Charles Town, but the fires continued.[132] Similarly, Edmund Ruffin wrote in his diary of his fears because Colonel Smith "thinks that if any rescue [of Brown] is attempted, it will begin by setting fire to the town."[133] Others might question whether the slaves and free blacks were capable of violent actions in support of freedom, but the people of Jefferson County were fearful of the possibilities.

The people closely associated with Brown continued to insist that not only was it vital for blacks to fight for their freedom but that they had the right. When the Civil War came, Frederick Douglass continually urged Lincoln to use black troops.

The first field commission awarded to a black man was presented, on direct orders from President Lincoln, to a Jefferson County native, Martin Delany.[134] Delany served as a major in the 104th United States Colored Troops, instructing other black officers.[135] And what of the other blacks associated with the raid? Osborn Anderson enlisted in 1864 and became a noncommissioned recruitment officer for the army until he was mustered out in Washington at the close of the war. John A. Copeland's brother William was commissioned as a second lieutenant in a colored light artillery company. And Harriet Tubman was affiliated with James Montgomery's black regiment, the Second South Carolina Volunteers.[136]

Many of Brown's white colleagues volunteered to serve with black troops. Richard Hinton was with the First Kansas Colored Volunteer Infantry (after 1864 known as the Seventy-Ninth U.S.C.I.), the "first body of colored men lawfully enlisted to fight for the union." John Bowles was a lieutenant colonel in the same unit.[137] Thomas Wentworth Higginson served as a colonel in a South Carolina black regiment.[138] During 1863, Francis J. Merriam recruited black soldiers on the South Carolina Sea Islands.[139] Two of the raiders, Barclay Coppoc (who was killed during the war) and Edwin Coppoc (who was executed after the raid), had a brother, Rev. Joseph Coppoc, who was a major in a colored infantry.[140]

Long after the war and John Brown had faded from others' memories, Harpers Ferry evoked deep emotion among black Americans. For many white Southerners, however, the raid on Harpers Ferry had epitomized abolitionism and the North. At the time of the raid, white Southerners believed that unless the South resorted to extreme measures, other aggression could be expected.[141] As Frederick Douglass said in a stirring speech given at Harpers Ferry twenty-two years after the raid, "If John Brown did not end the war that ended slavery, he did, at least, begin the war that ended slavery. If we look over the dates, places, and men for which this honor is claimed, we shall find that not Carolina, but Virginia, not Fort Sumter, but Harper's [sic] Ferry and the arsenal, not Major Anderson, but John Brown began the war that ended American Slavery, and made this a free republic."[142]

The most noteworthy John Brown observance was held during the week of August 15 through 19, 1906, at Harpers Ferry to commemorate the anniversary of his birth as well as the battle of Osawatomie. As a tribute to the memory of Brown, members of the Niagara Movement, newly founded by W. E. B. Du Bois, decided that Harpers Ferry would be the appropriate place to hold their first public meeting.[143] At dawn, Du Bois led forty-four members of the Niagara Movement on a barefoot pilgrimage to Murphy's farm, where John Brown's fort (the engine house) had been relocated.[144]

John Brown not only worked for blacks; he worked with them. He hired them in his business, addressed them respectfully as Mr. or Mrs., broke bread with them, shared home and church, sought their advice and approval.[145] He was a man without color prejudice.[146] He did not just talk of freeing the slaves; he acted. He understood that sacrifice was necessary to awaken the conscience of the nation but that the sacrifice of any number of black men might have no effect.[147] Many blacks knew it too. Even so, when John Brown called for people to join him in a great and terrible act to arouse the conscience of the nation, local people did answer his call. While others may belittle the role of the local black community in the raid, many who live in Jefferson County do not. In 1929 blacks from Jefferson County founded the Green-Copeland American Legion Post in honor of two of the black raiders. Their sacrifice and courage is remembered to this day.

NOTES

1. Frederick Douglass, "John Brown and West Virginia," *West Virginia State College Bulletin* 40, no. 6 (November 1953): 20.

2. Richard J. Hinton, *John Brown and His Men, With Some Account of the Roads They Traveled to Reach Harper's Ferry* (New York: Funk and Wagnalls, 1894), 26, 31.

3. Ibid., 30.

4. Ibid., 25, 183; William Fellows, Charles Town guard, to *New York Sun* reporter, February 13, 1898, cited in Benjamin Quarles, *Allies for Freedom: Blacks and John Brown* (New York: Oxford University Press, 1974), 111.

5. W. E. B. Du Bois, *John Brown* (1909; repr. New York: International Publishers, 1962), 97.

6. Hinton, *His Men,* reprint edition (New York: Arno, 1968), 34, 172; John Brown, *The Life and Letters of John Brown, Liberator of Kansas, and Martyr of Virginia,* ed.

Franklin B. Sanborn (1885; repr., New York: Negro Universities Press, 1969), 468, cited in Jean Libby, *Black Voices from Harpers Ferry* (Berkeley, CA: West Coast Printing Center, 1979), 147; Wilbur H. Siebert, *The Underground Railroad from Slavery to Freedom* (New York: Arno Press, 1968), 118.

7. F. Vernon Aler, *Aler's History of Martinsburg and Berkeley County, West Virginia* (Hagerstown, MD: printed for the author by Mail Publishing Company, 1888), 200.

8. Jerry M. Johnson III, *Johnsontown, West Virginia, Heritage Year Book* (self-published, 1987), 3.

9. Joint Committee of Hopewell Friends, *Hopewell Friends History, 1734–1934, Frederick County, Virginia* (Strasburg, VA: Shenandoah Publishing House, 1936), 12–98; Rufus M. Jones, *The Later Periods of Quakerism*, vol. 1. (London: Macmillan and Co. 1921), 388, cited in Larry D. Gragg, *Migration in Early America: The Virginia Quaker Experience* (Ann Arbor: University Microfilms International Research Press, 1980), 4.

10. Cassandra Smith-Parker, "Harpers Ferry National Historic Park, National Park Service," in *Afro-American History Interpretation at Selected National Parks*, comp. Department of History, Howard University, September 1978, Joseph E. Harris, project director, 17. In 1850, Jefferson County's population was 15,357 (10,476 white; 4,341 slaves; 540 free Negroes). The county had four main towns. Harpers Ferry was the largest, followed by Shepherdstown, Charles Town, and Bolivar.

11. Ibid., 17. In the Harpers Ferry–Bolivar area, whites outnumbered blacks nine to one, with approximately two hundred people of color in the two towns. Libby, *Black Voices*, 87.

12. Melinda Day, Shepherd College Oral History Project, no. 91–13.

13. David Larson, Shepherd College Oral History Project, no. 91–5.

14. James Fisher, Shepherd College Oral History Project no. 91–3.

15. Thomas Hahn, *Towpath Guide to the Chesapeake and Ohio Canal: Georgetown Tidelock to Cumberland*, 13th ed. (Shepherdstown, WV: American Canal and Transportation Center), 5, cited in Libby, *Black Voices*, 93.

16. *Shepherdstown Register* 1, no. 41 (September 3, 1850). On March 10, 1835, the "general assembly [*sic*]" incorporated "The Virginia Slave Insurance Company" at Charles Town (Legislative Petition B 308/10819). When the Fugitive Slave Bill was being debated in Congress a "faithful synopsis" was printed in the *Shepherdstown Register* because it was considered to be "a matter of peculiar importance in this section of the state."

17. James Redpath, *The Public Life of Capt. John Brown with an Auto-Biography of His Childhood and Youth* (Boston: Thayer and Eldridge, 1860), 203–5, cited in Du Bois, *John Brown*, 199–200.

18. Frank A. Rollin [Mrs. Whipple], *Life and Public Services of Martin R. Delany, Sub-assistant Commissioner Bureau Relief of Refugees, Freedmen, and of Abandoned Lands, and late Major 104th U.S. Colored Troops* (Boston: Lee and Shepard, 1883), 85–90, cited in Du Bois, *John Brown*, 254–55, repr. in Hinton, *His Men* (1968), 715.

19. James Surkamp, project director, *Delany: To Be More Than Equal*, teaching kit (SI, 1989), 6, 12, 13.

Local Involvement in the Raid on Harpers Ferry

20. Tilden G. Edelstein, *Strange Enthusiasm: A Life of Thomas Wentworth Higginson* (New Haven: Yale University, 1968); Stephen B. Oates, *To Purge This Land with Blood: A Biography of John Brown* (New York: Harper and Row, 1970), both cited in Jeffrey Rossbach, *Ambivalent Conspirators: John Brown, The Secret Six, and a Theory of Slave Violence* (Philadelphia: University of Pennsylvania Press, 1982), 8. Just before joining John Brown at the Kennedy farm, Frank J. Merriam visited Haiti to study the effects of its revolution on the "Negro character." Merriam returned to Haiti in the summer of 1860, hoping to organize a revolution of American slaves and to create a black nation in the Gulf states, islands in the Caribbean, and portions of South America. Hinton, *His Men* (1968), 571, 575.

21. Quarles, *Allies,* 13.

22. Ibid., 69.

23. George G. Gill's statement, as repr. in Hinton, *His Men* (1968), 710.

24. Du Bois, *John Brown,* 114.

25. Ibid., 243–44; Hinton, *His Men* (1968), 171–72.

26. Du Bois, *John Brown,* 247–48; Brown's outline of his plan to Sanborn, February 23, 1858, cited in Rossbach, *Ambivalent Conspirators,* 142.

27. Exhibit at Harpers Ferry National Historic Park, John Brown Museum, February 1991. Harpers Ferry passed a town ordinance in 1851 that ordered a ten o'clock curfew for slaves and free blacks. Curfew violators were subject to arrest, a fine, and ten lashes.

28. Du Bois, *John Brown,* 110, 294.

29. Ibid., 247–48; Hinton, *His Men* (1968),673–75; Redpath, *Public Life,* 203–5, cited in Wilbur H. Siebert, *The Underground Railroad from Slavery to Freedom* (New York: Arno Press, 1968), 167.

30. Du Bois, *John Brown,* 205.

31. Hinton, *His Men* (1968), 178.

32. Ibid. At the time of the raid, Delany was in West Africa exploring the Niger Valley with the hope of encouraging American black emigration to the region.

33. Ibid., 180.

34. Quarles, *Allies,* 76.

35. Du Bois, *John Brown,* 295.

36. Frederick Douglass, *Life of Frederick Douglass* (Boston: 1881), 280–81, 318–19; Hinton, *His Men* (1894), 30–32, cited in Siebert, *Underground Railroad,* 166, 339.

37. Frederick Douglass, *Life and Times of Frederick Douglass, Written by Himself* (Boston: DeWolfe & Fiske, 1892), part 2, ch. 8, 337–43, cited in Du Bois, *John Brown,* 105; Douglass, *Life,* ch. 10, 383–85, cited in Hinton, *His Men* (1968), 28.

38. Du Bois, *John Brown,* 109–10, 344.

39. Libby, *Black Voices,* 75.

40. Quarles, *Allies,* 77; Hinton, *His Men* (1968), 170, 246, 249. Thomas Henry was also connected with the Underground Railroad and the AME church. Thomas Henry was accused of assisting John Brown, and although he tried to deny any complicity with Brown, Henry was forced to flee after the raid.

41. Du Bois, *John Brown,* 292.

HANNAH GEFFERT

42. Hinton, *His Men* (1894), 249.

43. Douglass, "John Brown and West Virginia," 21–22.

44. Du Bois, *John Brown*, 280; Hinton, *His Men* (1968), 505.

45. Quarles, *Allies*, 76–77.

46. Hinton, *His Men* (1968), 507–8.

47. Du Bois, *John Brown*, 282; Hinton, *His Men* (1968), 267–68. Six men of color had been recruited by Lewis Hayden in Boston; but only one, John Anderson, a free-man, reached Harpers Ferry. Whether Anderson took part in the fight or returned to Boston or was killed at Harpers Ferry is unclear. The local Colored Elks suggest that John Anderson was killed at the rifle works battle. His name, however, is listed on the memorial to John Brown's men at the family farm in North Elba, New York, "as a Negro raider who escaped."

48. Du Bois, *John Brown*, 280, 281.

49. Quarles, *Allies*, 6; Du Bois, *John Brown*, 282; Hinton, *His Men* (1968), 505.

50. Hinton, *His Men* (1968), 266, 310. Dangerfield Newby had attempted to buy her from her owner, Jesse Jennings. Jennings had promised to sell Harriet and one child for one thousand dollars but then refused. Immediately after the raid, Harriet was sold and sent to Louisiana.

51. Du Bois, *John Brown*, 281.

52. Hinton, *His Men* (1968), 257.

53. Cook's information to Brown included the location of a sword presented by Frederick the Great to George Washington and a brace of pistols given Washington by General Lafayette. Understanding the symbolic importance of the relics, Brown had instructed Cook to become acquainted with Col. Lewis Washington, the owner of these trophies and a great-grandnephew of George Washington. Lewis Washington lived at Beall Air, near Halltown, about four miles west of Harpers Ferry near the Charles Town Road. It was Cook's idea to take Washington's sword and pistols, and he called on him to find out where he kept them. But it would be a black man, Osborn Anderson, to whom Washington would surrender Frederick the Great's sword and Lafayette's pistols, with which John Brown commanded his men at Harpers Ferry. Millard Kessler Bushong, *Historic Jefferson County* (Boyce, VA: Carr Publishing, 1972), 173, 175; Hinton, *His Men* (1968), 293, 468; *Weekly Anglo-African* (April 28, 1860), cited in Libby, *Black Voices*, 185.

54. Hinton, *His Men* (1968), 252.

55. Quarles, *Allies*, 51, 79; Brown, *Life*, 468.

56. Rossbach, *Ambivalent Conspirators*, 4. In a further attempt to discredit Brown, Forbes also had contact with J. McCune Smith of New York City, who was opposed to any black freedom movement that was not initiated and led by blacks. Brown had sought and gained the acquaintance of J. McCune Smith, but Smith rejected Brown's efforts. Smith and his followers favored a "separate and violent resistance" and "wanted no help from white men." Du Bois, *John Brown*, 97–98; Hinton, *His Men*, 162–63; Quarles, *Allies*, 53.

57. John Brown and Kagi, interview by Hinton, in Redpath, *Public Life*, repr. in Hinton, *His Men* (1968), 674.

41

58. Rossbach, *Ambivalent Conspirators,* 200.

59. Quarles, *Allies,* 82–83.

60. Franklin B. Sanborn, *Recollections of Seventy Years,* 2 vols. (Boston, 1909), 1:184; Sanborn, "The Virginia Campaign of John Brown," *Atlantic Monthly,* April 1875, 453; Hinton, "Old John Brown and the Men of Harper's Ferry," *Times* (London), August 1890, 824, cited in Quarles, *Allies,* 82–83.

61. Hinton, *His Men* (1968), 264–65, 270.

62. Benjamin A. Matthews, "Harper's Ferry and John Brown," *Storer Sentinel,* 1909, cited in Libby, *Black Voices,* 101.

63. John E. Cook's statement, repr. in Hinton, *His Men* (1968), 712.

64. Martin Delany, *Blake: The Huts of America* (Boston: Beacon Press, 1970), 119–21.

65. Cook's statement, in Hinton, 712.

66. Hinton, *His Men* (1968), 272–73.

67. Du Bois, *John Brown,* 314.

68. Hinton, *His Men* (1968), 294–95; Cook's statement, in Hinton, 713–14; Osborne P. Anderson, *A Voice from Harper's Ferry: A Narrative of Events at Harper's Ferry with Incidents Prior and Subsequent to the Capture of Captain John Brown and His Men* (1861; repr., Freeport, NY: Books for Libraries Press, 1972), repr. in Libby, *Black Voices,* 37.

69. Elijah Avey, *The Capture and Execution of John Brown,* cited in Libby, *Black Voices,* 102; Mr. Graham, interview by Dr. Featherstonehaugh, 1892, cited in Hinton, *His Men* (1968), 305; Cook's statement, in Hinton, 713.

70. John E. R. Dangerfield, "John Brown at Harper's Ferry," *Century,* June 1885, cited in Hinton, *His Men* (1968), 300.

71. Hinton, *His Men* (1968), 288; Cook's statement, in Hinton, 700–718, cited in Du Bois, *John Brown,* 314–15; Anderson, *Voice,* repr. in Libby, *Black Voices,* 37.

72. Hinton, *His Men* (1968), 550; Anderson, *Voice,* in Libby, *Black Voices,* 60.

73. Hinton, *His Men* (1968), 293; Cook's statement, in Hinton, 710.

74. Anderson, *Voice,* in Libby, *Black Voices,* 34.

75. Hinton, *His Men* (1968), 298.

76. Thomas Drew, comp., *The John Brown Invasion* (1892; repr., Freeport, NY: Books for Libraries Press, 1972), 6, cited in Libby, *Black Voices,* 104–5.

77. Hinton, *His Men* (1968), 516.

78. Anderson, *Voice,* in Libby, *Black Voices,* 52.

79. Hinton, *His Men* (1968), 291.

80. *Baltimore Weekly Sun,* October 22, 1859, cited in Bushong, *Jefferson County,* 187.

81. Quarles, *Allies,* 100–101; Hinton, *His Men* (1968), 295, 511, 530.

82. D. E. Henderson to unknown, cited in Libby, *Black Voices,* 138.

83. Thomas Higginson, *Cheerful Yesterday* (New York: Arno Press, 1968), 229.

84. Jennie Chambers, "What a School-Girl Saw of John Brown's Raid," *Harper's Monthly Magazine* 104 (January 1902); "Reminiscence of Thomas Allstadt," *Springfield Sunday Republican,* Boyd B. Stutler Collection, West Virginia State Archives, Charleston, cited in Libby, *Black Voices,* 121–22 (in this source the name is given as "Phil Lucker").

85. Anderson, *Voice,* in Libby, *Black Voices,* 60.

86. Ibid., 34.

87. *Shepherdstown Register,* November 12, 1859, cited in Quarles, *Allies,* 100.

88. Anderson, *Voice,* in Libby, *Black Voices,* 35, 59.

89. Hinton, *His Men* (1968), 298; Anderson, *Voice,* in Libby, *Black Voices,* 38, 40.

90. *Baltimore Weekly Sun,* October 22, 1859, cited in Bushong, *Jefferson County,* 180.

91. Libby, *Black Voices,* 91.

92. Anderson, *Voice,* in Libby, *Black Voices,* 61; Hinton, *His Men* (1968), 388. Col. Robert Baylor, the local commander, cited five more deaths among Brown's men at the end of Monday's fighting than can be accounted for, or four if one counts John Anderson as being present.

93. Anderson, *Voice,* in Libby, *Black Voices,* 60.

94. Thomas C. Miller and Hu Maxwell, *West Virginia and Its People* (New York: Lewis Historical, 1913), 307, cited in Libby, *Black Voices,* 94.

95. I. H. Betz, "Some Historic Houses of York County," *York (PA) Gazette,* October 5, 1912, cited in Libby, *Black Voices,* 170–71.

96. Libby, *Black Voices,* 177.

97. Ibid., 140–41.

98. *Virginia Free Press,* January 19, 1860, cited in Libby, *Black Voices,* 141.

99. *Shepherdstown Register,* January 28, 1860, repr. from *Auburn (NY) Advance,* January 18, 1860, cited in Libby, *Black Voices,* 141.

100. Mary Ellen Pleasant's statement appears in Earl Conrad, "She was a friend of John Brown," *Negro World Digest* 1 (1940): 9, cited in Libby, *Black Voices,* 102; manuscript, West Virginia University Archives, cited in Frederick Douglass, "John Brown and West Virginia," *Virginia State College Bulletin* 40, no. 6 (November 1953): 2.

101. Hinton, *His Men* (1968), 580.

102. Ibid., 511, 581. It was not until 1882 that John Brown Jr. was able to retrieve the bones of his brothers Oliver and Watson and bring them home to be buried next to their father. Watson Brown's skeleton had been on exhibit at the Winchester Medical School until it was taken to Indiana in 1862 by a Union surgeon. When the medical college was burned to the ground by the Union army, the remains of Copeland and Green were lost. Forty years after Harpers Ferry, the bodies of Dangerfield Newby and Lewis S. Leary were finally given a decent burial on John Brown's North Elba farm. Heyward Shepherd was buried with military honors in Winchester. Quarles, *Allies,* 103, 142, 173; Hinton, *His Men* (1968), 310, 581.

103. Hinton, *His Men* (1968), 325.

104. Quarles, *Allies,* 107.

105. Ibid., 159.

106. Exhibit at Harpers Ferry National Historic Park, John Brown Museum, February 1991.

107. Quarles, *Allies,* 106.

108. Story collected by Libby from a descendent of Samuel Strider, who presented the local militia's surrender terms to Brown; Richard Webb, ed., *The Life and Letters*

of Captain John Brown (1861; repr., Westport, CT: Negro Universities Press, 1972), 163, cited in Libby, *Black Voices,* 156.

109. Quarles, *Allies,* 106.

110. Libby, *Black Voices,* 119.

111. A. R. H. Ranson "Reminiscences of the Civil War by a Confederate Staff Officer," *Shawnee Review* 21 (October 1913): 439.

112. Exhibit at Harpers Ferry National Historic Park, John Brown Museum, February 1991.

113. *New York Herald,* October 26, 1859, cited in Libby, *Black Voices,* 100.

114. Andrew Hunter. "John Brown's Raid," *Publications of the Southern History Association* 1, no. 3 (1897): 177.

115. Hinton, *His Men* (1968), 103, 458, 507–8. Those supporters of Brown who wrote for the newspapers included Wendell Phillips of the *New York Tribune;* James Redpath of the *Missouri Democrat;* William Hutchinson, S. F. Tappan, and James M. Winchell of the *New York Times;* Hugh Young of the *New York Tribune* and Pennsylvania papers; and Anderson of the *Boston Advertiser.* Hinton had written for the *Boston Traveler* and the *Chicago Tribune.* And John Henry Kagi, who died at Harpers Ferry, had contributed articles to the *New York Evening Post* and *Tribune,* the *Washington National Era,* the *Kansas Tribune,* the *Lawrence (KS) Republican,* the *Chicago Tribune,* and the *Cleveland Leader.*

116. Alexander Boteler, "Recollections of the John Brown Raid," *Century,* July 1883, 399–411, cited in Quarles, *Allies,* 104.

117. Anderson, *Voice,* in Libby, *Black Voices,* 59.

118. Meeting in Toronto, reported in *Weekly Anglo-African,* April 28, 1860, cited in Libby, *Black Voices,* 185.

119. Brown, *Life,* 571–72, cited in Libby, *Black Voices,* 106.

120. Bushong, *Jefferson County,* 181.

121. Hinton, *His Men* (1968), 299.

122. These included the Alexandria Riflemen, Alexandria Artillery, Mt. Vernon Guards, Richmond Howitzers, Richmond Grays, Morgan Continentals, Petersburg Artillery, Upper Fauquier Cavalry, Lower Fauquier Cavalry, Virginia Rifles, Petersburg Guards, Petersburg Grays, Wheeling Rifles, Virginia State Wheeling Fencibles, and cadets from Virginia Military Institute. Bushong, *Jefferson County,* 197.

123. Quarles, *Allies,* 108.

124. Ibid.

125. Correspondence of the *Baltimore American,* cited in Libby, *Black Voices,* 176; Oswald Garrison Villard, *John Brown, 1800–1859: A Biography Fifty Years After* (1920; repr., New York: Alfred A. Knopf, 1943), 520, cited in Robert L. Bates, *The Story of Smithfield (Middleway), Jefferson County, West Virginia* (Lexington, VA: 1958), 135–36.

126. Quarles, *Allies,* 108.

127. Correspondence of the *Baltimore American,* in Libby, *Black Voices,* 176; Villard, *John Brown,* 520, in Bates, *Smithfield,* 135–36.

128. Archives of Virginia, Legislative Petitions, B 468/19846, Jefferson County, January 12, 1860.

129. Correspondence of the *Baltimore American,* printed in the *Dollar Pennsylvanian* (Philadelphia), November 26, 1859, cited in Libby, *Black Voices,* 176.

130. J. W. Ware to Governor Wise, November 1859, Boyd B. Stutler Collection, West Virginia State Archives, Charleston, cited in Libby, *Black Voices,* 175–76.

131. Quarles, *Allies,* 108.

132. Bushong, *Historic Jefferson County,* 197.

133. William K. Scarborough, ed. *The Diary of Edmund Ruffin* (Baton Rouge: Louisiana State University Press, 1972), 363.

134. Surkamp, *Delany,* 9.

135. Victor Ullman, *Martin R. Delany: The Beginning of Black Nationalism* (Boston: Beacon Press, 1971), 295.

136. Hinton, *His Men* (1894), 505, 568; Villard, *John Brown;* Anderson, *Voice,* 2d ed. (Washington: J. D. Enos, 1893); biographical sketch of Anderson, repr. in Libby, *Black Voices,* 201–2; Earl Conrad, *Harriet Tubman* (Washington, DC: Associated Publishers, 1943), 170, cited in Libby, *Black Voices,* 203.

137. Hinton, *His Men* (1968), 48.

138. Rossbach, *Ambivalent Conspirators,* 274.

139. Camp 3d Regt., SC Infantry, July 7, 1863, cited in Hinton, *His Men* (1968), 576.

140. Libby, *Black Voices,* 203; Hinton, *His Men* (1968), 491. Barclay Coppoc and Charles Tidd died in service. Tidd, Luke F. Parsons, Charles W. Moffett, and Richard Realf, all of whom attended the Chatham Convention, were commissioned officers. Lt. Col. Richard Metternich, who was to have gone with Hinton to rescue Stevens and Hazlett (two of Brown's Harpers Ferry raiders), died in Texas.

141. Du Bois, *John Brown,* 355.

142. Frederick Douglass, speech at Storer College, Harpers Ferry, May 30, 1882 (correctly, 1881), cited in Du Bois, *John Brown,* 353. Douglass's speech was given outside Lincoln Hall as part of the celebration of the fourteenth anniversary of Storer College.

143. *Spirit of Jefferson* (Charles Town), August 14, 1906, 5.

144. W. E. B. Du Bois, *The Autobiography of W.E.B. DuBois* (New York: International Publishers, 1968), 251.

145. Du Bois, *John Brown,* 99.

146. Quarles, *Allies,* 13.

147. Reminiscences of J. M. Jones, in James Cleland Hamilton, *John Brown in Canada: A Monograph* (Toronto, 1894), repr. from *Canadian Magazine,* December 1894, 16, cited in Du Bois, *John Brown,* 263.

HOW REV. THOMAS W. HENRY OF
THE AME CHURCH MET JOHN BROWN

JEAN LIBBY

It was a cold November morning in Baltimore in 1859 when Rev. Thomas W. Henry, a sixty-five-year-old minister in the African Methodist Episcopal Church, picked up the *Baltimore Sun* and found himself on the front page:

SUSPECTED SYMPATHIZERS WITH BROWN

Among Brown's papers was found an abstract of a letter in Brown's handwriting, in which the name of Thomas Henry, for many years a colored clergyman of Hagerstown Md., and long suspected of improper intercourse and intimacy with the abolitionists of the North, is significantly mentioned. The Hagerstown Herald states that Henry has, within the last six months, sold off his property and left the State. Brown's allusion to him shows pretty conclusively that he has been one of his confidential friends.[1]

Taken by surprise at the story—Henry had neither met Brown nor participated in the planning of the raid—Henry spent the next ten days in Baltimore seeking advice alternately from his former owner, Judge John Thomson Mason, and black abolitionists George T. Watkins and his cousin, writer Frances Ellen Watkins (later Frances Watkins Harper), who was deeply involved with John Brown's plans. A recent widower, Henry was in Baltimore arranging board and tuition for his teenage son at Watkins's school on Tessier Street, near the Orchard Street AME Church, an active station on the Underground Railroad.[2]

A series of letters ensued between Judge Mason and Governor Wise of Virginia, who also received two letters from two Maryland whites, insisting that "the finger of suspicion has been almost universally pointed to this negro as being privy to and aiding the escape" of slaves for twenty years and that his son Rev. John R. Henry "made a sudden trip to Harrisburg" (where an abortive rescue of John Brown was underway) from his Havre de Grace pulpit right after the raid.[3]

In the interim, Thomas Henry had agreed to a plan proposed by Senator Reverdy Johnson (D-MD), the recent victorious attorney in *Dred Scott v. Sandford*. Henry was to confront John Brown in the Charles Town jail and ask him face to face to confirm Henry's contention that the two had never met.[4] Instead, the minister secretly left Baltimore by train on November 19, assisted by the wife of Brother William Smith, a lay AME minister, who entertained the police with food and stories of Henry's imminent return to her home.

Frances Ellen Watkins was meeting in Philadelphia in November 1859 with William Still, Lucretia Mott, and John Brown's wife, Mary Day Brown. Mrs. Brown was making plans to bring her husband's body home after his December 2 execution. Watkins was best known by John Brown's family and friends as the author of the poem "Bury Me in a Free Land," which Oliver Brown had brought to Chambersburg before the raid.[5] Watkins was one of the earliest donors to Mary Day Brown, assisting her with money on November 14, and she wrote directly to Brown in jail on November 25.[6] Her advice, and that of her cousin George, prevailed in persuading the elderly minister that if he went to Charles Town, he would probably not be allowed to return.

Rev. Thomas Henry remained in the North throughout the Civil War, during which one of his sons served in the Maryland Band Brigade and his youngest son, left in Baltimore, died. Thirteen years after Brown's death,

Henry wrote an autobiography in which he described the events surrounding his escape North and that "good old saint," John Brown. It is the only known primary source on the raid by a contemporary local black resident. He was eagerly pursuing newspaper stories about the raid when his name turned up among John Brown's papers. Henry considered it very natural that the "good old saint" would have "merely a memorandum to find me with."[7]

John Brown came to the areas of Henry's rural ministry. In the summer of 1859, Henry had served as minister in the western Maryland community directly across from Harpers Ferry, where Brown had established his army headquarters. In 1845 he had been pastor at the St. James AME Church in Chambersburg, Pennsylvania, where John Brown's army gathered before the raid. In 1857, Henry had held a revival at St. James Church. One of its members, Joseph R. Winters, owned the land next to the quarry where John Brown and Frederick Douglass held their secret meeting in August 1859.[8] Another St. James member, Henry Watson, hosted Douglass in Chambersburg. Douglass describes Watson as housing the black members of John Brown's army as they came in, ready to be taken by wagon at night from Chambersburg to the Kennedy farmhouse in Maryland, Brown's staging headquarters for the raid, rented in the summer of 1859.[9] It was certainly in Chambersburg that John Brown, looking for "reliable friends" among the black population, was told about Thomas Henry of Hagerstown, which was halfway between Brown's two headquarters. In a letter probably written on July 12, Brown told his Chambersburg command leader, John Kagi:

> Look for letters directed to John Henrie, at Chambersburg, directed I. Smith & Sons. . . . See Mr. Henry Watson at Chambersburg and find out if the Tribune comes on. Have Mr. Watson and his *reliable* friends get ready to receive company. Get Mr. Watson to make you acquainted with his reliable friends, but do not appear to be in any wise thick with them, and *do not often be seen with any such men.* Get Mr. Watson to find out, *if he can,* a trusty man, or men, to stop with at Hagerstown (if any such there be), as Mr. Thomas Henrie has gone from there.[10]

It is reasonable to wonder why historians have not included the events surrounding Thomas W. Henry in studies of Brown. There are several explanations. First, the letter from Brown to Kagi was found in Brown's carpetbag, which was confiscated from the Maryland farmhouse and given to Virginia authorities after the raid. The letter was published in local papers but then lost when all the Brown material was hidden during the Civil War. It was rediscovered in 1893. One of the earliest Brown biographers, Richard Hinton, subsequently "explained away" the name by writing that John Kagi (whose middle name was Henry) had used the alias John Henrie while gathering arms in Chambersburg. Brown had used the same spelling, Henrie, in his letter to Kagi about Thomas Henry. Hinton—a coconspirator with Brown in Hagerstown at the time of the raid—said Brown was referring cryptically to Aaron Stevens.[11]

Second, later historians ignored both Henry Watson and Thomas Henry— or Henrie—until 1974, when Benjamin Quarles wrote *Allies for Freedom.* Quarles found the corroborating front-page newspaper report in the *Baltimore Sun;* and in the Library of Congress he found letters that Judge John Thomson Mason wrote to Governor Wise about the AME minister, whose character and whereabouts he vouched for according to Maryland laws regarding the monitoring of free persons of color. Although Henry was free in 1859, Mason's father had been the executor for Richard Barnes. A local historical association, Franklin County Heritage, Inc., published the letter again in full in 1977, researching further details on Henry Watson, who fought in the U.S. Colored Troops in the Civil War.[12]

Third, there was still no corroborating primary source from Thomas Henry's viewpoint, since the *Autobiography of Rev. Thomas W. Henry of the A.M.E. Church,* published in pamphlet form by the AME Book Rooms in 1872, was not known. Even the church's publishing house lost the record. Henry and his connection to Brown's raid was mentioned, but not fully described, in two other AME ministerial autobiographies, which were subsequently microfilmed and indexed in the historic black biography project in 1991.[13]

Indeed, Rev. Thomas W. Henry was not lost; scholars were. The only known copy of the original work found its way to the Moorland-Spingarn Collection at Howard University in Washington, D.C.[14] This African American primary source was not only important in relation to John Brown's raid, but—since Henry had been enslaved from 1794 to 1821—it was an unknown slave narrative as well. Thomas Henry wrote much more than the story of his escape from arrest because of suspected complicity with John Brown, or even of his rural ministry. He was a blacksmith in his youth, and during his ministry was a pastor in slave ironworking communities. His is the only written social history of this experience from within this laboring group of men and women enslaved in southern ironworks until the 1860s.[15] Ultimately, on the 200th anniversary of Thomas Henry's birth, my transcribed, documented, and illustrated edition was published by the University Press of Mississippi, with a foreword by the Maryland chief archivist, Edward C. Papenfuse.[16]

Although Henry was not involved in the raid on Harpers Ferry, it is interesting to ask why he was recommended to John Brown as a "trusty man" by members of the St. James Church, for whom he was pastor in 1845 and presiding elder in 1856. Thomas W. Henry was born in 1794. That year, his owner, Richard Barnes, was the largest slave owner in St. Mary's County, Maryland. At his death in 1804, Barnes willed all those in bondage to him to be freed, but his executor, John T. Mason (related to Virginian George Mason of the American Revolution and the father of Judge John T. Mason), arranged to have the younger members of the group bound as apprentices to cover the expense of caring for infants and the aged. At first Mason moved the entire enslaved group to his home in Georgetown (he had been appointed attorney for Washington, D.C., by Thomas Jefferson).[17] By 1820 he had moved the group to Montpelier, the Barnes family home in western Maryland, near Hagerstown. Tom's parents, Tom and Jenny, had been freed in 1811, but Mason, as executor of the will, allowed them to remain on the plantation in order to raise their own children. A provision of the Barnes will was that all those manumitted would be required to take the last name Barnes. Henry does not discuss this matter, or why he determinedly kept his family name, Henry, or its origin. His certificate of freedom in 1821, when he was legally twenty-one but actually twenty-seven years old, is in the name Thomas Barnes. By the 1830 census, he is known as Tom Henry, blacksmith; in 1840 and 1850, he is Thomas Henry, clergyman.

After his manumission, Henry returned to Hagerstown, where he married sixteen-year-old Catherine Craig, a slave living nearby. Catherine's owner had promised that he would free her when she turned thirty-one, but Henry, seeing his children born into perpetual slavery, purchased her and two of their four children in 1827 for nine hundred dollars. Henry did not have enough money to pay for the two oldest children, who were probably twins, and they were sold away. The fact that Rev. Henry placed this experience at the very end of his narrative, where African American autobiographers often revealed what was most important or painful, is evidence of his bitterness about it.

During his childhood, the slaves at Barnes's plantation were permitted to receive religious instruction from a Jesuit mission in Leonardtown. Once provided with this rudimentary education, Henry continued to teach himself using the Bible and the Methodist *Book of Discipline* after his conversion. He converted to Methodism at a camp meeting, encouraged by the family of his employer at the forge, an antislavery German Methodist to whom he was apprenticed.

Henry was ordained as a lay minister in the Methodist Episcopal Church in 1828, then broke away in 1834 over the issue of slave-owning church officials. He then joined the African Methodist Episcopal Church, which was undergoing rapid growth among free blacks in Maryland, Pennsylvania, and New Jersey. He became well known for his preaching and singing abilities in the rural areas of western Maryland, where whites sometimes came to hear him. His autobiographical narrative, written years later, describes the growing restrictions on integrated gatherings before the Civil War.

The AME circuits followed the route of the National Road in Maryland and Pennsylvania. Thomas Henry was part of the second generation of AME ministers, who built small congregations and stabilized them, traveling hundreds of miles by horse and staying at the homes of parishioners. These black congregations in western Maryland were the base for the Underground Railroad connection in western Pennsylvania that John Brown was looking for in his search for "Mr. Thomas Henrie of Hagerstown." Ambassador Ronald D. Palmer, born in Uniontown, Pennsylvania, and a descendant of a local U.S.C.T. soldier, states that "Reverend Henry's direct role in the Underground Railroad is not established," but the letters from whites accusing him of being involved with the UGRR "support the view that probably the Uniontown churches and those in the Monongehela River valley leading to Pittsburgh and the northwest were linked closely with the Maryland churches pastored by Reverend Henry."[18] These written routes were intended by Brown to support the slaves he would lead from the South.

Henry was a scrapper, often getting involved in or even creating controversies among congregation members. The church bishops sent him to discipline members and ministers. He was a "mountain man," rejected by the urban Washington congregation that is now the Metropolitan AME, the flagship church of the denomination. Henry used his white connections from his early years as a slave both for legal protection and for authority in areas of his ministry, when he acted as a mediator between the white and black communities. In

How Rev. Henry Met John Brown

Washington his white associates belonged to the Foundry Methodist Church. In Henry's time, these white Methodists were solid citizens, professionals, and businessmen, unlike the large slave owners, who were more likely to be Episcopalians. Further, in 1827, Rev. Henry was an agent for the American Colonization Society, before Maryland began establishing its own organization to resettle manumitted people in Liberia. He interacted in this regard with white ironworks owners John McPherson and John J. Merrick, whom he mentions favorably in his *Autobiography;* however, he does not mention the American Colonization Society, its work, or his own role as an official agent.[19]

Henry lived with his family in western Maryland, just below the Mason-Dixon Line. In 1845 the AME bishops assigned Henry to the Caroline District of the Pennsylvania circuit, which included St. James AME in Chambersburg. Many of the AME churches in Chambersburg, Lancaster, and the surrounding region had been originally organized by the first generation of AME leaders: Richard Allen, Daniel Coker, and James Champion.[20] This was Henry's first assignment in a free state. In order to travel back and forth between Maryland and Pennsylvania, he needed permission from the authorities in Maryland. He obtained that permission through the intervention of John Thomson Mason, the son of John T. Mason, who had been the executor responsible for Henry after the death of Richard Barnes in 1804. John Thomson Mason was by this time (1845) a thirty-year-old member of the Maryland legislature. He would later become a federal judge. This connection to John Thompson Mason would continue and later become even more crucial for Thomas Henry. Indeed, it would be the same Judge Mason who would help Henry in 1859 when he was under investigation for his connection to John Brown. At that time, Judge Mason would introduce Thomas Henry to Reverdy Johnson and would also write to Governor Wise, effusively praising his good character. In this letter to Wise, Mason praised Henry as a man "of good character, except so far as it may have been affected by the suspicion which usually attaches itself to all itinerant colored clergymen."[21]

Henry's assignment to Pennsylvania in 1845 brought him in contact with Martin R. Delany, the black nationalist leader who convened John Brown's convention in Chatham, Ontario, in 1858. Delany was an early member of St. James AME in Chambersburg. While Delany's childhood association with John Brown's jailer in Charles Town is well known, his relationship to the owner of the boarding house in Chambersburg where John Kagi managed the arms shipments coming to the local warehouses, is not. Joseph Ritner, governor of Pennsylvania, had assisted Delany in a legal matter in the 1840s. Mary Ritner, who owned the boardinghouse at 225 King Street, was the widowed daughter-in-law of the former governor.[22]

Delany was active in the congregation, which had been founded in 1811. Members of his family remained in Chambersburg after Delany moved to Pittsburgh, where he published a newspaper until he moved to Boston to attend Harvard University medical school—the first African American to do so. Despite being forced to leave Harvard because of opposition from white students, Delany eventually became a physician. He later moved to Canada, where he provided medical care for fugitive slaves and other blacks who sought more secure freedom under the protective mantle of Queen Victoria. While in Canada, he helped avert a cholera epidemic by educating the Chatham community about the need for better sanitation. He was also an editor of the *Provincial Freeman,* published by Isaac Shadd and Mary Ann Shadd Cary, whose offices housed the convention over which Delany presided in May 1858 at the behest of John Brown. During this period, Frances Watkins also wrote regularly for the *Provincial Freeman.*[23]

After the death of his wife, Catherine Craig Henry, in 1857, Rev. Henry was assigned to AME circuits on Maryland's Eastern Shore and in western Pennsylvania. Thus, in 1857 and 1858, when Brown was planning his raid at meetings in Canada and making contacts in Chambersburg, Henry would have had no opportunity to interact with Brown or any of the other conspirators. By the time John Brown arrived in Chambersburg, Henry had been transferred to Talbot County. As a recent widower, Henry was struggling to raise his youngest son, Louis M. Henry. At the same time he had to deal with suspicious whites looking hard at a new free black minister from the independent black church. During this period, Henry brought his teenage son to board with AME minister William Smith in Baltimore and enrolled him in the school of black abolitionist Rev. George T. Watkins, also AME.

Although Rev. Thomas Henry was associated with prominent abolitionists in Baltimore, who were directly connected with Brown, he does not state whether he would have assisted Brown's raid. Still, his lack of surprise at Brown's interest in him (which recognized his leadership in the community) suggests that he participated in abolition efforts in Maryland and Pennsylvania, including aiding fugitives. It was probably church members who gave Brown Henry's name as "a trusty man." John Brown learned that "Mr.

How Rev. Henry Met John Brown

Thomas Henrie has gone from there" when he stayed at the Washington Hotel in Hagerstown on June 30, 1859 (where he signed the register as I. Smith & Sons of New York).[24]

Showing remarkable trust in a system that denied him citizenship, Thomas Henry insisted that he would go to Virginia and confront John Brown. This was the only way he felt he could prove the truth of his denial of any connection to Brown. However, Henry's AME friends convinced him to instead head north to a free state at once rather than jeopardize his liberty by going to the jail at Charles Town. While Maryland officials were searching for Henry to extradite him to Virginia, his friends used delaying tactics to protect him. Mrs. William Smith invited police into her home and fed them, pretending that Henry would be returning shortly. Meanwhile, Henry was on his way to the railroad station. Henry's train passage was purchased with the help of a white Freemason. Like many AME leaders, Henry was a Prince Hall Mason. Henry's statement, "because he knew I was the widow's son," at the close of his escape narrative is a coded message identifying him as a Mason:

> The Sunday before I left, I went to down to Short street to see a friend named Benjamin Sayles, who I requested to take me to the Philadelphia depot on the following Monday morning. He was too busy to come for me on Monday, but came Tuesday morning, and took me to the depot and left me there, seeming to be anxious to rid himself of me. At that time a colored person could not leave the city of Baltimore unless he was vouched for by some responsible white person. I looked around and saw a very fine looking gentleman coming toward me. He asked me if I wanted to get on the cars, and I said that I did. He told me not to go to the office, but to give him my baggage and get in the cars, and pay my fare after the cars had left the city. I was informed that, in about ten minutes after I left Brother Smith's house, two officers came for me. Brother Smith's wife told them that I put up there, and might be in after a while. They loafed around the house until midday, by which time I was nearly in Philadelphia. When we got about six miles from Baltimore, the conductor came around for the tickets. He did not ask me for a ticket, but asked if I was going to Philadelphia. I told him I was, and he asked me for two dollars, which paid my fare. The gentleman that I had met at the depot had made this little friendly arrangement for me, as he knew that I was the widow's son.[25]

It was in Philadelphia that Thomas W. Henry finally met John Brown. Henry was part of a demonstration of African Americans at the train station when "John Brown's corpse" went through the state. Mary Day Brown was in Philadelphia waiting to accompany her husband's funeral train; donations totalling one hundred dollars were collected from among the black mourners.[26] Local newspapers reported that there was a near riot. After the Civil War, Henry recalled this meeting. In his words, the "good old saint" John Brown was "led by a supernatural hand to go into Virginia with about twenty men and subdue the State. . . . Look, for instance, at the fertile hills of Charles Town, W. Va., literally stained with blood."[27]

Rev. Thomas W. Henry was posted to Binghamton, New York, on the Elmira Circuit, by Christmas 1859. He later returned to Philadelphia, married the widow of another minister, and, following the Civil War, spent the remainder of his ministry near Baltimore. By 1868, Henry was the oldest presiding elder in the Baltimore Conference, and although he attempted to retire, he was unable to receive a promised annuity from the denomination he had served for thirty years. He was a part of the past among ministers or leaders who sought the elimination of spirituals and other reminders of slavery.[28] Henry, who was known for his old-fashioned insistence on plain dress in church (no bonnets or jewelry), seems bitter at times in his narrative about a lack of appreciation for the country preachers who came up from slavery. Perhaps his obituary in the *Hagerstown Mail Weekly*, May 4, 1877, when his body was returned from Washington to his home for burial, says it best:

BURIAL OF AN AGED COLORED PREACHER

Mr. Henry was a strong-minded colored man, and was greatly devoted to the freedom of his race, and he had the gratification of living long enough to see it accomplished, with all its other rights extended to them.

NOTES

1. *Baltimore Sun*, November 10, 1859, 1.

2. Carmen A. Weber, "Orchard Street Church Archaeological Monitoring," Baltimore Center for Urban Archaeology Research Series, Report no. 4 (October 1984). This building is now the Baltimore headquarters of the National Urban League. Delfield S. Yoes III, "Baltimore Urban League Orchard Church Proposal," *Baltimore Afro-American*, February 11, 1989.

3. Letter, "Edward R. Beatty relative to slave Henry in Maryland Nov. 14 1859." Beatty worked in the surveyor's office in Baltimore. Another letter, "'C' to Governor Wise," November 11, 1859, was mailed from Havre de Grace, a port city in Chesapeake Bay where the mouth of the Susquehanna River flows from Pennsylvania. Rev. John R. Henry, age twenty-nine, had recently been ordained and posted there. Wise Collection, AC4671 (both documents), Library of Congress.

4. Thomas W. Henry, *From Slavery to Salvation: The Autobiography of Rev. Thomas W. Henry of the A.M.E. Church*, ed. Jean Libby (1872 [anon. pamphlet]; Jackson: University Press of Mississippi, 1994), 53; Paul Finkelman, *Dred Scott v. Sandford: A Brief History with Documents* (Boston: Bedford Books, 1997).

5. This poem also provided solace for the raiders scheduled for execution after Brown, for whom negotiations were under way to have their remains returned to their original homes in Northern states or the abolition school operated by Marcus and Rebecca Spring in New Jersey. The black raiders' bodies were instead brought to the Winchester, Virginia, medical school, as was that of Brown's son Watson.

6. Benjamin Quarles, *Allies for Freedom: Blacks and John Brown* (New York: Oxford University Press, 1974), 113–14, 142–43, 145.

7. Henry, *Slavery to Salvation*, 52.

8. Edna Christian Knapper, "Joe Winters," *Public Opinion* (Chambersburg, PA), January 17, 1956. The late Mrs. Knapper, who knew Winters as a child, learned of the Brown association from Winters's daughter, who taught Sunday School at St. James. Knapper later researched the land records for the location and ownership. Interviews by the author, 1978, 1979, Chambersburg.

9. Douglass, *Life*, 314–21. See also Anderson, *Voice* (1861).

10. "In the hand of old Brown, and was probably intended for Kagi, alias I. Henrie, Esq." State of Virginia, *Calendar of Virginia State Papers and Other Manuscripts, 1652–1869; Preserved in the Capitol at Richmond*. Vol. 11, *January 1, 1836, to April 15, 1869*, ed. H. W. Flournoy (Richmond, 1893; microfilm, Boston Public Library); emphasis Brown's.

11. Richard J. Hinton, *John Brown and His Men, With Some Account of the Roads They Traveled to Reach Harper's Ferry* (New York: Funk and Wagnalls, 1894), 246–47.

12. Virginia Ott Stake, *John Brown in Chambersburg* (Chambersburg, PA: Franklin County Heritage, 1977), 42.

13. Alexander W. Wayman, *Cyclopedia of African Methodism*, (1882; repr., St. Charles, MO: St. Charles City-County Library District, 2000); Wayman, *My Recollections of African M.E. Ministers, or Forty Years' Experience in the African Methodist Episcopal Church* (Philadelphia: AME Bookrooms, 1881); Randall K. Burkett, Nancy Hall Burkett, and Henry Louis Gates Jr., eds., *Black Biography, 1790–1950: A Cumulative Index,* 3 vols. (Alexandria, VA: Chadwyck-Healey, 1991).

14. The late Dorothy Porter Wesley, archivist at the Moorland-Spingarn Research Center at Howard University, remembered cataloging the pamphlet *Autobiography of Rev. Thomas W. Henry of the A.M.E. Church*, dated 1872, and hoped that it would be rediscovered and analyzed. Pers. comm. from her friend, archivist Charlotte Price, of

Cape Cod, Massachusetts, 1996. See Dorothy Porter Wesley, ed., *Early Negro Writing: 1760–1837* (1971; repr., Black Classic Press, 1995).

15. Ronald L. Lewis, *Coal, Iron, and Slaves: Industrial Slavery in Maryland and Virginia, 1715–1865* (Westport, CT: Greenwood Press, 1979).

16. Henry's *Autobiography* was rediscovered by the author/editor Jean Libby in 1978.

17. Twelve male slaves under age twenty-six are listed as working in "manufacture" in the 1810 census for Georgetown. Libby, "Historical Essay" in Henry, *Slavery to Salvation,* 69.

18. Ronald D. Palmer, "Western Pennsylvania and the United States Colored Troops Regiments in the Civil War," *Westmoreland History* (Westmoreland County Historical Society, Greensburg, PA) 3, no. 3 (1997): 52. Palmer's theory is sustained by new findings of UGRR activity in Franklin County by local historians.

19. "The Colonizing System," Hagerstown *Torchlight,* November 29, 1827. This notice was found by historical researcher Marsha Fuller. See also Penelope Campbell, *Maryland in Africa; The Maryland State Colonization Society, 1831–1857* (Urbana: University of Illinois Press, 1971). The name Thomas W. Henry does not appear in the microfilmed records of the Maryland Colonization Society in Annapolis.

20. Leroy Hopkins, "Bethel African Methodist Church (Lancaster): Prolegomenon to Social History." *Journal of the Lancaster County Historical Society* 90, no. 4: 205–36.

21. John T. Mason to Henry Wise, November 10, 1859, Wise Collection, AC4695, Library of Congress.

22. Stake, *John Brown in Chambersburg.*

23. Frances E. W. Harper, *Minnie's Sacrifice; Sowing and Reaping; Trial and Triumph: Three Rediscovered Novels,* ed. Frances Smith Foster (Boston: Beacon Press, 1994), xv.

24. Hotel register, Western Maryland Room, Washington County Free Library, Hagerstown, MD. The original was saved from destruction by archivist John C. Frye in 1981. It had been bound as a county report.

25. Henry, *Slavery to Salvation,* 53–54. William Smith, a porter, and Benjamin Sales, a waiter, are listed in the Baltimore city directory of 1860 at the addresses given by Henry in his autobiography. The "widow's son" later became the name of the Masonic lodge in Washington, D.C. Henry uses this code to indicate to some of his readers his membership in the Masons and so as not to announce it to the AME leadership, who discouraged such membership.

26. Quarles, *Allies,* 145.

27. Robert Gordon, "A Mournful Trip," *Adirondack Life* 15, no. 1 (1984): 16–18, 29–32; Henry, *Slavery to Salvation,* 52.

28. Although AME church leaders, particularly Bishop Daniel Payne, discouraged Afrocentric displays of spiritual fervor, as they were reminiscent of slavery days, the congregations kept them alive—even voting to remove Payne as pastor of Bethel AME church in Baltimore over the issue. Bishop Payne also discouraged Masonic membership, a cornerstone of early AME leadership, because he felt it substituted another hierarchy that might create more loyalty than that to the denomination.

PART TWO

John Brown Defined

JOHN BROWN AS FOUNDER

America's Violent Confrontation with Its First Principles

SCOTT JOHN HAMMOND

We hold these truths to be self-evident, that all men are created equal.

—*Declaration of Independence*

No man in America has ever stood up so persistently and effectively for the dignity of human nature, knowing himself for a man, and the equal of any and all government. In that sense he was the most American of us all.

—*Henry David Thoreau, "A Plea for Captain John Brown"*

Was John Brown simply an episode, or was he an eternal truth?

—*W. E. B. Du Bois,* John Brown

John Brown moves at an angle through our history, a transfigured personage who is deemed a force of nature, an avenging angel wielding the scourge of God, a fearsome vessel of pure fanaticism that is seductive in the abstract as well as a terrifyingly demonic power in the flesh. Some would call him a tragic hero, flawed only in his insistence on purity in thought and action coupled with a mystical detachment from the political realities of his day; and some would see in him a prototerrorist, a criminal mind living on the lunatic fringe of history, condemned by rational people in both the North and South. Lincoln, in spite of his deep opposition to slavery, saw in Brown's raid the very archetype of lawless violence and was quick to distance both himself and his party from such obviously treasonous actions. For example, directing his remarks to Southern whites in a speech at the Cooper Union Institute on February 27, 1860, Lincoln declared: "You charge that we stir up insurrections among your slaves. We deny it; and what is your proof? Harper's [*sic*] Ferry! John Brown! John Brown is no Republican, and you have [yet] to implicate a single Republican in his Harper's [*sic*] Ferry enterprise."[1] Conversely, Emerson praised Brown and remarked that Brown would elevate the gallows to a symbol of martyrdom on the same order and import as the Cross. It was, and perhaps still is, difficult for one to be objective or neutral about Osawatomie Brown: one was either with him or against him.

What we know of Brown's life fuels all these interpretations. As a lover of freedom steeled by a devotion to strict Calvinism, Brown appears to have been a practitioner of the Christian ethic framed by the imperative of universal love and compassion for others, especially those who suffer under the yoke of oppression and injustice.[2] For in loving and caring for "the least" of his fellow human beings, he epitomized the purity of a love of human freedom that often comes from a sense of oneness with higher moral ends.[3] Nonetheless, this is the same John Brown who, in the course of one night, assumed the visage of the Night Rider and personally directed and participated in the murder of five defenseless men. Since these men were supporters of slavery, and some of them had previously committed violence against Free State settlers, Brown's decision to kill them is perceived by some as part of his greater mission on behalf of even more defenseless slaves. Still, the manner in which Brown summarily executed these five resembles that of the vicious terrorist more than that of the righteous warrior, and the Pottawatomie Massacre chills the blood of even the most ardent foe of oppression.[4]

These aspects of Brown's psyche reflect something about our own political soul—our "political psyche" writ large.[5] If Brown embodies the essence of us all, then it might be conceded that Brown's more pathological qualities replicate a profound dissonance within our general political and social culture. We must consider the inevitable consequences inherent within a sociopolitical condition fractured by the collision between the ideals of democratic liberty

SCOTT JOHN HAMMOND

and the appalling realities of slavery and racism. No American will impugn the principles of liberty and equality, for however they are construed or comprehended, the structuring principles of the American polity are derived from a noble vision and an aspiration for a free and dignified humanity. The presence of slavery in a country committed, at least in principle, to freedom is the worst possible incidence of ideational failure. Brown's fractured self is an embodiment of the tangled forces of light and darkness that grappled for the republic's soul; his character and actions demonstrate this, and in so doing, make him no different from the ruptured essence of our collective political self-consciousness. The Pottawatomie slaughter represents a symptom of the deeper malady, just as the abuse of any slave by an overseer represents the same type of symptomatic manifestation. In contrast to Brown's avenging violence in Kansas, the incident at Harpers Ferry was driven by a spirit imbued with the transfiguring fire of the idea of universal freedom, in the same manner as the Underground Railroad or the individual dissent of the most famous resident of Walden Pond. Both America and Brown reveal this self-negating duality.

That Brown could be so moved to action by the tragedy of his times further amplifies his character and conviction. Most citizens, absorbed in the daily process and considerations of private interest and obligation, ignore or suppress the maladies of the deeper social structure. The affairs of the state frequently demand too much concentration and emotional investment for the average citizen. Nevertheless, there will always be those among us who, like Brown, seriously regard the structuring principles of a political culture with unabashed sincerity and are thus impelled to hold our institutions and practices accountable to our own higher ideas and political ideals.

Brown judged society according to the laws of God, and he saw with a piercing clarity that neither the ruling political doctrine nor, more important, the commandments of Providence were being properly revered. Nothing could absolve us from the sin of slavery, and the distinctions between righteousness and evil were easily and sharply drawn. No ambiguity, no "gray in gray," no compromise or allowance would be tolerated; either one was with the warriors for freedom and divine righteousness or among the profane legions who served on behalf of sinful oppression. For Brown, unlike most of his fellow Americans, the only solution was an obvious one—brook no sympathy for or concession to the minions of evil, and unconditionally submit without hesitation or diffidence to the Higher Authority, never relenting until total emancipation was achieved or sublime retribution judiciously dispensed. This is what drove John

Brown to act with such intensity of conviction, which magnified every hidden idiosyncrasy. Hence, Brown is at once liberator and fanatic, messiah and monster, the very incarnation of the conflicted American political soul.

This leads us to a more direct consideration of the notion of foundations and founding. The act of founding involves at least an abstract comprehension of those first principles that constitute a political soul and the resolve to forward those principles in an undiluted form. Founding may develop over time, evolving almost imperceptibly through the growth of institutions and their practices, coupled with the slow accretion of tradition, law, custom, and political principles. Founding may also occur rapidly, within a comparatively brief period.

Part of the act of founding involves formation of new ideas or the adoption of high ideas advanced by predecessors and then effective application of those ideas. For all our recognition of the power of material forces pulsing throughout the structure of society or the awareness of the extensive influence of a pre-established language and sociopolitical mind-set, it is still the individual who must *think* ideas; it is the group that must freely and deliberatively accept them, and it is the activist who must ascend beyond immediate necessity to apply them, regardless of resistance. Upon examining those individuals who are noted for participating in an act of founding, we notice something unique that separates them from the ordinary politician, activist, or statesman. This is explained with considerable clarity by Machiavelli, who typically adds the ingredient of realpolitik to his observations of founding and reformative leadership. Given the fact that all founders and reformers will inevitably encounter resistance from those enemies who "profit from the old order," and assuming that a purely good leader will "bring about his own ruin among so many who are not good," Machiavelli notes that a lawgiver or prophet must go forth armed and prepared for struggle.[6] Machiavelli's idea of a founder is consonant with the idea of virtu, or grandeur of soul—a character of extraordinary proportions, defined in terms of "ingenuity, skill, and excellence."[7] Machiavelli seeks a type of transcending leadership, attaching a significant martial quality to his model founders. Even Moses, a religious founder, employs the might of God against Pharaoh in order to liberate the enslaved Israelites, something that those who follow the New Testament model of the suffering Christ would unequivocally reject.

Brown's actions are like those of a prophet-warrior. However, Machiavelli's armed prophet is also a conqueror; failure is associated with those who attempt to establish founding law without the enforcing power of arms. Brown does not seem to conform easily to the prophet-warrior model, for his arms were poor, his numbers few, and his plan thwarted by overextension and local hostility. Moses was at least able to extricate the Israelite slaves from their Egyptian oppressors. Moses conquered by overcoming the power of Egypt and then *founded* both a religion and a nation through the transmission of the Law of God. It is an understatement to say that Brown's achievement falls far short of this mark.

But if one considers the substance of Brown's commitment (the emancipation of the enslaved) and the method of Brown's action (confrontation with the sinful oppressor on behalf of the oppressed), Brown's character and actions do approximate the Machiavellian hero-founder. Furthermore, although he does not conquer in the physical or political sense, he does emerge triumphant. Brown was defeated but martyred, and in the end emancipation came for his people through the violence that he had prophesied.[8] In a sobering moment of synchronicity, Lincoln's retrospective utterance in his second inaugural address, that "until every drop of blood drawn with the lash, shall be paid by another drawn with the sword," echoes Brown's last testimony.[9] Two years earlier, Lincoln, at Gettysburg, had referred to a "new birth of freedom," and thus implicitly defined a new act of founding in the context and terms of the emancipation. From the blood and ashes of the war against slavery, the nation would be re-formed; Brown, who did not survive to witness the nation's second birth, nonetheless prophesied the act in his words. The nation was literally made anew but in a way that reaffirmed more completely the first principles of the republic. This represents an act of founding, and Brown's strike at Harpers Ferry was the prophetic prelude. Even though John Brown is distinct from Machiavelli's legendary types in a number of ways, he certainly shares in the role of founding/reforming visionary. Indeed, Lincoln, generally regarded as the heroic and tragic, even Christlike figure of the Civil War, resembles Brown in the end, only on a larger scale and from the comparatively more acceptable authority of his office. For Lincoln used violence to preserve the Union and purge the new nation of slavery. In his second inaugural address, he finally admits what he most likely knew from the beginning, that slavery was "somehow the cause of the war," and in so doing, for a brief moment toward the end of that war, the Great Emancipator shows himself akin to the Prophet of Osawatomie.

An alternative discussion of the founder-legislator is found in Rousseau's *Social Contract*. The Rousseauian founder is less applicable to the case of John

Brown than the Machiavellian model. Rousseau's founder-legislator possesses a "superior intelligence" and is capable of "beholding all the passions of human beings without experiencing them."[10] It is unlikely that Brown possessed a superior intelligence, and Brown's personality was far from the dispassionate character that Rousseau requires of his legislator. Furthermore, Rousseau's concept of the founder is identical to the concept of the first lawgiver and by no means resembles a prophet-warrior. Martial skill is not a requisite quality of Rousseau's founder, for Rousseau is always careful to mark an acute distinction between government based on consent and authority imposed by force. Only the former can be legitimate and only if it is established as a government based on law. Thus, Rousseau's idea of the legislator is more compatible with the character and ideas of Lincoln than of Brown, for both agreed that law based on higher principle (for Rousseau, the general will; for Lincoln, the Declaration of Independence) is part of the proper act of founding. There is also a sense in Rousseau that the founder-legislator is an actor in the first foundation of the polity and not simply a reformer attempting to reshape or reassert first principles. Additionally, even though the Rousseauian founder acts outside the normal processes of institutions and with an authority that is based solely on genius and devoid of any power, the act of founding is compatible with ordinary politics. The founder is indeed extraordinary but does not seize power and acts wholly within the concept of law. Clearly, Rousseau's founding act is antithetical to those alluded to by Machiavelli or to the actions exemplified by Brown.[11]

At another level, however, there is a similarity between Brown and Rousseau's founder. Rousseau's founder is an individual of superhuman qualities; indeed, Rousseau's description compares the creation of human first laws to the actions of gods. Rousseau's ideal founder is not afraid to act in a way that would challenge "human nature" itself.[12] Brown seems to act against the natural order, but he does not intend to "change" human nature so much as to salvage it and even to save us from it. As a Calvinist, Brown undoubtedly believed that our nature is fixed by original sin; hence, he departed from Rousseau in yet another way. Brown fought against our sinful nature on behalf of redemption. Again, this seems to depart from Rousseau, but one must note that Rousseau's overall view of human nature was not much different from that of Calvin. Rousseau and Calvin both argued that humanity exists in a fallen condition, and although we cannot return to our original innocence, we can recover something of it through the affirmation of freedom and morality. For Calvin

SCOTT JOHN HAMMOND

and John Brown, that higher state could be achieved through the Redeemer; for Rousseau, redemption is possible through the Social Contract. Both Rousseau and Brown sought a kind of recovery and affirmation of a better state of existence, and both insisted that in order to achieve such a goal, we must struggle mightily against our corrupted natures in order to reform and ennoble our humanity.

It should also be emphasized that the element of consent is vital to Rousseau. Brown's actions cannot admit of either direct or indirect consent of the governed for a number of reasons; most obvious of these is that Brown governed no one and possessed no legal or political authority, and that Brown was wholly dissociated from normal political channels. Even so, Brown acted in a way that relates indirectly to the notion of consensual governance. Brown sought neither the approval nor the consent of the populace, for the majority of the populace ignored, permitted, supported, or participated in the possession of human beings. More importantly, the law of God is not based on consent, but like Rousseau's general will, it is always right. Additionally, a minority of the population, both the enslaved victims and the various types of free dissenters and abolitionists, had been effectively deprived of their fundamental right to consent. The only rule that the slave knew was the rule of force, and the only rule that the abolitionist experienced was ultimately deemed immoral. The case of John Brown and his small group of followers and sympathizers exemplifies the latter, and it is compatible with Rousseau's theory of consent and resistance.

Even if Brown is not a founder-legislator in the strict Rousseauian sense, there are at least two arguments in the *Social Contract* that provide theoretical and moral support for Brown's extreme actions. First, Rousseau follows Locke in affirming that the notion of consent unequivocally requires unanimity.[13] A political culture that either legitimizes or permits slavery violates this fundamental principle of universal consent. No one consents to be a slave; the enslaved population constitutes an excluded group that indicates a government based (partially) on force that is thus (wholly) illegitimate. Lincoln saw this as well and employed a similar argument in one of his many criticisms directed at the continued allowance of slavery.[14] Even if one counters this argument by *incorrectly* objecting that Rousseau would not have included a slave population when considering the origins of the social contract, one would still have to take into account the abolitionists who, in acting against slavery from first principles, withdrew their consent to be governed by the current instrument. The unanimity that Rousseau demanded in theory never existed in practice under a regime that allowed slavery; thus, according to these standards, the Constitution, if it did indeed support or permit slavery (an issue that is in itself open to further analysis and argument within a different context) *was therefore not legitimate.* The founding act had occurred under an initial condition that was shaped by a great error.

This directs us back to our second point. Rousseau states without ambiguity that slavery is in every instance illegitimate and immoral. Freedom cannot be surrendered or usurped, for to "renounce liberty is to renounce being a man, to surrender the rights of humanity and even its duties."[15] Thus, slavery can never be rendered legitimate or permitted by a government or any portion of its population. Rousseau makes this clear in the cases of both voluntary and involuntary submission. Slavery can be based neither on a voluntary arrangement nor on coercion or conquest. In the case of the former, one who agrees to be a slave is "out of one's mind," for it is madness to "renounce one's very humanity." Of course, American slavery was anything but voluntary, and for Rousseau, this form of slavery is equally inhumane. Even if one is conquered during the progress of war, the individuals of the subdued army and state should not be enslaved, even if the victor claims a right to hold them in slavery owing to a decision to spare their lives. The conqueror has no right to either kill or enslave a subdued army or population. Despite the bloodletting that occurs during war, Rousseau argues that war is really between things or abstractions and not people, between states that deploy armies composed of individuals agreeing to obey as soldiers, and not between individual citizens of such states. Once the fighting has ceased and the conflict is resolved, the subdued soldier becomes like any other citizen, a free individual; thus, he cannot rightfully be killed, enslaved, or held in any kind of captivity by the conquering power. As Rousseau powerfully states, "So, from whatever aspect we regard the question, the right of slavery is null and void, not only as being illegitimate, but also because it is absurd and meaningless. The words *slave* and *right* contradict each other, and are mutually exclusive. It will always be equally foolish for a man to say to a man or people: 'I make with you a convention wholly at your expense, and wholly to my advantage; I shall keep it as long as I like, and you will keep it as long as I like.'"[16] Thus, not only is a social contract left unformed if it does not include the affirmation of *every* voice that is present within the polity, it is also morally incompatible given the presence of an enslaved group regardless of how the enslavement

SCOTT JOHN HAMMOND

came about. In refusing to seek the consent of the majority, Brown chose to act on behalf of those who had been excluded from the founding act of consent and against a government that under Rousseau's definition can only be interpreted as illegitimate. Surely an analysis of Brown's actions from this perspective can better illuminate the questions that revolve around the accusation of his "lawlessness."

The notion of founding entails far more than establishment of institutions or governmental charters; it also, and above all, includes critical political and social reform in the pursuit of the higher principles of a given political culture. If we are to accept, along with such martyred luminaries as Lincoln and King, the proposition that the first principles of the American founding are to be understood as the guarantee of both individual liberty *and* the advance of political and legal equality, and if we add to this Rousseau's theoretical demolition of any claim to the alleged right to own human beings as property, then we can see in Brown's holy war against slavery an act that does indeed resonate with the spirit of the founding movement.

Returning to Machiavelli for further insight, we read in his *Discourses* that, given the inevitability of change in human affairs and the inexorable caprice of fortune that can have an effect on us all, it is necessary from time to time to return a republic to its "original principles." Republics contain the background elements of that "original goodness" on which a nation's "growth and reputation" depend, and it is altogether necessary that, should corruption ensue, it is then incumbent on citizens either to work toward restoration or toward the destruction of the degenerate order "unless something intervenes to bring it back to its normal condition." For Machiavelli, this could occur either through an "extrinsic act" or "internal prudence," but in any event, the stimulus for reconciliation with the founding principles is a critical requirement for the healthy development of states. Machiavelli argues that internal reform should be peaceful, involving the actions of a great statesman or the enactment of a new set of reforming laws that succeed in leading to the reinvigoration of the original ideals, or both. However, Machiavelli acknowledges the possible need to employ force in internal matters in order to compel the more recalcitrant defenders of the corrupt regime back into the fold of the higher law, and such actions require a personage of courage and vision. The ideal founder, as described by Machiavelli, possesses the quality of "simple virtue . . . without depending upon any law that incites him to the infliction of extreme punishments; and yet his good example has such an influence that

John Brown as Founder

the good men strive to imitate him, and the wicked are ashamed to lead a life so contrary to his example."[17]

By comparison, Brown falls short of the mark because the most excellent founder remains a giant of the proportions of a Gandhi or a King, a rare individual who can peacefully found or reform along higher principles and, in so doing, inspire friends and shame enemies; yet we can say that Brown meets at least some of the requirements of Machiavelli's founder. Pacifism aside, when "internal prudence" does not succeed on its own, Machiavelli refers to specific historical examples of the elimination of Rome's enemies in order to restimulate or reinitiate the inner goodness of the original beginning or founding. Lincoln was reluctantly forced to resort to war on a scale that greatly eclipsed the guerrilla actions of Brown, and both were driven by the knowledge that, as Lincoln averred in his second inaugural address, the "republican cloth [had] been soiled." The stain of corruption needed to be removed, but Lincoln's abiding reverence for law would not allow him to move as Brown had.[18] Eventually, events proved that such respect for the law was not equal to the task of eradicating the degenerate influence of bondage. Brown knew that fact from the beginning, and his contribution to the refounding of America is seen as much in the realization of this as in the fact that his disadvantaged position would inevitably lead to his ambiguous martyrdom.

Significantly, Brown made one major attempt to assume the mantle of legislator. The provisional constitution that was drafted and signed at the antislavery convention in Chatham, Ontario, was intended to provide the foundations for the new society that Brown envisioned establishing in the South after his successful liberation of the slaves and, as such, emulates the type of effort associated with a founder-legislator. In the Chatham document, Brown once again shares something in common with Lincoln in the latter's reaffirmation of the first principles established within the Declaration of Independence. Brown included in the Chatham document a statement that his provisional constitution was not meant to dissolve the federal constitution, but only to reaffirm the principles of the American Revolution through amendment and modification.[19] The banner of the Spirit of '76 was to serve as the flag of the provisional government, thus echoing Lincoln's belief that the true founding of the nation began in the struggle for liberty and equality during the Revolution. In addition to the expression of higher political ideals, Brown also provided plans for framing a new government for the freed slaves and their allies, a proposed political system that, to many, was original and

SCOTT JOHN HAMMOND

revolutionary. The Brown document departed dramatically from all previous constitutional examples because of such features as a supreme court that was to be elected by the widest possible popular vote; government officials who were "to serve without pay" and be removed and punished upon misconduct; extensive public reclamation of all property that was formerly acquired at the expense of the slaves; protection of female prisoners from violation; and plans for the "moral instruction" of the new citizens. Here again, Brown comes close to Rousseau's concept of the founder: a lawgiver who attempts to make human nature anew, one who is committed through law more than through force to the moral elevation of the human spirit. This is an example of Brown designing a more democratic government aimed toward human advancement and intended to restore the principles of the original American founding. Brown's actions at this point in his struggle are reminiscent of such similar moments as the Seneca Falls convention in 1848 that produced the "Declaration and Sentiments" and the Port Huron assembly in 1961 that provided the American left with a radically new voice on behalf of a greater participatory democracy. None of these documents contained the force of law, but they are typically American, rooted in the tradition of constitutional government and connected by the belief that the principles of reason and the proscriptions of prudence should frame government. Brown's actions at Chatham are also similar to the steps taken at the convention of 1776, and once his supporters had signed the document, Brown felt prepared to enter the field of battle, knowing that his deeds were formally supported by written principles and political ideals as well as by his steadfast religious faith. At Chatham, Brown exchanged arms for pen and ink and, like Jefferson and Madison, attempted to establish a new order for humanity through law.

In essence, the political notion forwarded by the American founding is freedom. Nonetheless, in the American story liberty and captivity were born as twins. At the very point when the colonists were beginning the first motions toward more democratic forms of governance, nearly every affirmation for liberty, equality, and the natural rights of human beings was being rendered half-formed or hollow by the virulent presence of slavery. The first principles of American political culture were doomed to incomplete actualization even within the colonial crucible that formed the American notion of freedom. Thus, it would require nothing less than war leading to a second act of founding in order to remove the negating factor of slavery and to redirect the polity toward its ideational and practical completion and reconciliation.

Some might argue that, in fact, the American founding consists of two separate foundings, one based on the egalitarianism of the Declaration of Independence and the other rooted in hierarchy, paternalism, and slavery. In response, one can turn to Lincoln's approach to the American founding, for he traced the birth of the republic back to the Declaration of Independence and its binary doctrine of liberty and equality. Many of the signers may not have considered African slaves as being among those covered by the principles of the document, but the *idea* of human equality was established without any specified qualifications, and thus the principles behind the founding immediately collided with contemporary examples of inequality and bondage. The Declaration does not say, "all men are created equal only if they are males of European descent"; rather, it employs the term *man* as a generic and inclusive concept. Hence, the notion of equality was fully and openly affirmed in the founding act. Arguments linking the "necessity" for slavery to the support of the "more civilized liberty of gentlemen" did not emerge until well after the founding and did not fully develop until the abolitionist movement openly attacked the institution. None of the slaveholding founders argued for any notion of liberty as a function of possessing slaves—and even in the drafting of the Constitution, the concessions to slavery won by the slaveholders were based on immediate economic and direct political interests and were not based on principle or a notion of the proper order of things. Slavery is not an element of the *founding idea,* no matter how one interprets that idea; the founding documents came to be associated with justifications of slavery only in response to the abolitionists' challenge and long after the Revolution had been fought and the republic established. There is no mention in 1776 or 1787 of any notion of liberty dependent on an enslaved underclass, and not until well into the nineteenth century was there a justification of slavery as the natural consequence of the liberties expressed in the Declaration of Independence and the Bill of Rights.

In turning back to Harpers Ferry, we must also raise the following question: Why weren't more people of conscience moved to arms, as was John Brown? This can be partially explained by the close connection between abolition and nonviolent moral suasion, as in the case of William Lloyd Garrison and the Transcendentalists, but that connection notwithstanding, it is still remarkable that, after conceding the pacifism of most free opponents of slavery, we cannot remember another case that resembles or emulates the Harpers Ferry raid. This might be the best evidence on behalf of the case for

SCOTT JOHN HAMMOND

Brown as founder, for his was an act consistent both with the tenets of scripture and with the political principles of the polity within which he lived. It was committed out of the purest motivations, it was directed to the achievement of the goal of purging the pathology responsible for the republic's social and cultural ills, and it anticipated the violent methods in which slavery was finally abolished. John Brown acted from high principles against evil, and while his methods were decidedly flawed, the moral necessity of his act of resistance remains evident. Although Brown's raid on Harpers Ferry was ultimately unsuccessful, he exemplifies the true spirit of just liberty; and while he contributed neither new law to support democracy nor any new concept to develop the idea of freedom, his deeds accelerated its progress. Thomas Jefferson proclaimed the egalitarian creed when he drafted the Declaration, but he was unable to renounce his own status as master or overcome his idiosyncratic ideas about racial difference.[20] Abraham Lincoln sincerely and eloquently reaffirmed this creed on a higher and more authentically universal level at Gettysburg, but he was unable to act immediately and abolish the pernicious institution. John Brown, however, perhaps more than any founder since Thomas Paine, fully incorporated the creed into his actions and lived the idea of equality and racial friendship with unparalleled purity and ardor. John Brown compels us to think of him as a founder—one who, unlike Jefferson and Lincoln, appears to live and act on the fringes of society, but one who, on closer examination, springs from its very center.

Measuring the character and relevance of any historical figure is a task that lends itself to a certain degree of ambiguity. Figures such as Jefferson, Lincoln, and King have all been assessed differently by their champions and critics, and interpretations of their character and descriptions of their heroism as well as their lesser acts have all undergone continual redefinition. Yet they remain, for us, heroes all the same, for in spite of any inadequacies, they reflect the perpetual quest for the affirmation of higher political principle and remain among the great movers who helped shape the conscience and the development of the republic.

John Brown differs from these men because he shaped nothing tangible, at least nothing that we can point to today as the direct creation of his actions or product of his influence. However, he is similar to them because he represents the pursuit of high ideas consistent with action. In some aspects, John Brown is more relevant than they, for in his perpetually frustrated zeal for freedom and justice, he embodies the core of the American story; we see in the growth of the nation writ large the same constant buffeting between the idea of freedom and the reality of its interminable frustration that created a similar tension in the turbulent psyche of the Osawatomie Prophet. That tension was felt by the Sage of Monticello and was manifested in the visage of the Melancholy President, but it was *incarnate* in John Brown, and through that incarnation, the hope and dread of the American soul became flesh.

If some can embrace as a great hero the figure of Robert E. Lee, the defender of a commonwealth that included slavery as an accepted institution, then is it implausible to recognize heroism in the more astonishing figure of Brown? Lee never supported secession until the deed was committed, yet he chose to renounce his commission and past loyalties after years of distinction under arms only in order to side with his state. Other distinguished Southern warriors, such as David Farragut of Tennessee and Winfield Scott, Lee's fellow Virginian, went with the North, but Lee reluctantly followed the Old Dominion into the Confederacy. Is it fair to say that whereas Lee chose his homeland, Brown chose humanity? To his credit, Lee worried over the possibility of siding against his family and friends, thus exhibiting a tenderness for his communal roots and native land that is not as evident in Brown, so is it fair to argue that Lee chose to defend the hearth while Brown chose to fight for an abstraction? Whose abstraction is more meaningful: Lee's insistence on abiding with Virginia right or wrong or Brown's devotion to a people sealed in bondage? We must bear in mind that, in spite of his protestations, Lee owned slaves, and his wife owned even more than he did.[21] Regardless of the answer to these questions, popular history has made its judgments, and Lee is known (by most) today as a gentleman warrior, acting from duty and on principle, while Brown is considered (by many) as the guerrilla fanatic, blinded by undignified zeal and without honor. But we must ask which of the two acted on the higher principle, which violated the greater law, which one carries more blood on his hands, and who between them is a more genuinely American hero? If it is madness to conduct a private, unruly, and suicidal war against an enemy that one perceives as the very cause of sinful oppression, then what state of mind could cause a man of principle to lead thousands into death out of questionable loyalty to a political system that acknowledges oppression as a venerable institution? Who acted on the real spirit of liberty as expressed in the motto *Sic semper tyrannis?* Without intending to detract from the achievement of either man, it is still instructive to compare the actions and motivations of these past contemporaries, one widely deemed a hero, the other, quite often, a villain. At Harpers Ferry, these two men of different principles fatally met, and it is primarily on principle that their legacies stand before us today.

If we are to judge heroes on the principles that they attempt to advance, then we must develop a more comprehensive sense of the value and purity of those ideals that stir one to action. By any measure, John Brown represents the more startling manifestation of the murky dynamics that course within the continual process of the unfolding and founding of America's first principles; thus, he represents an individual of heroic, if still frightening, proportions who speaks powerfully to us today as we continue to confront our higher purposes as a political culture and democratic nation. Perhaps for this reason he is the most typical founder of all: the most consistently idealistic, the most existentially frustrated, the most American.

NOTES

1. "Speech of Abraham Lincoln at the Cooper Union Institute," February 27, 1860, quoted in Edward Stone, ed., *Incident at Harper's Ferry* (Englewood Cliffs, NJ: Prentice-Hall, 1956), 210.

2. "John Brown loved his neighbor as himself. He could not endure, therefore, to see his neighbor poor, unfortunate, or oppressed." "This was the man. His family is the world. What legacy did he leave? It was soon seen that his voice was a call to the great final battle with slavery" W. E. B. Du Bois, *John Brown* (1909; repr., New York: International Publishers, 1962), 374, 373–74.

3. "Inasmuch as ye have done it unto one of the least of these, my brethren, ye have done it unto me." Matthew 25:40 (King James Version).

4. See Alice Nichols, *Bleeding Kansas* (New York: University of Oxford Press, 1954), 115. "The whole community was shocked by the brutal massacre. . . . The cold-blooded ferocity of these dark deeds committed on the night of 24 May was to be unsurpassed in all the bloody years that were to write Bleeding Kansas into the history books." Nichols argues that Brown was actually a "bit player" in Kansas, and she treats Brown's legend as "fiction [made into] history and [Brown as] a saint [made into] a madman" (115).

5. Any attempt to understand the psyche of a historical figure as distant as Brown or to identify and describe a political psyche with any accuracy is admittedly problematic. What is argued here is the possibility that Brown's actions stemmed from a deeper social pathology that was the result of the inner systemic tension between a democratically oriented polity and the institutionalization of oppression.

6. Niccolò Machiavelli, *The Prince and the Discourses* (New York: Modern Library, 1950), 21, 56.

7. This definition of *virtu* is borrowed from Michael Morgan's commentary in *Classics of Moral and Political Theory* (Indianapolis: Hacket Publishers, 1992), 490.

8. "I John Brown am now quite *certain* that the crimes of this *guilty land: will* never be purged *away;* but with Blood. I had *as I now think: vainly* flattered myself that without *very much* bloodshed: it might be done." John Brown, "a prophetic note written by Brown on the day of his execution predicting the establishment of abolition through bloodshed," John Brown Papers, Chicago Historical Society.

9. "If God wills that it continue, until all the wealth piled up by the bond-man's two hundred and fifty years of unrequited toil shall be sunk, and until every drop of blood drawn by the lash, shall be paid by another drawn by the sword, as was said three thousand years ago, so still it must be said, 'the judgments of the Lord are true and righteous altogether.'" Abraham Lincoln, "Second Inaugural Address," in *Abraham Lincoln: Speeches and Writings,* 2 vols. (New York: Library of America, 1989), 2:687.

10. Jean-Jacques Rousseau, *The Social Contract and the Discourses,* ed. G. D. H. Cole (New York: Dent-Dutton/Everyman Library, 1973), 194.

11. Ibid., 194–97.

12. Ibid., 194.

13. Ibid., 173–75.

14. Lincoln, *Speeches,* 1:328.

15. Rousseau, *Social Contract,* 170.

16. Ibid., 169–72.

17. Machiavelli, *Prince,* 397–402.

18. Lincoln, *Speeches,* 2:687. Also see Lincoln, "Address to Young Men's Lyceum of Springfield, Illinois" (January 27, 1838), in *Speeches,* 1:28–36.

19. Stephen B. Oates, *To Purge This Land with Blood: A Biography of John Brown,* rev. ed. (Amherst: University of Massachusetts Press, 1985), 245–47.

20. Paul Finkelman, *Slavery and the Founders: Race and Liberty in the Age of Jefferson* (Armonk, NY: M. E. Sharpe, 1996).

21. My gratitude to Paul Finkelman for his helpful comments on Lee's position regarding his family's slaves.

SCOTT JOHN HAMMOND

five

JOHN BROWN AND THE
LEGACY OF MARTYRDOM

EYAL NAVEH

THE NONCONSENSUAL HERITAGE OF JOHN BROWN

A tourist visiting the historical site of John Brown's raid at Harpers Ferry is in for a surprise. The famous engine house where the fighting and the capture took place has been moved about two hundred yards from its original location and stands neglected and deserted—in sharp contrast to many other historical monuments commemorating events that took place in this area. Moreover, the only stone monument on the spot is a boulder that was placed there in 1932 by the United Daughters of the Confederacy and the Sons of Confederate Veterans as a memorial to Heyward Shepherd, a free African American killed by the raiders. Ironically, these children of the Confederacy commemorated this black man in the following words:

ON THE NIGHT OF OCTOBER 16, 1859
HEYWARD SHEPHERD, AN INDUSTRIOUS

AND RESPECTED COLORED FREEMAN,
WAS MORTALLY WOUNDED BY JOHN
BROWN'S RAIDERS. IN PURSUANCE
OF HIS DUTIES AS AN EMPLOYEE OF
THE BALTIMORE AND OHIO RAILROAD
COMPANY, HE BECAME THE FIRST
VICTIM OF THIS ATTEMPTED
INSURRECTION.

THIS BOULDER IS ERECTED BY
THE UNITED DAUGHTERS OF THE
CONFEDERACY AND THE SONS OF
CONFEDERATE VETERANS AS A
MEMORIAL TO HEYWARD SHEPHERD,
EXEMPLIFYING THE CHARACTER AND
FAITHFULNESS OF THOUSANDS OF
NEGROES WHO, UNDER MANY
TEMPTATIONS THROUGHOUT
SUBSEQUENT YEARS OF WAR, SO
CONDUCTED THEMSELVES THAT
NO STAIN WAS LEFT UPON A RECORD
WHICH IS THE PECULIAR HERITAGE
OF THE AMERICAN PEOPLE, AND AN
EVERLASTING TRIBUTE TO THE BEST
IN BOTH RACES.

Full comprehension of this inscription would require an essay-length analysis, which is beyond the scope of my topic. Clearly, however, John Brown, who had intended to free African American slaves in this raid, was perceived by Southern whites as a violent killer. Consequently, the victim of the shooting, who happened to be an African American freeman, served those who saw the whole raid as a crime against peaceful, harmonious race relations. Obviously, this boulder could not stand as the sole monument to the historical significance of the Harpers Ferry raid; indeed, the National Park Service has placed a wooden plaque next to the boulder, which states that the memory of the event is still controversial, generating conflicting interpretations of its meaning. Under the headline "A Different Interpretation," the plaque quotes W. E. B. Du Bois, the famous African American leader who was a

EYAL NAVEH

radical critic of what he defined as American racism and imperialism. Du Bois praised John Brown's attempt to free the slaves and commemorated him as a freedom fighter and a pioneer of slave emancipation.

These two monuments, with their diametrically opposed messages, indicate beyond doubt John Brown's strikingly nonconsensual heritage. His image has never gained that holistic representation necessary to transform a flesh-and-blood individual into the sublime, revered mythical figure so essential to the historical collective memory. Instead, it has given rise to a multiplicity of representations with conflicting meanings that have been highlighted in many public discourses.

Artists and intellectuals, journalists and politicians, as well as religious and community leaders have all kept the memory of John Brown alive since his execution more than 140 years ago. Plays, movies, fictional works, poems, pictures, and sculptures, as well as historical monographs, have recalled the dramatic story of John Brown. But the figure that emerges from all these media is always ambiguous, controversial, even paradoxical. John Brown exemplifies the best and the worst of human nature. His actions reflect the highest form of altruistic idealism on one hand, and malicious, egoistic fanaticism on the other. As a result, John Brown failed to become a revered, mythical, all-American hero.

If Brown had been killed at Harpers Ferry, the whole attempt to turn him into a martyr would have come to nothing. But his last six weeks, from his capture through his trial and execution and up to his burial, created the potential to transform him into an unequivocal martyr for the cause of emancipation, the abolition of slavery, and freedom. Brown himself leapt at the opportunity, immediately beginning to portray himself in mythical terms as a martyred saint willing to die for a glorious cause. As historian Bertram Wyatt-Brown has written, Brown consciously developed that "mysterious desire not to succeed in the ordinary sense but to sow sectional discord by making the whole enterprise, and himself in particular, a human sacrifice to the cause of freedom."[1]

Up until the Civil War, Brown's friends and followers reinforced this image by portraying his trial and execution as an epilogue underlining the positive, true lessons to be learned from his controversial activities. By ignoring his violent actions and using the circumstances of his capture and death to represent him as a martyr, they attempted to engrave a positive image on the historical consciousness of the American people. This image, they hoped, would make him an inspirational symbol of victory, thus turning his apparent defeat into triumph.

No doubt to certain contemporary admirers, he is the ultimate martyr for the abolitionist cause; and no doubt within the context of the Civil War, his image in the North was exalted and sublime. Overall, however, the monumental endeavor to develop a general legacy of abolitionist martyrdom around the figure of John Brown collapsed shortly after the end of the Civil War. His martyr image diminished over time and even became identified with a number of un-American values.

Here I seek to account for this failure through a historical examination of Brown's legacy of martyrdom. By briefly reviewing the original significance of the martyr image in monotheistic religions and by examining the rhetorical devices used to integrate that image in modern times, I will offer some explanation for the ambiguous outcome of John Brown's attempt at martyrdom. I hope to demonstrate that the diminishing effect of John Brown's image as a national martyr was due to two interrelated reasons: first, the changing historical context, and second, the incongruity of the initial rhetoric of martyrdom adopted by Brown and his supporters with the general American political culture.

In the long run, Brown's legacy of martyrdom has remained significant to extremist critics of American society from both the radical left and the radical right. Brown has provided inspiration to militant black movements, communist intellectuals and politicians, anarchist groups, and ethnic outsiders, as well as, more recently, right-wing antiabortion fanatics claiming to be following in his footsteps. The fact that only these extremist individuals and movements have drawn on the Brown legacy is a further indication of his inability to serve as a focus of consensus and unification. Despite many efforts to portray him as having made an enduring sacrifice for a sublime cause that would improve the values and mores of American society, his image has remained ambiguous and controversial, appealing basically to marginal and eccentric elements of society.

JOHN BROWN AND THE ROOT PARADIGM OF MARTYRDOM

Charles Joyner has argued that John Brown embraced the root paradigm of martyrdom.[2] This is obviously true. The root paradigm provides a familiar repertoire of values, symbols, concepts, normative behavior, and rituals de-

EYAL NAVEH

signed to invest meaning in a dramatic and tragic narrative of the struggle, suffering, sacrifice, and death of the hero, thereby exalting him to martyrdom. Archaic and pagan legends, Bible stories, apocryphal Jewish books, and above all the New Testament and Christian martyrology provided a body of stories and created the root paradigm of the martyred hero. Despite differences in plot, these stories as a root paradigm share similar patterns and structures.

The significance of the paradigm derives above all from its ability to articulate binary contrasts: that the essence of a situation is the opposite of what it appears; that the ultimate outcome of the story contradicts the apparent plot; that the villain of the story turns into a revered saint and martyr; that the forces of law and order ultimately prove to be villains. The hero dies but lives forever; he is apparently defeated but achieves supreme victory through his martyrdom. It is these binary contrasts that give rhetorical form and meaning to the narratives of martyred heroes.[3]

Besides the binary contrasts, most stories of martyrdom interpret the hero's tragic fate in terms of three different dimensions: individual, social, and cosmic. As a unique individual, the martyr suffers and often dies a terrible death because of absolute faith in and total devotion to the transcendental world that he has witnessed. The very word *martyr* means witness—an individual with the ability to penetrate the divine world and testify to a divine revelation. A supernatural power determines the course of his life and decides when he should be removed from the human world. During his lifetime, he delivers a divine message to all human beings, and through his suffering and sacrificial death, that message perpetuates itself over the ages. As a unique individual, the martyr overcomes his physical existence and through the process of suffering and death he undergoes a transfiguration into pure spirit.

Socially, the martyr sacrifices himself for the sake of a certain collective: community, nation, class, city, ethnic group, even universal humankind. Innocent of any real crime, he suffers for a cause that has meaning for the collective to which he belongs. In sanctifying him, this society endows his death and suffering with significance, imprinting them in its collective memory. Being pure and innocent, the martyr dies not for his own sins, but to atone for the sins of his society, tempering God's wrath against it and thereby saving it from destruction. The martyr's blood bonds the society together, and his death expiates society's crimes.

Finally, the whole paradigm is part of a cosmic plan. The martyr appears as a messiah, analogous to the Son of God, who is to return at the end of

John Brown and the Legacy of Martyrdom

history to redeem humankind and proclaim the coming of the millennium. His tragic fate is part of the apocalyptic period often described as a premillennial reign of evil. He is a herald of redemption who appears in the final stage of history in order to wage war against the evil cohorts of Satan. As such a herald, he endures a terrible fate, but his sacrifice is part of the divine design, for humanity must fulfill its quota of suffering and sorrow until God's purpose is achieved. Every martyr's death undermines Satan's domination, bringing humanity's redemption closer. In his death, the martyr becomes a player in the cosmic drama that will lead ultimately to the establishment of the Kingdom of Heaven on earth.

Thus, as a root paradigm the martyr's story invests meaning in the hero's tragic fate by using binary contrasts. The martyr-hero is an individual who, having witnessed a divine revelation and having the capacity to transform his body by self-spiritualization, suffers and dies on behalf of his community and in atonement for all sinners. As a herald of redemption who fights the forces of evil in the last historical period of the apocalypse, he advances humankind's salvation.

JOHN BROWN AND THE RHETORIC OF MARTYRDOM

Initially, John Brown's rhetoric of martyrdom uses many elements of this root paradigm. As an individual, Brown portrayed himself in his letters from jail as a unique, mysterious disciple of Christ, driven by a divine passion. "You know that Christ once armed Peter, so also in my case I think he put a sword in my hand," he wrote to a Quaker woman from jail. On November 25, 1859, he wrote to his aged cousin: "I have a strong impression that God has given me power and faculties . . . whether my death may not be vastly more valuable than my life is I think quite beyond all human foresight."[4] When one of his captors asked who had sent him to Harpers Ferry, he eventually answered, "No man sent me here. It was my own prompting and that of my Maker." To another officer he clearly stated that he considered himself an instrument of God.[5]

In his messages from jail, Brown stressed the social aspect of the root paradigm. He died for American society. He considered his death as a necessary sacrifice designed to purge and purify the American people. "Without the shedding of blood there is no remission of sin," he reiterated to his followers, thus portraying his death as a necessary atonement for the nation's sin of slavery.[6]

By comparing his fate to that of Christ, John Brown invested his own trial and execution with cosmic meaning. When asked by a local reporter if he was ready to meet death, he replied: "I am entirely ready so far as I know. I feel no shame on account of my doom. Jesus of Nazareth was doomed in like manner. Why should I not be?"[7] His last statement was phrased in the same cosmic terms. Just before going to the gallows, he handed his jailer a piece of paper with his famous prophecy of wrath against the American redeemer nation, which had deviated from its mission: "I John Brown am now quite *certain* that the crimes of this *guilty land: will* never be purged *away:* but with Blood."[8]

The manufacture of John Brown as martyr began from the moment of his execution. As Paul Finkelman has shown, the raw material for this project consisted of Brown's letters from jail, his statement before the judges at his trial, "his stoic behavior at the gallows, and the efforts of anti-slavery activists to exploit his execution for the greater cause." John Brown was more valuable to the abolitionist cause as a dead, romantic martyr than as a living fugitive or fanatic murderer.[9] However, in order to transcend his circle of close friends and supporters and become a perpetual source of national inspiration, Brown's martyrdom had to coalesce with American political culture at large.

Ralph W. Emerson, Henry D. Thoreau, Wendell Phillips, and William L. Garrison all tried to apply the repertoire of martyrdom to the image of John Brown and to integrate it with the American mission of redemption. Despite reservations among Northern conservatives, Democrats, and even Republicans, that attempt achieved a certain degree of success. Throughout 1860 and up to the Civil War, Brown was portrayed as someone who had not really died but had joined God in battle against the sin of slavery. Exploiting this contrast between apparent physical death and perpetual spiritual life, George William Curtis proclaimed in Rochester, Massachusetts, on December 12, 1859, that "John Brown was not buried but planted. He will spring up hundredfold."[10] A few months later, on July 4, 1860, Henry David Thoreau said in a speech delivered in North Elba, New York, "John Brown was the only one who has not died. He is more alive than ever he was. . . . He is no longer working in secret. He works in public and in the clearest light that shines on this land."[11]

John Brown was depicted as a saint who fought the sinful regime of the South, a martyr for freedom both in the limited sense of African American emancipation and in the large sense of freedom from tyranny and injustice all over the country.

Death kill not. In later time,
(O, slow but all accomplishing!)
Thy shouted name abroad shall ring
Wherever right makes war sublime.[12]

This verse, written by William Dean Howells in December 1859, had prophetic significance: the Civil War engulfed the nation a year and a half later, thus turning John Brown into the herald of an apocalyptic moment in the history of the United States. In fact, the Civil War enlarged the context of Brown's martyrdom. First, it provided the dramatic and tragic setting that made the root paradigm of martyrdom a meaningful story to many Americans. The destruction and bloodshed of the war, the assassination of President Lincoln at the end of the conflict, the Union's victory and the emancipation of the slaves, the atmosphere of national suffering and bereavement—all these helped turn John Brown into a mythical soldier presaging this whole baptism of blood. Between the deaths of John Brown and Abraham Lincoln, the two famous martyrs, nearly 360,000 soldiers gave their lives for the Union, the country, the republic, the freedom of man (over 198,000 died fighting for the Confederacy).[13] Thus, the figure of John Brown seemed to transcend its particular historical setting, and his image as a martyr was integrated into the public memory of the Union as one whose "body lies a-mouldering in the grave, / But his soul goes marching on."

The Civil War created a propitious atmosphere for applying many elements of the root paradigm of martyrdom to the image of John Brown. The Virginia court became the seat of the criminals. The Southern white officers who had executed Brown turned into rebels, and John Brown was, by the same token, converted into a mythical soldier who had preceded the Union soldiers in fighting Southern tyranny. Law and order had been violated by those who hanged John Brown as a criminal; in the eyes of the North, the traitor became the true patriot, while the executioner became the great traitor. The Civil War's redemptive significance for the Union, for African Americans, for the republican form of government, and for humanity in general was part of the cultural context that imbued the whole tragedy with meaning.

Henry C. Wright viewed John Brown, the dying soldiers, the slaves, and Abraham Lincoln as interrelated in their sacrifice for the sake of American society, as "[i]ndividuals who had deliberately chosen to suffer rather than to inflict suffering, die rather than kill."[14] This statement, although completely wrong in Brown's case, made sense in the dramatic and tragic context of the war, which gave the whole gesture of martyrdom social, national, humanistic, and even universal and cosmic meaning. "Let not the American people weep for Lincoln," wrote the French author Victor Hugo, "this martyr has his place between John Brown and Jesus Christ as the third redeemer of humanity."[15]

THE FAILURE OF JOHN BROWN'S LEGACY OF MARTYRDOM

But the war ended and the dramatic atmosphere that had kept John Brown's martyrdom meaningful ebbed away. A mood of conciliation between North and South replaced the war spirit. Many Americans began to view the war not as a redemptive battle between the forces of good and evil, but rather as a tragic fraternal conflict. Some even began to doubt whether the immense tragedy and suffering had been necessary. In order to endure in this changing atmosphere, Brown's martyr image had to be integrated into a less dramatic cultural system, a more traditional American political culture that did not view death and sacrifice as normative values in themselves.

Indeed, those who sought to create a lasting martyr image for John Brown began to stress certain typical elements in order to portray him as an American national archetype. New England Transcendentalists saw him as a man of great common sense guided by a higher law, a representative of American national character and moral community. Many sympathetic writers emphasized Brown's Puritan background, his kinship to the Founding Fathers, his pioneering experience on the Western frontier, his humble yet independent career as a self-made man, his love of liberty, and his simple, authentic religious faith. Many compared him to Catholic saints, Jewish prophets, Old Testament figures, or Protestant martyrs.

African American leaders stressed Brown's commitment to freedom. "He began the war which ended slavery," declared Frederick Douglass, who admired him but had refused to join his raid.[16] He always viewed Brown as an ideal against which he measured himself. For most African Americans, John Brown's raid was only the beginning of a long journey toward legal equality; later, African American leaders would emphasize in their tributes to him that he had merely started the long battle for freedom. W. E. B. Du Bois concluded his biography of Brown with Brown's declaration: "Now is the day to strike for a free nation. It will cost something, even blood and suffering, but it will not cost as much as waiting."[17]

Many Americans, however, deplored blood and suffering, so Brown's supporters had to develop a few mythical images to keep his memory alive. An imaginative painting by an unknown artist portrayed John Brown's last moment in a way that stressed the common myth of a last stand, which is part of the root paradigm of martyrdom. A classical iconography of Brown's head served to transform a man of flesh and blood into a universal embodiment of the ideal human being. Paintings, monuments, sculptures, medals, and other figurative artifacts of John Brown were numerous and well known. His grave became another medium of legend. Contemporaries ascribed a certain cosmic significance to the fact that he was buried at the foot of a huge boulder out in the open amid vast mountains: Merged forever with the authentic forces of American nature, he had been transformed from a human being into a cosmic, transcendental force.

Certain groups—for example, Northern liberals and radicals, Union veterans, former abolitionists, and certainly African Americans—had a sincere interest in turning Brown into an enduring martyr even after the Civil War had ended and the political atmosphere changed. But that change made their task more difficult. It enabled Brown's enemies to resume their rhetorical attacks, in which they reminded many Americans that John Brown had acted against large segments of American society, provoking hostility that had enlarged the gap between North and South and had ultimately led to the tragedy of the Civil War. The demise of the war spirit encouraged an interpretation of his activities as completely incompatible with American norms and values, thereby undermining his image as a martyr.

Oddly, the discourse that sought to negate Brown's image followed the same root paradigm, but in the opposite direction: it portrayed John Brown as the very antithesis of a martyr. As an individual, he emerged as a villain driven by avarice, lust, and a thirst for blood, rather than as the recipient of a divine revelation. His whole career bore witness to the dark and carnal instincts of man rather than to any divine truth. "He met and established confidential relations with men who plotted against the life of the nation and planned how to provoke a revolution," wrote historian Hill Peebles Wilson. "Out of his negotiations with them came money, munitions of war, mutual planning for revolution, and a dream of an empire." Wilson, whose focus on the history of Bleeding Kansas led him to attempt to debunk Brown's martyr image, claimed that Brown's quest for martyrdom "was just another device to acquire pecuniary assistance for his family whenever favorable opportunity presented itself."[18]

Socially, the negative rhetoric claimed that far from bonding the community together, John Brown intensified national conflict by increasing the gap between North and South. To white Southerners, he was a traitor whose raid had threatened their very existence. His execution had created a false martyr image that seduced the North. Historian John Burgess expressed this feeling when he wrote that a "prayer meeting for the soul of John Brown . . . in the North should appear to the people of the South to be evidence of the wickedness which knew no bounds."[19] Northern historian and former abolitionist Sydney Howard Gay asserted that, after the Harpers Ferry raid, "the intention to divide the Union at any moment became a universal Southern idea."[20] Although each side blamed the other for the war, both the Northern and Southern versions agreed that John Brown's raid and his posthumous image created belligerent feelings between the two sides. Brown's detractors viewed him as a false martyr because he had promoted fragmentation and disintegration instead of social cohesion and unification in American society.

With respect to the sin of slavery, Brown's foes claimed that his death could not atone for the crimes of the nation because in the bloody events in Kansas he himself had figured as a terrorist and a criminal with a price on his head. Even many Americans who had welcomed the abolition of slavery at the end of the war saw Brown's actions as unnecessary and counterproductive. They preferred Abraham Lincoln in the role of the great martyr who had atoned for the nation's sins in his life and death.

The transformation of the Civil War from a holy crusade into a tragic conflict robbed Brown's image of its cosmic significance as a forerunner of national redemption. The mythical overtones that had worked so well in wartime rhetoric foundered on myth-breaking iconoclasm after the war. Some writers ridiculed the picture of Brown's last stand, claiming that the scene had never taken place; others disputed the origin of the Union song about John Brown, asserting that it was actually about a different John Brown, a sergeant from the Massachusetts Seventh Regiment.[21] For those who refused to attribute any sacred meaning to the Civil War, Brown's actions had no cosmic significance whatsoever, while those who continued to interpret the war in terms of biblical eschatology saw Lincoln rather than John Brown as an enduring martyr.

The rhetoric that rejected the image of John Brown as a national martyr denied any binary contrasts that his supporters had emphasized. He had been a criminal while alive and remained so after his execution. Viewed as a tragic conflict, the Civil War did not turn the patriot into a traitor and the traitor

John Brown and the Legacy of Martyrdom

into a patriot. Both North and South had heroes and patriots like Abraham Lincoln and Robert E. Lee, and criminals and traitors like John Brown and John Wilkes Booth. The war did not produce any cosmic transformation. It abolished an institution that some believed would have disappeared anyway. It reaffirmed the authority of the Union and suppressed the rebellion, but it did not transform American society. Race relations did not change in any major way after the failure of Reconstruction. The complete social and political change that could have integrated John Brown into the martyr root paradigm by emphasizing the binary contrasts of his story simply never came to pass.

For radical opponents of the American status quo, however, Brown's career remained meaningful, and consequently his martyr image was highly significant as well. "The spirit of John Brown moves on in social reform," declared an African American historian late in 1959, during the centennial commemoration of the execution. "Does not the spirit of the Grangers, the Populists, of Eugene V. Debs, of the Muckrakers, of Robert La Follette, of Huey Long and Henry Wallace suggest the ghost of John Brown?"[22] For most Americans, the answer was no. The Kansas state legislature's request to have Brown's statue placed in the National Hall of Fame in Washington, D.C., was never granted.[23] In the 1940 Hollywood film *Santa Fe Trail,* John Brown is portrayed as a violent and eccentric outsider rather than a peace-loving, patriotic, typical American. An African American newspaper in Chicago complained that the centennial of John Brown's raid had passed almost without notice.[24] Only a conspicuous few still saw him as an enduring martyr of human freedom.

I have offered here a brief explanation of this outcome based on an examination of the rhetoric that either constructed or debunked the martyrdom of John Brown. He was a martyr within the dramatic context of the Civil War. But his image transcended his time and place only for particular groups who radically opposed the American status quo. While reverent biographers have depicted Brown as an eternal martyr, hostile writers have portrayed him as an un-American adventurer and criminal. "What infinite variety of opinions may exist of a man who on one hand is compared to Socrates and Christ, and on the other hand to Orsiniad and Wilkes Booth," wrote James Ford Rhodes in his monumental *History of the United States.* In a more subjective tone, he concluded, "the comparison of [Brown to] Socrates and Christ strikes a discordant note. The apostle of truth and the apostle of peace are immeasurably remote from the man whose work of reform consisted in shedding blood."[25]

Clearly, Brown's use of violent means to achieve his aim, together with his exaggerated emphasis on blood, sacrifice, and death, contradicted basic American values. In the long run, his martyrdom could not overcome this contradiction, and consequently the American public in general has evaluated his image in very divided terms of praise and condemnation, exaltation and scorn. For this reason, too, radical foes of the American system that resort to violence to express their opposition find in John Brown's character and legacy of martyrdom a source of inspiration and support.

NOTES

1. Bertram Wyatt-Brown, "'A Volcano beneath a Mountain of Snow': John Brown and the Problem of Interpretation," in *His Soul Goes Marching On: Responses to John Brown and the Harpers Ferry Raid,* ed. Paul Finkelman (Charlottesville: University Press of Virginia, 1995), 27.

2. Charles Joyner, "'Guilty of Holiest Crime': The Passion of John Brown," in Finkelman, *Soul,* 296–334.

3. Bruce A. Rosenberg, *Custer and the Epic of Defeat* (University Park: Pennsylvania State University Press, 1974), 217.

4. John Brown, *The Life and Letters of John Brown, Liberator of Kansas, and Martyr of Virginia,* ed. Franklin B. Sanborn (1885; repr., New York: Negro Universities Press, 1969), 582, 604.

5. Quoted in Robert Penn Warren, *John Brown: The Making of a Martyr* (New York: Payson and Clark, 1929), 382, 392.

6. Brown, *Life,* 620.

7. *Charlestown (WV) Independent Democrat,* [no date], quoted in Oswald Garrison Villard, *John Brown, 1800–1859: A Biography Fifty Years After* (1920; repr., New York: Knopf, 1943), 545.

8. John Brown, "A prophetic note written by Brown on the day of his execution predicting the establishment of abolition through bloodshed," John Brown Papers, Chicago Historical Society. Brown defined this blood in a conversation with F. B. Sanborn in January 1857: "I have always been delighted with the doctrine that all men are created equal . . . it is like the Saviours' comand, 'Thou shalt love thy neighbor as thyself,' . . . That is the doctrine, sir; and rather than have that fail in the world, or in these States, 't would be better for a whole generation to die a violent death." Brown, *Life,* 620.

9. Paul Finkelman, "Manufacturing Martyrdom: The Antislavery Response to John Brown's Raid," in Finkelman, *Soul,* 46.

10. Quoted in Villard, *John Brown,* 564.

11. Henry David Thoreau, *The Writings of Henry David Thoreau,* 11 vols. (Boston: Houghton, Mifflin and Company, 1894), 10:237, 248.

12. William Dean Howells, "Old Brown," *Ohio Archaeological and Historical Review* 30 (1921): 181.

13. United States Civil War Center, "Statistical Summary: America's Major Wars," http://www.cwc.lsu.edu/cwc/other/stats/warcost.htm.

14. Quoted in Lewis Perry, *Radical Abolitionism: Anarchy and the Government of God in Antislavery Thought* (Ithaca, NY: Cornell University Press, 1974), 279–80.

15. Quoted in Boyd B. Stutler, "Abraham Lincoln and John Brown," *Civil War History* 8 (September 1962): 229.

16. Frederick Douglass, "John Brown," an address given at the fourteenth anniversary of Storer College, Harpers Ferry, West Virginia, May 30, 1881, in *John Brown: The Making of a Revolutionary: The Story of John Brown in His Own Words and in the Words of Those Who Knew Him,* ed. Louis Ruchames (New York: Grosset and Dunlap, 1969), 298.

17. W. E. B. Du Bois, *John Brown* (1909; repr., New York: International Publishers, 1962), 289.

18. Hill Peebles Wilson, *John Brown, Soldier of Fortune: A Critique* (1913; repr., Boston: Cornhill Company, 1918), 406, 231.

19. John W. Burgess, *The Civil War and the Constitution 1859–1865,* 2 vols. (New York: Charles Scribner's Sons, 1901), 1:42.

20. William Cullen Bryant and Sydney Howard Gay, *A Popular History of the United States,* 4 vols. (New York: Charles Scribner's Sons, 1881), 4:431.

21. For the refutation of the last-stand story, see Captain John Avis (John Brown's jailer and executioner), to editor, *Southern Historical Society Papers* 13 (1885): 341–42; *American Mercury* 1 (1924): 273. On the origins of the Union song "John Brown's Body," see George Kimball, "Origins of the John Brown Song," *New England Magazine* 20, no. 4 (December 1889): 371–76.

22. Benjamin Quarles, ed., *Blacks on John Brown* (Urbana: University of Illinois Press, 1972), 137.

23. Wilson, *John Brown,* 399–400.

24. Editorial in *Chicago Defender,* repr. in Quarles, *Blacks,* 124.

25. James Ford Rhodes, *History of the United States from the Compromise of 1850,* vol. 2. (1893; New York: Harper and Brothers, 1920), 2:414–15.

EYAL NAVEH

Plate 1. "The United States armory or musket factory at Harpers Ferry, Virginia, from Magazine Hill," from Edward Beyer's *Album on Virginia,* 1857. (Courtesy of Historic Photo Collection, Harpers Ferry National Historical Park, Harpers Ferry, West Virginia, HF-0959.)

Plate 2. Although most images of John Brown show him with a long, flowing beard, for almost fifty-eight of his fifty-nine years he went beardless. Biographers Richard J. Hinton and John Redpath first saw Brown with his long beard on June 28, 1858, in Lawrence, Kansas; he had grown it to disguise himself since he had a price on his head. This portrait was photographed in 1858, before the raid on Harpers Ferry. (Courtesy of Historic Photo Collection, Harpers Ferry National Historical Park, Harpers Ferry, West Virginia, HF-0789.)

Plate 3. The bearded John Brown became the familiar iconographic image, one that could be used for either positive or negative propaganda. Photographers: Black and Batchelder, May 1859. (Courtesy of Library of Congress, Prints and Photographs Division, LC-USZ62-2472.)

Plate 4. In this commemorative image, John Brown looks somewhat smug and self-satisfied. He holds a copy of the *New York Tribune,* Horace Greeley's antislavery newspaper; in the background is a map of Bleeding Kansas. In 1859 artists E. B. and E. C. Kellogg produced this lithograph anonymously for an audience of Brown supporters, but in 1860, when Brown's actions at Harpers Ferry had gained public support in the North, they began signing copies. (Courtesy of Library of Congress, Prints and Photographs Division, LC-USZ62-89569.)

Plate 5. A month after the Harpers Ferry raid, *Harper's Weekly* depicts slaves determined to resist John Brown and his followers. These political cartoons effectively undercut the heroic aspects of Brown's efforts by making fun of his methods. Although published in New York, the magazine was soft on slavery because of its large Southern readership. David Hunter Strother, "Effect of John Brown's Invasion at the South," cover of *Harper's Weekly*, November 19, 1859, 737. (Courtesy of Library of Congress, Prints and Photographs Division, LC-USZ62-79478.)

Plate 6. A sinister John Brown offers one of the one thousand pikes that he had brought with him to Harpers Ferry in order to arm the slaves, who could then fight against their white masters to gain their freedom. But as in the *Harper's Weekly* cartoon of November 19 (plate 5), this slave refuses to join Brown. *Harper's Weekly,* November 26, 1859.

A PREMATURE MOVEMENT.

JOHN BROWN. "Here! Take this, and follow me. My name's Brown."
CUFFEE. "Please God! Mr. Brown, dat is onpossible. We ain't done seedin' yit at our house."

JOHN BROWN

Plate 7. An 1863 print depicts John Brown as a compassionate martyr, pausing to kiss a black child held by a Madonna-like slave woman. Sinister guards surround him; overhead flies the Virginia state flag, whose motto, ironically, is *Sic semper tyrannis. John Brown. Meeting the slave woman and her child on the steps of Charlestown Jail on his way to execution.* From the original painting by Louis Ransom. Currier and Ives, 1863. (Courtesy of Library of Congress, Prints and Photographs Division, LC-USZ62-2890.)

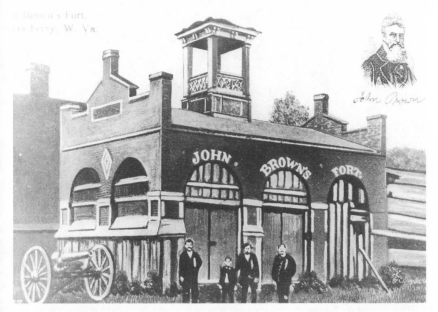

Plate 8. As depicted on a contemporary postcard, by the 1880s the John Brown Fort in Harpers Ferry had become a tourist attraction and a cultural icon. (Courtesy of the Harpers Ferry National Historical Park, Harpers Ferry, West Virginia, HF-8.)

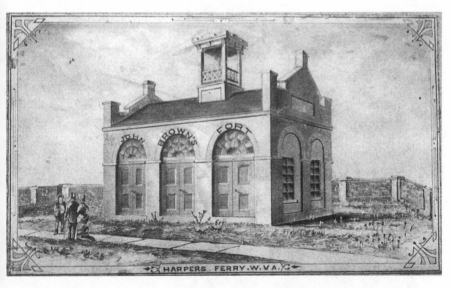

Plate 9. During the 1880s the John Brown Fort became so popular a cultural icon that Thomas Savery, who had purchased the fort, scavenged bricks from it, had silver engravings of the fort attached to the bricks, and gave them away as souvenirs. (Brick in museum collection at Harpers Ferry National Historical Park; photograph by Paul A. Shackel.)

Plate 10. By the mid-1890s the John Brown Fort had become a symbol of racial equality for African Americans. Photo of the John Brown Fort on the Murphy farm with members of the Pilgrim Party from the National League of Colored Women, 1896. (Courtesy of the Harpers Ferry National Historical Park, Harpers Ferry, West Virginia, HF-599.)

Plate 11. A Storer College class meets in front of the John Brown Fort in the 1940s. The fort was located on the Storer campus in Harpers Ferry, West Virginia, from 1910 to 1968. (Courtesy of the Harpers Ferry National Historical Park, Harpers Ferry, West Virginia, HF-581.)

Plate 12. In this idealized portrait, Brown leads a family of slaves that he had liberated in Missouri in 1859. He is taking them toward Detroit and freedom in Canada. Mural by Arthur S. Covey in the post office in Torrington, Connecticut (John Brown's birthplace), 1937. Photograph by Robert Fenton Houser. (Collection of the Torrington Historical Society, Torrington, Connecticut.)

Plate 13. In John Steuart Curry's Kansas statehouse mural (ca. 1937–42), a fanatical John Brown brings the apocalypse to Kansas and to the country. This cause-effect relationship suggests tragic overtones because of the dead bodies of Union and Confederate soldiers at Brown's feet. *The Tragic Prelude: John Brown* by John Steuart Curry, state capitol, Topeka, Kansas, 1937–42. (Courtesy of the Kansas State Historical Society.)

Plate 14. Unlike John Steuart Curry's apocalyptic image (plate 13), Mexican muralist Diego Rivera's mural depicts John Brown as a more positive catalyst for change. Appearing as a hanged martyr, Brown looks into the future and sees the Emancipation Proclamation. Detail of *Portrait of America* by Diego Rivera, New Workers School, New York City, 1933 (destroyed). From International Ladies Garment Workers Union, *Rivera Murals* (pamphlet, 1942). (Collection of Jean Libby.)

six

JOHN BROWN AS
"LAWLESS FANATIC"

A Usable Past for the Postwar South

CHARLES J. HOLDEN

Stephen Oates writes that John Brown, for all the discussion of his sanity, was at least canny enough to gauge the white Southern reaction to Brown's adventures across the Mason-Dixon Line. Brown, being a Northerner and an abolitionist, understood that he merely had to "step into Dixie with a gun, announce that he was there to free the blacks, and the effect on the South would be cataclysmic." Oates then adds, "He was right."[1] The same could be said for John Brown's appearance in postwar Southern histories. Mere mention of John Brown sets loose torrents of vitriol from postwar Southern writers—the description of Brown as "this fiend in human shape" being only a more extreme variation on the theme.[2]

The defeat of the Confederacy threw questions of power into chaos. By the end of the century, the self-proclaimed New South boasted of, more than it achieved, industrialization, an improving educational system, and progress toward national reunification.[3] Yet the South still also adhered to older, conservative ideals more assumed than explored by historians. These include firm beliefs in racial and gender hierarchy, wariness about industrialization, fears of democratization and majoritarian rule, and lingering states' rights sentiment against an increasingly powerful central government.[4]

These older conservative values abound in post–Civil War historical writing on John Brown. The meaning and use of Brown's legacy in the postwar white South is nearly absent in historical scholarship. Oates notes that in the South "a counterlegend" arose regarding John Brown, although Oates does mention Robert Penn Warren's 1929 biography of Brown.[5] Writers of the Southern conservative tradition—figures Charles Reagan Wilson describes as having a "hierarchical, paternalistic, moralistic, non-materialistic conception of the good society"—made frequent references to John Brown.[6] In memoirs and in publications such as *The Southern Historical Society Papers* and *The Confederate Veteran*, conservatives shaped the Southern interpretation of John Brown and inserted into the New South political and social principles of the Old.[7]

Postwar Southern writers used John Brown and the raid on Harpers Ferry to make a range of assertions representing different aspects of the proslavery defense. To paraphrase the arguments of slavery's defenders: the institution of slavery produced a noble planter class and contented slaves, it made model laborers out of backward Africans—under white tutelage, and it civilized and Christianized heathen savages.

Former Confederate officer A. R. H. Ranson, born and raised just outside Harpers Ferry, began his 1913 reminiscences with a historical sketch of plantation life in the valley leading up to Brown's raid. Ranson described the planter class on the eve of John Brown's raid: "I knew of no more refined, cultivated, and hospitable people anywhere." He maintained that slavery had created a leisured, educated, genteel class, a fact that abolitionists refused to accept because "they were simply ignorant of the subject. . . . Bad men are brutal often, and some slave-owners were brutal; but that they were brutal as a class, I deny."[8]

The explanation of a bad slave owner among an otherwise virtuous slave-owning class was crucial to the proslavery ideology. Ranson and other planters, both before and after the war, did not perceive the cruel master as a contradiction of the proslavery ideology. Southern conservatives believed that sin, for instance, or the inherent weakness of human nature, rather than the in-

CHARLES J. HOLDEN

stitution of slavery itself, explained the brutal slave owner. Proslavery Christians struggled to understand why antislavery Christians could not comprehend what to them was a simple, theologically sound explanation.

Accordingly, Ranson remembered race relations under this paternalistic rule as peaceful and intimate. Like many former slave owners, Ranson asserted the view that slaves were faithful during the war and accepted emancipation reluctantly. He recalled the slave-master relationship as one built on affection and kindness: "That kindness was the rule was fully proved during the civil war [*sic*]; for when all [white] men had gone to the front, and only the women and negroes [*sic*] were left, the negroes were the only protectors and supporters the women had, and it is a historical fact that they performed their duties faithfully to the end, and not one single instance of outrage has been recorded" (429–30). Clearly, not all Southern white men went to the front, and seldom were Southern white women left entirely alone with slaves for any length of time. Nowhere was this more the case than in Ranson's embattled corner of Virginia (soon to become West Virginia), which saw some of the heaviest fighting. Ranson further recalled how one slave "followed" him throughout the war and "though given his freedom twice by our being captured, refused to be free and came back to me. And why should not this be so? I was the best friend he had in the world and he knew it." Slavery made slaves "docile, gentle, and easy-going," and according to Ranson's recollections, they "loved to laugh and dance and sing songs." His slaves had "warm clothing, plenty of wholesome food, and a good doctor when ill" (430–32).

No sooner does John Brown appear in Ranson's memoirs than this simplistic, idyllic picture of the slave plantation becomes complicated and muddied. The Monday following Brown's Sunday night raid, and prior to his hearing the news, Ranson was overseeing the slaves' field work when he noticed that "the men often turned their eyes on me as I followed behind them in their work,—a thing I had never observed in them before." He referred to their looks as "stolen glances" that made him "feel uncomfortable and doubtful" (439). Peculiar behavior among "best friends," one would have to say.

Ranson tried another frequently used white Southern argument in defense of slavery and later in defense of segregation—that only white Southerners understood the mysterious ways of the African American. John Brown, Ranson explained, mistakenly assumed that the slaves wanted freedom and "would gladly and instantly embrace the first opportunity which was presented them."

John Brown as "Lawless Fanatic"

Brown, Ranson wrote, misunderstood the true character of the slave and the true conditions of slavery. Indeed, Ranson reminded his readers: the "negro . . . in that section at least, [was] comfortable and happy, [and] there was such a thing as love between master and slave. . . . As a consequence, not one slave joined him [Brown] at Harper's [sic] Ferry" (445).

Ranson, however, reveals an inconsistent memory of life in western Virginia. His discussion of emancipation explains that when the Union armies finally took control of the region, "the negro saw his opportunity and embraced it," but earlier when Brown had attempted his invasion, the slaves "had sense enough to see the utter folly of his attempt and turned their backs upon him to a man" (446). Here Ranson himself concludes that it was not for love of a master's kind care that the slaves in Harpers Ferry did not rise to greet Brown. The slaves recognized an impending disaster and wisely stayed away. Following the war, Ranson's slaves also apparently had a different notion of loyalty to Ranson's family than he tries to maintain. He earlier defended their obedience during the war, noting that "not one single instance of outrage" occurred. His memoirs, however, reveal that while perhaps not misbehaving, his slaves also did not remain on the Ranson farm. When Ranson returned from the war he was surprised and a little hurt to find that only "one able-bodied negro" remained (446).

In 1906 the Southern Historical Society published an episode from the war written by William Preston Cabell. Cabell recalls how in March 1864 the women of Richmond saved former Governor Henry A. Wise from Yankee marauders anxious to capture Wise for his role in hanging John Brown. Like Ranson, Cabell portrays the scene in lush antebellum colors, replete with scenes of a noble, genteel planter class; loyal slaves; and zealous, murderous Northerners.

Part of the genteel scenes include descriptions of then Brigadier General Wise traveling to his daughter's plantation, Eastwood, south of Richmond. On his arrival a feast commenced, and at the evening's end Wise rested his head "on snowy pillows . . . in a Christian bed, with linen, lavender-scented sheets, and warm, soft blankets, to dream of days gone by."[9] This scene was shattered the next morning by reports that the Union army was advancing toward Richmond. One group of Yankees under Col. Ulric Dahlgren was specifically intent on capturing General Wise as "the man that hanged John Brown." Cabell reports that along the way, Union soldiers paid "a burly,

CHARLES J. HOLDEN

black negro man" ten dollars to guide them through the ferry crossings of the James River. The man evidently did not know the depth of the crossing, and a handful of Union soldiers and horses drowned. Dahlgren took the black man back to the shore and had him hanged: "The neighbors [Virginians] allowed this coal-black corpse to hang there for a week as an object lesson to impress the slaves of the vicinage with a new idea of Northern feeling toward the blacks" (356). With the rise of lynching in the early 1900s fast becoming a national disgrace, and with much of the blame pointed at the white South, this story about the Union army's actions provides a provocative, contrasting image.

At Eastwood, loyal slaves "Uncle Ephraim" and "Tom . . . one of the most courtly and graceful butlers," helped Wise escape. Shifting the scene to the next plantation, Cabell adds "Aunt Lou" and "Uncle Charles" to his list of devoted slaves. With the arrival of Dahlgren's men, "the old black 'mammy,' Aunt Lou" hid the children while Uncle Charles, who was "as true and loyal as 'Aunt Lou,'" humbly "begged the bluejackets not to burn and destroy the property of his master and mistress" (357).

In addition to giving him the opportunity to establish and praise the loyalty of slaves, the story of the search for General Wise allowed Cabell to invoke the traditional Southern myth of ideal womanhood. Having failed to capture Wise at Eastwood, Dahlgren and his troops scampered down the road to the next plantation where they encountered one of the Old South's finest ladies, Sarah Bruce Seddon, the wife of Confederate secretary of war James Seddon. After Dahlgren introduced himself to Sarah Seddon, she immediately charmed him by recalling, "[Y]our father was an old beau of mine." This, Cabell continues, "seemed to strike a tender chord, and the Colonel at once doffed his hat and promised Mrs. Seddon protection." Sarah Seddon then ordered Uncle Charles to bring some wine, and "quickly the hostile invader was converted into an amiable guest, whose brain was soon exhilarated by the gracious diplomacy and finesse of his father's quondam sweetheart." Cabell concludes the entire episode by noting that through this "device and strategy," Sarah Seddon detained Dahlgren and allowed Wise to ride to Richmond and notify James Seddon and the other Confederate authorities of the impending danger to Richmond (356).

Gender ideology in the Old South and during the war placed white women within subordinate, yet not powerless, roles.[10] Sarah Seddon combined the femininity, intelligence, bravery, and loyalty central to the notion of ideal

John Brown as "Lawless Fanatic"

womanhood as it was established in the Old South. Cabell's lesson is not subtle: these ideals contained the power to save, literally, the capital of the Confederacy, as well as General Wise, "the man that hanged John Brown."

Along the same lines, LaSalle Corbell Pickett, the wife of Gen. George Pickett, enjoyed some popularity after the war with a string of romanticized, genteel pseudohistories of the South. Her recollections of John Brown, inspired by a chance meeting with Robert E. Lee, appear in her 1917 autobiography *What Happened to Me.* LaSalle Corbell and her father shared a train ride from Richmond with Lee shortly after Brown's raid. At one point, she recalls Lee asking her father what the slaves' reaction to Brown's hanging would be. Her father replied: "Well, I've thought of that, too, Colonel, and I've asked my foreman, who is a representative of his race, if he did not think we ought to hang old John Brown. He looked at me earnestly for a while then, shaking his head slowly, said, 'I knows, Marse Dae, dat po' Marse John done en bruk de law, killin' all dem mens; but den, Marse Dae, even if po' Marse John did bre'k de law, don't you think, suh, dat hangin' him would be a li[']l abrupt?'"[11] Pickett then adds that Lee laughed and replied, "'I think that just about expresses the sentiment not only of the colored people but of many others.' They agreed that John Brown was an honest, earnest, courageous old man and that his friends ought to put him where he would be cared for" (85). Corbell's "foreman" appears as a kindly, contented slave who under his master's tutelage has a clear sense of right and wrong, as well as hierarchy and compassion. These were precisely the virtues trumpeted by proslavery writers for decades before and after the war.[12] The "foreman" disapproved of John Brown for breaking the law; he made no mention of Brown's mission to free slaves, and in the end he wanted Brown cared for, not executed.

At a 1911 reunion of the Army of Northern Virginia, Winfield Peters's speech used racial themes that are extreme, but not uncommon, in their characterizations. Recounting Brown's activities in Kansas in 1856, Peters found Brown's reasons for the murder of his proslavery victims significant. Brown ordered their deaths because the slaveholders were "making model laborers, harmless and happy, out of savage negroes, with cannibals for daddies." This, he continues, "in the satanic minds of Brown and his Puritan abolition co-conspirators, was a crime against the cardinal virtues!"[13]

James McNeilly, editor of the *Confederate Veteran,* the magazine of the Union of Confederate Veterans, struck a similar chord in 1917. McNeilly claims that the South had inherited the institution of slavery only after it was "forced upon her originally by the rapacity of England and by the activities of northeastern slave traders." The South, he asserts, opened its arms to "the victims of this rapacity, black savages from Africa[,] and in two centuries had given them a measure of Christianity and civilization." In addition, slavery made slaves "the best-cared-for and most contented body of laborers in the world." McNeilly's interpretation of slavery features John Brown as the "real spirit" of Northern fanaticism. His "object was to free the negroes even at the price of destroying the Union and arousing the slaves to the butchery of the master's family."[14]

White Southerners argued long and hard that their reasons for secession involved far more than the preservation of the peculiar institution. It is hard to imagine states' rights or constitutional matters coming to blows in the mid-1800s *without* slavery in the midst of these debates. Nonetheless, white Southerners, in their historical writing, remained steadfast in their insistence that the South rose for other causes. These included the traditional Southern conservative distrust of democracy at home and fears of centralization of power in the nation. Discussions on John Brown allowed spokesmen for the Old South to lament these perceived evils.

Famous for his 1861 statement that slavery was the "cornerstone" of the new Confederacy, Alexander Stephens, former vice president of the Southern nation, used the Kansas exploits of John Brown to argue differently after the war. Stephens wrote a two-volume history arguing that secession struck a blow against the centralization of political power by Northern fanatics. According to Stephens, following Brown's 1856 activities, President James Buchanan missed a chance to put down "these mischievous malcontents." Stephens asserts that there existed at that time, "a very large majority . . . devotedly attached to the Union under the Constitution . . . who were resolved to maintain, if possible, the Federal system against all attempts, whether covert or open, at Centralism or Consolidation."[15]

Other Southerners, meanwhile, shared Stephens's postwar interpretation and continued to apologize for or explain away his "cornerstone" statement. J. William Jones offered a remarkable refutation of the claim that "'the South' had declared slavery to be the 'corner-stone' of the Confederacy." He instead asserts that the views of those who had supported the cornerstone argument were "very far from being those of 'the South.'" In short, Jones, and by extension those arguing secession strictly from constitutional grounds, were

John Brown as "Lawless Fanatic"

forced to reject the prewar Alexander Stephens, the Confederate States' vice president, as one who did not speak for the South.[16]

James McNeilly explains in a 1916 essay that the North had gradually departed from the original, loose confederation of states and had thus made war inevitable. "But lo, the change!" McNeilly exclaims. With the outcome of the war, "the Federal government has become supreme." Southern whites, he insists, fought for the Constitution in its original construction. The Confederacy's defeat, he laments, "meant a radical revolution in the nature of our government from a Federal republic to a centralized nation." Thus, he adds, "Before we boast of the change that has been accomplished with us, we should remember that the history of liberty shows it in constant conflict with centralized power."[17]

In the same essay, McNeilly discusses how prominent Northern politicians such as William McKinley, Teddy Roosevelt, and Elihu Root continued through the years to make great shows of admiration for John Brown. Managing to avoid the issue of slavery almost entirely, McNeilly counters that to expect white Southerners to join in the John Brown celebrations "is asking us to confess that the abolitionists were right in refusing to be bound by the Constitution and in denying the equality of the Southern States" (130–31).

Former Confederate postmaster general John Reagan and John W. Daniel, a postwar senator from Virginia, both articulated the Southern conservative fear of democracy in writing about John Brown. They would have nodded in fast agreement to John C. Calhoun's suggestion that "a government based wholly on the numerical majority, would . . . certainly corrupt and debase the most patriotic and virtuous people."[18] Like many Southern conservatives, Reagan perceived in the movements for abolition and democracy threats of race-based violence and political tyranny. Brown, Reagan explains, backed by his "armed band of revolutionists," came to Virginia "for the purpose of inaugurating a servile war between the white and black people, with all the barbarism and cruelty which would of necessity be engendered by such a war." Once Northern politicians converted to abolitionism, efforts at compromise following Brown's raid at Harpers Ferry were met with "hooting and derision by the Republicans." Appeals to the North, Reagan writes, were answered by the taunt: "We are in the majority and you will have to submit."[19]

Writing on the eve of disfranchisement in 1889, John Daniel places John Brown's Harpers Ferry raid under a broader discussion of political democracy

CHARLES J. HOLDEN

and racial solidarity among whites. The South, he explains, rose in 1861 to protect access to the nation's political process for whites only. "Look further southward," Daniel advises his readers, "behold how the Latin races have commingled their blood with the aborigines and negroes, creating mongrel republics and empires, where society is debased and where governments, resting on no clear principles, swing like pendulums between the extremes of tyranny and license." White political solidarity, not slavery, unified the South in 1859 when John Brown came from Kansas with his "band of misguided men, and, murdering innocent citizens, invoked the insurrection of the slaves." Daniel argues that "it was not the property invested in the slave that stood in the way, for emancipation with compensation for them was then practicable . . . and was indeed offered." But, he continues, "free the slaves, they would become voters; becoming voters, they would predominate in numbers, and so predominating, what would become of white civilization?"[20]

Focusing more on the postwar threat to Southern white supremacy, Thomas M. Norwood, a senator from Georgia, offered in 1874 a woeful vision of life under Brown's legacy: "The white man and the black, the mulatto and the quadroon, the coolie and the Digger Indian, shall be gathered, a united family, in one unbroken circle, around one common soup bowl and using the same spoon, while shielded by the Stars and Stripes and regaled by the martial measure and inspiring strain of—John Brown's soul is marching on."[21]

At a dedication to the Virginia monument at Gettysburg, Leigh Robinson placed Robert E. Lee at Harpers Ferry, fighting against Northern forces and majoritarian rule. John Brown represented these forces, and as Lee and Brown squared off in 1859, "then and there were brought face to face the opposite ideals. No!—*the idol versus the ideal!*" Robinson continues: "One who shared the blood of the Revolutionary Lees did not have to strive mightily to read signs of a tradition of free government sacrificed to a chimera." In the aftermath of the Harpers Ferry raid, the North "fully realized that the way, with assurance, to make a majority permanent, was to make it geographical." Thus, Robinson concludes, "When liberty says: 'Death to robbers,' what more natural than for robbers to say: 'Then death to liberty.'"[22]

John Brown also provided an outlet for discussions of free labor and gender relations in the New South. Ranson's memoirs continued a traditional Southern conservative critique of free labor and industrialization from the days of

John Brown as "Lawless Fanatic"

George Fitzhugh and James Henry Hammond. Having asserted that Brown and his followers did not understand that the slave had lifelong care under the master, Ranson asks further, "How many laboring people, white or black, have this provision now?"[23] This was a timely question in 1913.

As Ranson published his memoirs, a bitter dispute between coal miners and mine owners gripped his home state of West Virginia. In Harpers Ferry it seemed that once again agitators were causing trouble among the local laborers. The *Charleston Labor Argus,* a paper that supported the Socialist Party, reminded the "coal barons" that "Southern slave barons hung John Brown and brought about the Civil War." It would be wise, the paper continues, for West Virginia's coal barons to take heed, or "they might start a revolution that will be equally disastrous to their interest." John Browns, the paper concludes, "are bad medicine for both aristocracy and plutocracy."[24]

As an Old South conservative, Ranson remained unimpressed by either side of the dispute and found in slavery an absence of labor strife that benefited the entire social hierarchy. Having already asserted slavery's advantages for the slave, Ranson writes that for the planter, "His butler, his coachman, his cook were all his property. They could not strike for higher wages, they could not give notice of leaving. They were there and there to stay." Slave labor freed the master to become a "better-educated man, a better-read man . . . he was a better-mannered man than the man of the present age."[25]

Similarly, James McNeilly argued in 1917 that the Confederacy fought to oppose the "false and fanatical theories of equality and liberty" represented by John Brown, a "noted thief and murderer." He then adds, "her defeat leaves it still in doubt whether the present regime of the trust or the labor union is to prevail over liberty, equality, and fraternity." Concluding with great irony, he proclaims that the South "fought 'that the government of the people, by the people, and for the people might not perish from the earth.' The South is proud of her record."[26] McNeilly's use of Lincoln's words and his claim that the Old South represented the legacy of the French Revolution—liberty, equality, fraternity—would no doubt have left many Southern conservatives of the 1850s gasping in disbelief.[27]

Donald Davidson, one of the sharpest Southern conservatives of the Great Depression–New Deal era, bluntly captured the persistent disdain the white South had for John Brown. In his essay "American Heroes," Davidson asks,

CHARLES J. HOLDEN

"John Brown may be memorialized both in Connecticut and Kansas, but who dares to propose that his name be honored south of the Mason and Dixon line?"[28] Davidson disapproved of the postwar movement within the South toward reunification under Northern ideals and industrialization. He painfully understood that this kind of reunification came at a cost to his view of the Southern identity. Davidson elsewhere asks simply (yet, one imagines, not without a little relish), "Why does Miss [Ellen] Glasgow, self-styled the 'social historian' of Virginia, propagate ideas that would be more quickly approved by Oswald Garrison Villard [a prominent Brown biographer] than by the descendants of [Virginia's] first families?"[29]

The dominant, conservative image of John Brown as a murderous, lawless, Yankee zealot created problems for New South advocates. Brown's career was too divisive along sectional lines as New South boosters sought reunification and Northern capital. The New South still supported the Old South's tradition of racial hierarchy, but too much emphasis on white supremacy brought out postwar defenders of slavery as the region lurched toward a free-labor system. Postwar nostalgia for slavery undermined the New South's efforts to garner Northern aid. Paul Gaston observes that all New South critiques of the Old South began with an investigation of slavery. Gaston continues: "one of the happiest discoveries of the New South spokesmen was the finding that the destruction of slavery was a great event not because it freed the blacks . . . but because it liberated the whites."[30]

This left John Brown to the Southern conservatives, who found much in Brown's story that could be used to defend and even advocate the principles of the Old South. Perhaps even more than newer intellectuals like Donald Davidson were aware, conservative Southern historical writing kept much of the Old South ideology very much alive.[31] The raid at Harpers Ferry, for example, was a successful event by conservative standards. The slaves did not rebel, although we might offer a different explanation today than the conservative argument for the slaves' contentment. Robert E. Lee and J. E. B. Stuart were victorious without raising the sticky issues of secession and broken vows to the Union. In the late 1800s and early 1900s, Northern industrialists cried out for law and order against labor agitation. Southern conservatives, who accepted, more than welcomed, industrialization, gladly refreshed Yankee memories of an earlier time when many Northerners appreciated John Brown's lawlessness—especially, Southerners felt, since it occurred somewhere other than in the North.

John Brown as "Lawless Fanatic"

The writing of postwar Southern conservatives merits closer evaluation. While the South was irrevocably changed by emancipation and Northern victory, the changes within the South, in the minds of many white Southerners, were still measured against its traditional conservatism. This vital intellectual force survived in the vast amount of historical writing after 1865. Here was a field left open for Southern conservatives. As Charles Reagan Wilson observes in *Baptized in Blood,* their work, such as that which deals with John Brown, teems with "doubtful history, but revealing rhetoric."[32]

NOTES

1. Stephen B. Oates, *To Purge This Land with Blood: A Biography of John Brown* (1970; rev. ed., Amherst: University of Massachusetts Press, 1985), ix.

2. John H. Paris, "The Soldier's History of the War," *Our Living and Our Dead* (New Bern, NC), December 1874, 1:302.

3. See Paul Gaston, *The New South Creed: A Study in Southern Mythmaking* (New York: Knopf, 1970); Gaines Foster, *The Ghosts of the Confederacy: Defeat, the Lost Cause, and the Emergence of the New South, 1865 to 1913* (New York: Oxford University Press, 1987).

4. For an enlightening comparison of Southern cities following the war, see Don Doyle, *New Men, New Cities, New South: Atlanta, Nashville, Charleston, Mobile, 1860–1910* (Chapel Hill: University of North Carolina Press, 1990). Doyle contrasts the fate of Atlanta and Nashville, which embraced the principles and direction of the New South, with Charleston and Mobile, which did not.

5. Stephen B. Oates, "John Brown and His Judges: A Critique of the Historical Literature," *Civil War History* 17 (March 1971): 5–24; Robert Penn Warren, *John Brown: The Making of a Martyr* (New York: Payson and Clarke, 1929).

6. Charles Reagan Wilson, *Baptized in Blood: The Religion of the Lost Cause, 1865–1920* (Athens: University of Georgia Press, 1980), 90.

7. Postwar Southern conservatives also contributed their share of a continuing defense against white Northern writers, including the self-appointed keepers of Brown's legacy. For instance, reviews in the *Southern Bivouac* and the *Confederate Veteran* of John Brown biographies by white Northern writers were nearly all negative and occasionally vicious. But one must be acknowledged before one can be rejected. Also, white Southern writers ignored almost completely W. E. B. Du Bois's 1909 pro-Brown biography, *John Brown.* For examples of the continued white Southern criticism of the pro-Brown, Northern interpretation, see "The Editor's Table," *Southern Bivouac* 1 (February 1886): 575; James H. McNeilly, "The Real John Brown," *Confederate Veteran* 14 (January 1916): 44.

8. A. H. R. Ranson, "Reminiscences of the Civil War by a Confederate Staff Officer," *Sewanee Review* 31 (October 1913): 429 (hereafter cited in text).

9. William Preston Cabell, "How Women Saved Richmond," *Southern Historical Society Papers* 34 (1906): 355 (hereafter cited in text).

10. See Drew Gilpin Faust, *Southern Stories: Slaveholders in Peace and War* (Columbia: University of Missouri Press, 1992); Elizabeth Fox-Genovese, *Within the Plantation Household: Black and White Women in the Old South* (Chapel Hill: University of North Carolina Press, 1988); Anne Firor Scott, *The Southern Lady: From Pedestal to Politics, 1830–1930* (Chicago: University of Chicago Press, 1970).

11. LaSalle Corbell Pickett, *What Happened to Me* (New York: Bretano's, 1917), 84–85 (hereafter cited in text).

12. Drew Gilpin Faust, ed., *The Ideology of Slavery: Proslavery Thought in the Antebellum South, 1830–1860* (Baton Rouge: Louisiana State University Press, 1981); Eugene Genovese, *The Slaveholders' Dilemma: Freedom and Progress in Southern Conservative Thought, 1820–1860* (Columbia: University of South Carolina Press, 1992); John David Smith, *An Old Creed for the New South: Proslavery Ideology and Historiography, 1865–1918* (Westport, CT: Greenwood Press, 1985).

13. Winfield Peters, "Lee and Stuart at Harper's Ferry," *Southern Historical Society Papers* 38 (1911): 373.

14. James McNeilly, "Why Did the Confederate States Fight?" *Confederate Veteran* 25 (September 1917): 398.

15. Alexander H. Stephens, *A Constitutional View of the Late War Between the States; Its Causes, Character, Conduct and Results Presented in a Series of Colloquies at Liberty Hall* (Philadelphia: National Publishing Company, 1868–70), 258.

16. J. William Jones, "Is the 'Eclectic History of the United States,' Written by Miss Thalheimer and Published by Van Antwerp, Bragg and Co., Cincinnati, a Fit Book to be Used in Our Schools?" *Southern Historical Society Papers* 12 (June 1884): 283.

17. James McNeilly, "The Defeat of the Confederacy—Was It a Blessing?" *Confederate Veteran* 24 (February 1916): 128 (hereafter cited in text).

18. John C. Calhoun, "A Disquisition on Government," in *Union and Liberty: The Political Philosophy of John C. Calhoun,* ed. Ross M. Lence (Indianapolis: Liberty Fund, 1992), 39.

19. John H. Reagan, *Memoirs, with Special Reference to Secession and the Civil War* (1906; repr., Austin: Pemberton Press, 1968), 90–91.

20. John W. Daniel, "The Life, Services and Character of Jefferson Davis: An Oration by John W. Daniel," *Southern Historical Society Papers* 17 (1889): 141–42. One historian describes Daniel as a "florid, limping Confederate veteran" who gave a consistent answer when the same question was applied to the people of the Philippines following the Spanish-American War. Daniel was strongly opposed to allowing "the mess of Asiatic pottage" into the American political process. Jack Temple Kirby, *Darkness at the Dawning: Race and Reform in the Progressive South* (Philadelphia: Lippincott, 1972), 115–16.

21. Quoted in Richard Weaver, *The Southern Tradition at Bay: A History of Postbellum Thought* (Washington, DC: Regnery Gateway, 1989), 158. Digger Indians were

primitive tribes located in what is now the southwest United States who had not gone beyond the root-gathering stage of development. Hence, for Norwood, the reference to their having a share of the "common soup bowl" represented as great a threat to white supremacy, as did the "quadroon" and the "coolie."

22. Leigh Robinson, "Dedication of Virginia Memorial at Gettysburg," *Southern Historical Society Papers* 42 (September 1917): 111; emphasis Robinson's.

23. Ranson, "Reminiscences," 445.

24. Quoted in Edward M. Steel, ed., *The Court Martial of Mother Jones* (Lexington: University Press of Kentucky, 1996), 236.

25. Ranson, "Reminiscences," 446.

26. McNeilly, "Why Did the Confederate States Fight?" 398.

27. See Eugene Genovese's discussion of James Henry Hammond in *Slaveholders' Dilemma*, 88–107.

28. Donald Davidson, *The Attack on Leviathan: Regionalism and Nationalism in the United States* (Chapel Hill: University of North Carolina Press, 1938), 221.

29. Donald Davidson, "A Mirror for Artists," in *I'll Take My Stand: The South and the Agrarian Tradition* (Baton Rouge: Louisiana State University Press, 1930), 58.

30. Gaston, *New South Creed,* 57.

31. Davidson's fellow Agrarian, Robert Penn Warren, hardly a reactionary for his time, incorporated into his biography of Brown many traditional Southern conservative views on states' rights and on slavery as a paternalistic, benign institution. It is, I would argue, more a statement of the continuing influence of this tradition than an indictment of his moral failures that Warren presented Brown's actions within these Southern views. In white Southern schools, churches, and newspapers, these views were put forward daily. It would have been remarkable indeed to find many white Southerners raised in this environment of the early 1900s having a change of heart upon their first reading of, for example, W. E. B. Du Bois's work, rightfully praised as it is now.

32. Wilson, *Baptized in Blood,* 165.

PART THREE

Behavioral Analyses of John Brown

seven

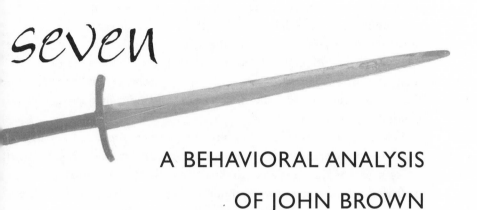

A BEHAVIORAL ANALYSIS

OF JOHN BROWN

Martyr or Terrorist?

JAMES N. GILBERT

The scholarly examination of the topic of terrorism has developed into a significant area of legal and criminological research. Academic and governmental studies pertaining to terrorist crimes and those who perpetrate them are now voluminous and continue to be actively pursued. Emerging as what appeared to be a new form of criminal deviance, the definition and cause of the "disease of the 70s" has challenged criminologists.[1] While most contemporary documented incidents continue to occur outside the United States, the fear of domestic terrorism, as recent events have illustrated, remains a legitimate concern. The public and researchers alike have in the past commonly assumed that this country would continue to be spared from acts that conform to our contemporary definition of terrorist activity. Terrorism was associated with a foreign environment and viewed as exceptional in the history of American criminal violence.[2]

But after February 26, 1993, when the New York World Trade Center was the target of a massive terrorist bombing, the attention of Americans became riveted upon the unique form of criminality that we have collectively termed terrorism. And of course this criminal act was followed by the far more deadly bombing in Oklahoma City and the attacks on the World Trade Center and the Pentagon on September 11, 2001. Although much of the media and public has treated these terrorist acts as precedent-setting domestic attacks, the history of terrorism in the United States actually dates to the founding of the nation.[3] Of the many such violent episodes in our earlier history, John Brown's attack on Harpers Ferry in October 1859 is comparable to these more recent acts in terms of national terror and consequent social and political upheaval.

In late 1859 John Brown and twenty-one followers attempted to rally and arm large numbers of slaves by attacking and briefly holding the United States arsenal at Harpers Ferry, Virginia (presently West Virginia). Captured by federal military forces and local militia, Brown was hastily tried and executed.[4] While the life and deeds of John Brown are immensely important for their impact on abolitionism and the American Civil War, this powerful historical figure is rarely defined as a terrorist. Instead, a vast collection of literature generally portrays Brown as either saint or madman. On one hand, there is the sympathetic traditional portrait of John Brown as an American hero of near mythical proportions. Such an image is certainly not viewed as criminally deviant, nor does it suggest the status of criminal folk hero. But while a minority historical judgment has questioned his sanity or the radical end-justification logic he appeared to employ, few even in this camp would declare his actions truly terrorist. Civil War and military historian John Hubbell reflects this multidimensional view. Stating that while John Brown was, "in fact, a combination of humility and arrogance, submission and aggression, murder and martyrdom," his true motivation may not have been calculated terroristic cause and effect, but "an unresolved resentment of his father; his hatred of slaveholders may have been the unconscious resolution of his anger."[5]

Thus, one can only question how and why this imagery has persisted throughout the decades. Is the terrorist label lacking due to the singular rationale of his crimes: the massive evil of slavery? Alternatively, are we correct in excluding Brown from the definition of terrorist because his actions simply fail to conform to contemporary elements that constitute such a criminal? For example, a similar definitional confusion currently exists regarding various violent attacks on abortion clinics and their personnel by those who,

JAMES N. GILBERT

like Brown, rationalize their violence by moral or religious conviction. Some would define convicted murderer Paul Hill as a domestic terrorist for his premeditated attack on an abortion doctor and an escort during the summer of 1994. Yet others would fail to define his actions as terroristic due to Hill's justification of his act as a "lesser evil."

In order to define Brown precisely as a terrorist rather than as a martyr, the meaning of terrorism must be explored. As with many singular, emotion-producing labels of criminality, terrorism is easier to describe than define. The *Vice President's Task Force on Combating Terrorism* describes terrorism as a phenomenon involving "the unlawful use of threat of violence against persons or property to further political or social objectives."[6] In a similar vein, the FBI's Terrorist Research and Analytical Center states that terroristic activity "is the unlawful use of force or violence against persons or property to intimidate or coerce a government, the civilian population, or any segment thereof, in furtherance of political or social objectives."[7] Both definitions agree with views commonly provided by various governments. This traditional bureaucratic view stresses a triad in which both property and people are potential targets with the necessary presence of illegal actions and social or political motivations as the causative agent.

Additional attempts to conceptualize the terrorist often focus on the perpetrator's motive rather than legal definitions. To this economist Bill Anderson links the economic viewpoint, stressing that fundamental principles of economic theory are the real, often hidden, motives of such crimes. Anderson believes that after we "peel away the ideological skins and fig leaves that terrorists use to justify their violence, we come to the core reason for their actions: the terrorists' own desire for power and influence. In other words, the terrorists are seeking wealth transfers and/or power (all of which can be defined as economic or political rents) through violent means because they are not willing to pay the cost of participating in the political process."[8]

Others prefer to explain away terrorism through an apologist approach, stressing the anger, hopelessness, and governmental violence brought against various victimized populations from which, inevitably, terrorists will be mobilized. Eqbal Ahmad, a research fellow at the Washington, D.C.–based Institute for Policy Studies, stresses this sympathetic theme when he links terrorism to government indifference to violence. He believes that individuals turn to terrorism to exercise "their need to be heard, the combination of anger and helplessness producing the impulse for retributive violence. The

A Behavioral Analysis of John Brown

experience of violence by a stronger party has historically turned victims into terrorists."[9] Thus, the apologist view firmly supports the recurring belief that terrorism is merely situational, constantly coming in and out of criminal focus according to prevailing political power or orientation. Sheikh Omar Abdel-Rahman clearly embraced the situational view when he claimed to be a victim rather than an alleged conspirator in the 1993 World Trade Center bombing. Angered over his conspiracy indictment and subsequent incarceration, he stated, "but what bothers me, and makes me feel bitter about the whole thing, is when a person who was called a freedom fighter then is now called, when the war is over, a terrorist."[10]

A final view, particularly popular in fictional portrayals of terrorists, suggests individual psychopathology as the chief cause of terrorism. As detailed by political philosopher and professor of religion Moshe Amon, one form of terroristic crime may originate within the disturbed minds of some perpetrators, triggering myths and fantasies that can be categorized as messianic or apocalyptic. The messianic terrorist ideology streams from a conviction that one has special insight that produces an individual state of enlightenment. Terrorists are then convinced that "they are the only ones who see the real world, and the only ones who are not affected by its depravity. It is their mission, therefore, to liberate the blind people of this world from the rule of the unjust."[11] Although this concept may be traced to early Hebrew origins, a more contemporary form is common among Latin American terrorists. Political scientist John Pottenger concludes, "The existence of social injustice and [the] individual's commitment to human liberation, demand that a radical change can turn the Christian into a revolutionary vanguard demonstrating that God not only intervenes in human history but He does so on the right side of the oppressed."[12]

Other psychological theorists believe that the most common type of terrorist has a psychopathic or sociopathic personality. The classic traits of the psychopath—impulsiveness, lack of guilt, inability to experience emotional depth, and manipulation—are perceived as ideally suited to the commission of terrorism. The ability to kill often large numbers of strangers without compunction or to manipulate others to unwittingly further criminal ends convinces many that the psychopathic personality is a requirement for terroristic action.[13]

With such definitions of terrorism in mind, how are we to view John Brown? After almost a century and a half, the actions of Brown have been

JAMES N. GILBERT

preserved with stark clarity, yet his personality and related psychological motivations can only be surmised. John Brown was fifty-nine years old when he was executed by the state of Virginia for treason, conspiring with blacks to produce insurrection, and murder in the first degree.[14] His criminal activities of record include embezzlement and assault with a deadly weapon against an Ohio sheriff in 1842. In 1856 a warrant was issued by a proslavery Kansas district court charging Brown with "organizing against slavery." A month later he and eight other men kidnapped and murdered five Kansans, including a constable and his two sons. The killings were particularly brutal: the victims were hacked to death by repeated sword blows. In December 1858 the state of Missouri and the federal government offered a reward for Brown's capture because he was the chief suspect in yet another criminal homicide. Finally, Brown's criminal activities culminated in the seizure of the federal armory at Harpers Ferry on October 16, 1859. A company of U.S. Marines captured him the following day, and history records his execution less than fifty days after his attack against the armory.[15]

The question of whether John Brown was indeed a terrorist must be based on a definitional standard that defies emotional or mythical distortion. The linkage of Brown's cause to the horrors of slavery circumvents the true nature of the man and of his crimes. According to Albert Parry, author of a bestselling work on the history of terror and revolutionary violence, terrorists and those who study them offer innumerable explanations of their violence; yet their motivations can be compacted into three main concepts:

1. Society is sick and cannot be cured by half measures of reform.
2. The state is in itself violent and can be countered and overcome only by violence.
3. The truth of the terrorist cause justifies any action that supports it. While some terrorists recognize no moral law, others have their own "higher" morality.[16]

Comparing John Brown's actions to these criteria produces an inescapable match. On many occasions Brown expressed his solid belief that society, particularly a society that would embrace slavery, was sick beyond its own cure. Brown had clearly given up on public policy reforms or legal remedies regarding slavery when he drafted his own constitution for the benefit of his followers. The document attempts to define his justifications for the upcoming

A Behavioral Analysis of John Brown

attack at Harpers Ferry and utterly rejects the legal and moral foundation of the United States: "Therefore, we citizens of the United States and the Oppressed People, who by a Recent Decision of the Supreme Court are declared to have no rights which the white man is bound to respect; together with all other people regarded by the laws thereof, do for the time being, ordain and establish for ourselves the following provisional constitution and ordinances, the better to protect our persons, property, lives, and liberties: and to govern our actions."[17]

As to the terroristic belief that violent government can only be overcome by violence, Brown's convictions were preserved for posterity by a note he handed to a jailer while being led to the gallows: "I John Brown am now quite *certain* that the crimes of this *guilty land: will* never be purged *away;* but with Blood. I had *as I now think: vainly* flattered myself that without *very much* bloodshed: it might be done."[18]

With similar conformity, Brown's beliefs and actions demonstrated his rigid "higher" morality, which served to justify numerous crimes, including multiple homicides. As described by historian Stephen Oates, "Brown knew the Missourians would come after him . . . yet he was not afraid of the consequences for God would keep and deliver him: God alone was his judge. Now that the work was done, he believed that he had been guided by a just and wrathful God."[19]

Brown's deeds conform to contemporary definitions of terrorism, and his psychological predispositions are consistent with the terrorist model. As observed by David Hubbard, founder of the Aberrant Behavior Center and psychiatric consultant to the Federal Bureau of Prisons, the actions and personality of the terrorist are not "merely bizarre and willfully antisocial; but a reflection of deep-seated personal and cultural pathologies."[20] Such behavioral pathology is commonly linked to the psychopathic personality or, less frequently, to some form of paranoia. Virtually unknown to mental health authorities during Brown's lifetime, the psychopathic personality is currently considered a relatively common criminal mental abnormality among violent offenders. Although psychopathic criminals account for a small percentage of overall lawbreakers, psychologist William McCord notes that they commit a disproportionate percentage of violent crime.[21] While psychopaths may be encountered within any violent criminal typology, they appear to be particularly well represented in various crimes of serial violence, confidence fraud, and terrorism.[22]

The concept of psychopathy focuses on the unsocialized criminal, who is devoid of conscience and consequently in repeated conflict with society; he or she fails to learn from prior experiences. As observed by Herbert Strean, professor of social work and psychotherapy researcher at Rutgers University, the psychopath is often arrogant, callous, and lacking in empathy and tends to offer plausible rationalizations for his or her reckless behavior.[23] While John Brown demonstrated a guilt-free conscience on many occasions, his calculating leadership in the kidnapping and murder of five people in Kansas provided beyond question his capacity to free himself of normal emotion. On the night of May 26, 1856, Brown led a small party of followers to the various cabins of his political enemies, which included Constable James Doyle and his sons. During what would later be termed the Pottawatomie Massacre, the Brown party systematically dragged the five unarmed and terrified men from their homes and murdered them in a frenzy of brutal violence. "About a hundred yards down the road Salmon and Owen [Brown's sons] fell on the Doyles with broadswords. They put up a struggle, striking out, trying to shield themselves from the slashing blades as they staggered back down the road. But in a few moments the grisly work was done. Brown, who must have watched the executions in a kind of trance, now walked over and shot Doyle in the forehead with a revolver, to make certain work of it."[24] When later questioned about his motives during the Kansas murders, Brown offered a classic messianic psychopathic rationalization. Without a trace of remorse, he stated that the victims all deserved to die as they "had committed murder in their hearts already, according to the Big Book . . . their killing had been decreed by Almighty God, ordained from eternity."[25]

While the violent acts of John Brown in Kansas and at Harpers Ferry were extreme, the episode is far from the sole example of deadly historical American terrorism. Some suggest American violence against the British before the Revolutionary War was our earliest example of terrorism; other authorities cite crimes committed in the name of the agrarian movement immediately following that war.[26] Although deadly crimes of violence, which we would now term terrorism, have occurred during virtually every decade of American history, certain periods are particularly noteworthy. The nineteenth century was unusually violent, with many terrorist acts; sensational crimes linked to radical social and political movements were common. Terrorism expert Robert Liston reports various slave uprisings throughout the century, of which Nat Turner's rebellion in 1831 is considered the most deadly. Turner and fellow slaves "marched from plantation to plantation in Virginia, sparing no one who owned slaves. . . . they left in their wake 59 slain whites—men, women, and even infants."[27] By the 1870s considerable terror was linked to radical labor groups such as the Molly Maguires. This group, formed in the coalfields of Pennsylvania, murdered at least fifteen of its enemies.

Terrorism accelerated during the latter half of the century as the European-based anarchistic movement gained American support. Arguing that capitalism and government control were essentially illegitimate, anarchists spread terror throughout the country, including major bombings in Chicago, Los Angeles, and San Francisco. The 1882 Chicago Haymarket bombing took place while police attempted to disperse a labor demonstration. As the police appeared, a powerful bomb was ignited that killed eleven people and wounded 110 others. In 1910 the *Los Angeles Times* building was bombed, killing twenty-one individuals. Finally, an explosive device killed ten and wounded forty people during a 1916 patriotic parade.[28]

Terrorism did not disappear after World War II, but the nature of the terrorist did. Moving away from radical labor origins, the focus of terror became more diffuse. The stereotypical anarchist bomb thrower was replaced by a diverse, multicultural collection of violent criminals, all having the sole objective of violent political or social change. Examples include the 1950s terrorist attacks on President Truman and the House of Representatives by Puerto Rican nationalists and, in the late 1960s and early 1970s, police killings linked to the Black Liberation Army and Black Panthers and the terrorist violence of the Weathermen.[29] The latter phase was marked by a unique transformation of terror in that white, middle-class youth became the mainstream American terrorist type. While the Weathermen faction of the Students for a Democratic Society emerged as the largest such group, many others existed and were responsible for a variety of criminal acts. As terrorism researchers and authors Christopher Dobson and Ronald Payne detail, by the mid-1970s it was estimated "that some 50 subversive groups were operational in the United States, involving the participation of up to 15,000 people."[30]

Accordingly, John Brown does not stand alone in the annals of American-based terrorism. Yet he obviously remains a unique, paradoxical example of a terrorist whom history has often viewed through rose-colored lenses. As opposed to alarm or disgust, the deeds of John Brown have moved some to great literary inspiration, such as Stephen Vincent Benét's epic poem *John Brown's Body*. Ralph Waldo Emerson, writing shortly before Brown's execution, referred to Brown as "the Saint, whose fate yet hangs in suspense, but whose martyrdom, if it shall be perfected, will make the gallows glorious like the Cross."[31] Other towering figures of the arts echo the purity of Brown while conveniently ignoring his murderous past. Henry David Thoreau wrote, "No man in America has ever stood up so persistently and effectively for the dignity of human nature, knowing himself for a man, and the equal of any and all governments. . . . He could not have been tried by a jury of his peers, because his peers did not exist."[32] Other, more contemporary sources, including scores of textbooks, continue to echo such laudatory sentiments, informing generation after generation of young Americans that John Brown was a genuine hero. Typical of many such high school and middle school American history texts, one leading book praises Brown through Emerson's words as "a new saint," while another considers him "a martyr and hero, as he walked resolutely to the scaffold."[33]

In a pragmatic sense, it is doubtful that the heroic legend of John Brown will ever include the terrorist truth of his crimes. As observed by guerrilla warfare essayist Walter Laqueur, "terrorism has long exercised a great fascination, especially at a safe distance . . . the fascination it exerts and the difficulty of interpreting it have the same roots: its unexpected, shocking and outrageous character."[34] While many American terrorists exert a continuing fascination, none have occupied the unique position of John Brown. By contemporary definition, he was undoubtedly a terrorist to his core, demonstrating repeatedly the various axioms from which we shape this unique crime. Brown quite purposely waged war for political and social change while simultaneously committing the most heinous crimes. As political scientist Charles Hazelip would say when defining a terrorist, he had "crossed over the blurred line of demarcation between crime and war where political terrorism begins."[35]

Yet John Brown's obsessive target, the focus of all his energy and murderous deeds, has by its nature absolved him from the cold label of *terrorist*. History and popular opinion have quite naturally found the greater criminality of slavery to far outweigh his illegal acts. The bold tactics at Harpers Ferry, coupled with his humanistic motives to free the Virginia slaves, compels us to forgive his disturbed personality and deadly past. The attack on a key government arsenal and armory, which in a contemporary context would horrify the nation, has been judged through the passage of time to be an inevitable, gallant first strike against the soon to be formed Southern Confederacy. When taken as a whole, and to the natural dismay of our justice system,

A Behavioral Analysis of John Brown

Brown's actions quite convincingly demonstrate that if the weight of moral sentiment is on one's side, terroristic violence can be absorbed into a nation's historiography in a positive sense. Dobson and Payne conclude, "the main aim of terror is to make murderers into heroes."[36] While many will continue to debate the magnitude of John Brown's terrorism, his heroic stature has been secured by the often paradoxical judgment of history.

NOTES

1. Robert Liston, *Terrorism* (Nashville: Thomas Nelson, 1977), 23.

2. Bernard Johnpoll, "Perspectives on Political Terrorism," in *Terrorism: Opposing Viewpoints,* ed. David L. Bender and Bruno Leone (St. Paul: Greenhaven Press, 1986), 30.

3. Walter Laqueur, *Terrorism* (Boston: Little, Brown, 1977), 79.

4. Elijah Avey, *The Capture and Execution of John Brown: A Tale of Martyrdom* (Elgin, IL: Brethren, 1906).

5. John T. Hubbell, "John Brown," *Timeline Forum* (Ohio Historical Society) 9, no. 2 (February–March, 1992): 25.

6. Bender and Leone, *Terrorism,* 17.

7. U.S. Department of Justice, *Terrorism in the United States, 1982–1992* (Washington, DC: Government Printing Office, 1992), 20.

8. Bill Anderson, "Economics—Not Oppression—Motivates Terrorism," in Bender and Leone, *Terrorism,* 66.

9. Eqbal Ahmad, "Terrorists Struggle against Oppressive Governments," in Bender and Leone, *Terrorism,* 60.

10. "The Talk of the Town," *New Yorker,* January 10, 1994, 25.

11. Moshe Amon, "The Unraveling of the Myth of Progress," in *The Morality of Terrorism: Religious and Secular Justifications,* ed. David Rapoport and Yonah Alexander (New York: Pergamon Press, 1982), 69.

12. John Pottenger, "Liberation Theology: Its Methodological Foundation for Violence," in Rapoport and Alexander, *Morality of Terrorism,* 117.

13. John Douglas, ed., *Crime Classification Manual* (New York: Lexington Books, 1992); Samuel Yochelson and Stanton Samenow, *The Criminal Personality: A Profile for Change* (New York: Jason Aronson, 1976).

14. Richard Boyer, *The Legend of John Brown: A Biography and a History* (New York: Knopf, 1973).

15. Avey, *Capture;* Eve Iger, *John Brown: His Soul Goes Marching On* (Reading, PA: Addison-Wesley, 1969); Truman Nelson, *The Old Man: John Brown at Harper's Ferry* (New York: Holt, Rinehart and Winston, 1973).

16. Albert Parry, *Terrorism: From Robespierre to Arafat* (New York: Vanguard Press, 1976), 12.

17. Oswald Garrison Villard, *John Brown, 1800–1859: A Biography Fifty Years After* (1920; repr. New York: Alfred A. Knopf, 1943), 334.

18. John Brown, "A prophetic note written by Brown on the day before his execution predicting the establishment of abolition through bloodshed," John Brown Papers, Chicago Historical Society.

19. Stephen B. Oates, *To Purge This Land with Blood: A Biography of John Brown* (1970; revised ed., Amherst: University of Massachusetts Press, 1985), 147.

20. David Hubbard, "Terrorism Is Criminal Activity," in Bender and Leone, *Terrorism*, 28.

21. William McCord, *The Psychopath and Milieu Therapy: A Longitudinal Study* (Orlando: Academic Press, 1982).

22. James Gilbert, *Criminal Investigation* (Upper Saddle River, NJ: Prentice Hall, 2004); Paul Weston and Kenneth Wells, *Criminal Investigation: Basic Perspectives* (Pacific Grove, CA: Brooks/Cole, 1991).

23. Herbert Strean, *The Experience of Psychotherapy: A Practitioner's Manual* (Metuchen, NJ: Scarecrow Press, 1973).

24. Oates, *Purge,* 135.

25. Ibid., 147; Oates, "God's Angry Man," *American History Illustrated* 20 (1986): 10–21.

26. Yonah Alexander, *International Terrorism* (New York: Praeger, 1976); Graeme Newman, *Understanding Violence* (New York: Harper and Row, 1979).

27. Liston, *Terrorism,* 90.

28. Alexander, *International Terrorism;* Parry, *Terrorism.* Many researchers suspect the actual Haymarket bombers were never caught, believing the wrongful conviction and execution of those arrested to be the work of antilabor agents provocateurs.

29. J. Bowyer Bell, *Transnational Terror* (Washington, DC: American Enterprise Institute for Public Policy Research, 1975); Newman, *Understanding Violence.*

30. Christopher Dobson and Ronald Payne, *The Terrorists: Their Weapons, Leaders, and Tactics* (New York: Facts on File, 1979), 60.

31. James Redpath, *The Public Life of Capt. John Brown with an Auto-Biography of His Childhood and Youth* (Boston: Thayer and Eldridge, 1860), 4.

32. Henry David Thoreau, "A Plea for Captain John Brown," in *Civil Disobedience and Other Essays,* ed. Philip Smith (New York: Dover, 1993), 40.

33. David King, Norman McRae, and Jaye Zola, *The United States and Its People* (Menlo Park, CA: Addison-Wesley, 1993), 297; Donald Ritchie and Albert Broussard, *American History: The Early Years to 1877* (New York: Glencoe/McGraw-Hill, 1999), 557.

34. Laqueur, *Terrorism,* 4.

35. Charles Hazelip, "Twelve Tenets of Terrorism: An Assessment of Theory and Practice" (PhD diss., Florida State University, 1980), 123.

36. Dobson and Payne, *Terrorists,* 3.

eight

A PSYCHOLOGICAL
EXAMINATION OF JOHN BROWN

KENNETH R. CARROLL

Still recovering from the wounds sustained in his capture, John Brown lay on a cot in the Jefferson County courtroom, just before the bench, rising occasionally to address the court.[1] Despite his frail health, and even while recumbent, he retained a commanding presence. His voice was strong and clear, and his bearing conveyed calm self-assurance. He was as serene and self-possessed as a man in such straits could possibly be. But as the evidence mounted, attorneys for the defense grew ever less serene. The court had assigned Charles J. Faulkner and Lawson Botts as counsel for Brown and his codefendants. Faulkner immediately begged off, so Botts's associate Thomas Green was appointed in his place. Neither wanted the job, but both felt duty-bound to accept and, by all accounts, did their level best. They were in a tight spot, made all the more uncomfortable by the principal defendant's unwillingness to accept their help. But on the trial's second day, quite unbidden, there came a ray of hope in the form of a telegram from an abolitionist newspaper editor in Akron, Ohio:

To C. J. Faulkner and Lawson Botts:

John Brown, leader of the insurrection at Harpers Ferry, and several of his family, have resided in this county for many years. Insanity is hereditary in that family. His mother's sister died with it, and a daughter of that sister has been two years in a Lunatic Asylum. A son and daughter of his mother's brother have also been confined in the lunatic asylum, and another son of that brother is now insane and under close restraint. These facts can be conclusively proven by witnesses residing here, who will doubtless attend the trial if desired.

A.H. Lewis[2]

This came as no great surprise to anyone. "Old John Brown had to be crazy," writes historian Robert McGlone. "That was the almost universal supposition after Brown's capture."[3] Many suspected that Brown was insane, and now here was some concrete evidence that offered a chance to save the old man from the gallows. When defense counsel tentatively suggested an insanity plea, however, Brown would have none of it. He regarded this effort in his behalf as "a miserable artifice and pretext." He readily acknowledged his family history of insanity but judged himself unaffected by it and proclaimed, "Insane persons, so far as my experience goes, have but little ability to judge of their own sanity; and if I am insane, of course I should think I know more than all the rest of the world. But I do not think so. I am perfectly unconscious of insanity, and I reject, so far as I am capable, any attempt to intervene in my behalf on that score." However flawed his logic, the defendant rejected the insanity plea and that was that.[4]

Brown expressed no confidence in Botts and Green, who were then permitted to withdraw from the case. An able team of Northern lawyers—Charles Hoyt of Boston, Samuel Chilton of Washington, and Henry Griswold of Cleveland—took over the defense. But despite their efforts, the trial's outcome was a forgone conclusion. After four days of testimony and forty-five minutes' deliberation, the jury returned guilty verdicts on all three counts: conspiring with Negroes to produce insurrection, treason, and murder in the first degree. Next morning Brown was sentenced to be hanged.

As soon as the verdict was announced, Virginia's governor, Henry A. Wise, was deluged with correspondence from across the country. Some writers, like New York mayor Fernando Wood, lauded the fairness of the trial but urged

A Psychological Examination of John Brown

clemency lest Brown be made a martyr. Other letters contained outrageous threats. But most were simple appeals for mercy. The governor read all this mail and sorted it into two large stacks, one labeled "Consider" and the other "Contemptible nonsense."[5]

Into the first pile went a curious group of documents. Young Charles Hoyt, one of Brown's defense attorneys, had traveled to Ohio to follow up on that telegram about Brown's familial insanity.[6] He returned with sworn affidavits from nineteen of Brown's former neighbors and associates, each attesting to his mental illness. Governor Wise read these carefully and gave the matter much thought. However, he himself had been among the small group of officials who interviewed Brown in the arsenal's engine house immediately upon his capture, and he was certain Brown was sane: "Remarkably sane," he said later, "if quick and clear perception, if assumed rational premises and consecutive reasoning from them . . . if memory and conception and practical common sense, and if composure and self-possession are evidence of a sound state of mind."[7] Still, he considered seriously the evidence of Brown's insanity and directed Dr. Francis Stribling, superintendent of Virginia's Western Lunatic Asylum at Staunton, to go to Charles Town and examine the prisoner. However, he soon thought better of it. Confident in his own judgment and disinclined to open an endless bitter controversy, Wise canceled the examination. The issue of Brown's mental health was quite unresolved when sentence was carried out as scheduled on December 2, 1859.

So it is still.

Was John Brown crazy? The question remains the focus of speculation and passionate debate. He certainly was not normal; few would dispute that. But controversy surrounds the nature of his abnormality and its effects on his actions. Was he gifted with vision or afflicted with mental illness? That neither of these precludes the other complicates the issue, and today opinion remains divided. Throughout the long debate, discussion of Brown's mental status has been colored by competing political and philosophical views, and that is no less true today than it was in 1859.

Can the issue be resolved definitively? Given the complex emotional and philosophic issues that surround it, the question of whether John Brown was mentally ill will perhaps never be answered in a manner satisfactory to all, and it may be presumptuous to try. Perhaps though, we can attempt to answer a somewhat more humble and specific question: If John Brown were examined by a modern psychiatrist or clinical psychologist, what would be

KENNETH R. CARROLL

the likely findings of such an examination, and what would the examiner conclude? This undertaking proposes to apply the discipline, methods, and tools of modern psychology to approximate that examination.

Naturally, assembling a psychological profile of a man who died almost a century and a half ago is a difficult proposition. Many contend that it is not possible to perform a useful evaluation without direct examination of the subject. But the undertaking is not without precedent. Modern psychologists are called on to perform "psychological autopsies" of recently deceased people, usually in conjunction with wrongful death litigation. Governments employ psychologists to provide psychological assessments of foreign leaders. Police psychologists produce profiles of criminals who have not yet been apprehended, and these outlines often prove uncannily accurate. On a more general level, the work of all scientists frequently involves making inferences about what cannot be seen on the basis of that which can be. A psychological assessment of John Brown is not beyond the pale of the modern science of psychology.

First, we must address the thorny issue of defining mental illness, a process fraught with philosophic, social, and political ramifications. Every person is a collection of idiosyncrasies, habits, predilections, temperament, passions, and beliefs. How can we judge that some such collections are pathological and others healthy, that some people are mentally well and others sick? When does an idea become a delusion, or passion become mania? When do personality quirks become symptoms? Can such determinations be made with any degree of confidence?

While these questions may seem so complex as to defy explication, those who work in psychiatry and psychology must make such determinations every day, like it or not. To guide us, we have developed and continue to refine diagnostic procedures. Though imperfect, they are the result of much research, experience, and consensus and are as close as we have yet come to an orderly and empirical system. It is a well-focused system, based not on theoretical speculation. It entails the careful search for specific symptoms, an assessment of their severity, and an effort to determine if the discovered symptoms fall into clusters suggesting known mental illnesses. This procedure, with its emphasis on symptoms and syndromes, has been described as the medical model because it applies to the investigation of mental disorder the same approach used to diagnose physical disease. The approach has been criticized by those who feel mental phenomena should not be regarded as

A Psychological Examination of John Brown

symptoms and can only be understood in the context of broad theories of development, personality, and experience. Typically, such critics reject the notion that behavioral abnormalities can be viewed as diseases and have devised, each with reference to his or her own theory, arcane and elaborate explanations of how psychological problems arise. However, a steadily accumulating body of evidence demonstrates beyond serious doubt that psychiatric disorder is heavily determined by biology, that the concept of disease is entirely appropriate, and that the medical model is the most useful way of understanding it. Even if critics' arguments are granted, the medical model is an elegant and useful system. It does not demand belief in theoretical constructs like ego, collective unconscious, or self-actualization. For diagnostic purposes, it does not ask how or why symptoms develop but only if they are present.

The standard reference guide in our field is the *Diagnostic and Statistical Manual of Mental Disorders* (4th ed.), by the American Psychiatric Association. DSM IV, as it is commonly known, is the culmination of a process begun in the nineteenth century to help gather and organize census information. Over the years, it has evolved into a comprehensive guide to psychiatric diagnosis. Briefly, it is a compendium of all recognized mental disorders, describing the essential features or symptoms of each, providing guidelines for assessing their severity, and specifying the criteria that must be met to warrant a particular diagnosis. DSM IV is not without its faults and its critics, but it stands as the most widely used and respected system of its kind. Its definition of mental illness, inelegant as it may be, is difficult to refute or refine:

> In DSM IV, each of the mental disorders is conceptualized as a clinically significant behavioral or psychological syndrome or pattern that occurs in an individual and that is associated with present distress (e.g., a painful symptom) or disability (i.e., impairment in one or more important areas of functioning) or with a significantly increased risk of suffering death, pain, disability, or an important loss of freedom. In addition, this syndrome or pattern must not be merely an expectable and culturally sanctioned response to an articular event, for example, the death of a loved one. Whatever its original cause, it must currently be considered a manifestation of a behavioral, psychological, or biological dysfunction in the individual. Neither deviant behavior (e.g., political, religious, or sexual) nor conflicts that

are primarily between the individual and society are mental disorders unless the deviance or conflict is a symptom of dysfunction in the individual, as described above.[8]

This definition and the systematic diagnostic decision rules outlined in DSM IV constitute the touchstone against which the evidence concerning John Brown will be measured.

The most direct evidence of Brown's mental condition is contained in the nineteen affidavits from Ohio.[9] Milton Lusk, Brown's own brother-in-law, asserted his belief "that the said Brown has been at all times more or less insane, disposed to enter upon wild and desperate projects and adventures, and incapable of deliberation or reasoning." Henry Baldwin, another affiant, felt that "when [Brown's] mind was fastened on *any* subject there was evidence of an aberration of mind" (emphasis mine). Edwin Wetmore recalled Brown telling him his adventures in Kansas. "From his [statements then?] and the whole manner and appearance of the man, he regarded him as demented and actually insane. His whole character became changed, he appeared fanatic and furious and incapable of reasoning or of listening to reason."[10]

Sylvester Cray swore he knew Brown "for about twenty years," and "for all that time, from his conduct and conversation, he has regarded him as insane." Ethan Alling praised Brown's integrity and "mild disposition" but lamented that "his mind has become diseased." Brown's cousin Gideon Mills had for twenty years "regarded him as subject to periods of insanity especially when from any cause his mind has been fixed for *any* length of time upon *any* subject" (emphasis mine). George Leach, who claimed to know Brown from boyhood "in all his social and business relations," attested that when he became aroused by "*any* subject and from *any* cause his mind was brought to dwell upon . . . he became greatly excited, and often as this affiant believes, completely insane" and "liable to attacks of mania" (emphasis mine). Leach said he "frequently saw [Brown] when excited for some time upon religious matters and also when excited in regard to his business matters when for long periods of time he has appeared to this affiant to be . . . incapable of reasoning."

James Weld tried to dissuade Brown from his plan to make war in Kansas, but Brown "explained that with a hundred men he could free Kansas and Missouri too and could then march to Washington and turn the President and his Cabinet out of doors, that he had no confidence in aid societies,

A Psychological Examination of John Brown

associations or anything else. The only thing to be done was to fight." Weld expressed admiration for "Mr. Browns [*sic*] courage and devotion to his beliefs, but I have no confidence in the sanity of his judgment."[11] David L. King was "slightly acquainted with John Brown from five to eighteen years and have considered him lacking a 'balance wheel.'" After a conversation with Brown, King "became convinced that on the subject of slavery he was crazy—he was armed to the teeth and remarked among other things that he was 'an instrument in the hands of God to free the slaves.'"

Dr. Jonathan Metcalf, a physician, said, "I have always [esteemed?] him subject to fits of insanity." After his last conversation with Brown, Metcalf "was beyond all doubt in my mind that he was [illegible word] insane on the subject of our conversation, which was for the most part upon matters relating to Kansas." L. Goodale said, "I have known John Brown for 15 years and never saw any business transaction conducted by him which indicated a sane mind. . . . Whenever under great mental excitement, he was clearly insane."

W. S. L. Otis, an attorney who taught a Bible class in which Brown participated, knew him well and praised his character, Christian devotion, and citizenship but declared him "constitutionally predisposed to insanity and would be likely to become insane under strong excitement."

Most of the affiants mentioned the significant history of mental illness in John Brown's family. Two of Brown's first cousins, Sylvester and Mills Thompson, provided the most detailed account and listed numerous relatives who were mentally ill. These included Brown's grandmother, mother, three aunts (including the mother of the affiants), a sister, a brother, five cousins, a niece, and two sons. Another affiant, O. L. Kendricks, was at the time superintendent of the Northern Ohio Lunatic Asylum and confirmed on the basis of his own knowledge and an examination of the institution's records that many of Brown's relatives were or had been inmates there.[12]

It has been suggested that Brown's friends and relatives, anxious to save his life, may have exaggerated or contrived their accounts of his symptoms.[13] This seems highly unlikely. To begin with, many of his neighbors had unhappy business dealings with Brown or had been insulted by him (or both) and would appear to have little motivation to lie on his behalf. Several affidavits include references to Brown's integrity, piety, and kind disposition, appended "in defense" of his character. Clearly these affiants attested to his mental illness reluctantly and apologetically and seem not to have grasped the fact that doing so was to Brown's benefit. Further, if any of the affiants were disposed to bend the truth for Brown's sake, they did not do a very good

KENNETH R. CARROLL

job of it. The testimony is not overwhelmingly conclusive. If they were to exaggerate or contrive their reports, why not add a few hallucinations and delusions? If they were determined to save Brown from the gallows, even at the cost of violating their oaths, they should have portrayed him as the madman of the public's imagination. They did not.

I have examined the affidavits as closely as I can and am struck most of all by their remarkable consistency. No bit of evidence introduced by any affiant is contradicted by or inconsistent with any evidence presented by any other affiant. Moreover, all the testimony is consistent with the knowledge base of psychiatry. No bizarre, bogus, or questionable symptoms are described, nor any peculiar anomalies, or unusual combinations of symptoms. There is nothing here to puzzle the modern psychologist. The symptoms described form a coherent picture.

What do these reports tell the clinician? First, there is the incontrovertible establishment of the family history of mental disorder. People of Brown's time were well aware that major mental illness is heavily determined by biological factors, which are heritable. The psychoanalytic tradition, which marked the better portion of the twentieth century, tended to ignore and obscure that fact, and it had to be rediscovered. But today no responsible psychiatrist or psychologist has any doubt about the crucial role of genetics in the development of mental illness.

Psychohistorians tend to focus their inquiries on the circumstances of their subjects' lives and the conditions and experiences that influenced them. These factors are important in understanding the development of character and disposition. But as predictors or explanations for the emergence of major mental illness, they are of little relevance. Experience plays a far smaller role in the development of major mental illness than does biology.

Brown's boyhood experiences, which have been much discussed, are best understood not as the causes of his emotional problems but as symptoms of underlying, genetically determined illness. To be sure, the presence of so much mental illness in Brown's family does not prove that he, too, was mentally ill, but it is of compelling importance and cannot be ignored. Especially since Brown clearly exhibited unusual behavior, the family history must influence the search for explanations.

The affiants use various terms for mental illness without clear definitions. No matter. As lay witnesses, their task is not to diagnose but to provide behavioral description, and this they do quite well. They describe a man who is emotionally unstable, who easily becomes overexcited, and not exclusively over

A Psychological Examination of John Brown

the issue of slavery. They describe a man who is grandiose, unrealistic, given to flights of fancy; capable of periods of enormous energy but a disorganized reckless planner, incapable of reason and often unable to control his emotions.

What do these signs suggest? Clearly, Brown is not mentally retarded. Though one affiant uses the term *demented,* which at the time was very loosely defined, Brown never gives evidence of the serious memory problems that are the central feature of the condition we today call dementia. There is no evidence of hallucinations. There are no signs of formal thought disorder. Brown is not schizophrenic. And though often "obsessed" with slavery, or other passions, he is not obsessive-compulsive. That disorder is marked by unwelcome intrusive thoughts (obsessions) or the overpowering drive to engage in repetitive ritualistic behaviors (compulsions) that are unwanted, recognized by the suffer as irrational, and a source of marked distress. He does not suffer from any of the anxiety disorders (formerly called neuroses). In fact, his reckless conduct reveals an unusual, probably pathological *absence* of anxiety. He certainly manifests features of various personality disorders, but that is insufficient to account for the severity of his symptoms or the apparent fluctuations in their intensity.

Several of the affiants use the word *mania* in their descriptions of Brown's behavior, and that is the term a modern psychologist would apply to the behavior they describe. Indeed, Brown was manic, probably suffering from what today is called bipolar disorder.

Other circumstances of Brown's life support the diagnosis. His numerous business failures are often mentioned. Surely, failure in business is not proof of mental illness. However, Brown's failures were many and varied—"fifteen business failures in four different states"—and not due simply to bad luck. He was prone to throw himself into grand projects with little forethought and without the advice of more experienced businessmen, or in direct defiance of such advice. He was often driven by wild theories that violated the "known laws of trade" and by his unshakable faith in the "infallible accuracy" of his calculations and expectations.[14] Moreover, although being a defendant in a civil suit does not constitute proof of mental illness, Brown found himself in this position at least a dozen times. The conclusion is unavoidable: He was not a man in good control of his life.[15]

Certainly he was grandiose. He believed himself gifted with divine inspiration, the font of radical ideas. Though he had no military experience, and in fact paid fines to avoid militia duty,[16] after a brief tour of European battlefields,

KENNETH R. CARROLL

he pronounced himself a military genius. As such, he discarded the age-old military dictum "Take the high ground" and confidently asserted that the perfect defensive position is a wooded ravine.[17] He had, in the most literal sense, a fortress mentality, reminiscent of modern-day survivalists and separatist cults. As far back as 1836, in a matter having nothing to do with slavery, he and his sons armed themselves and occupied a cabin on a piece of property he had signed over after defaulting on a loan. There they defied all comers until the sheriff arrived.[18] Later, after he threw himself into the abolitionist cause, he regaled Frederick Douglass with his dream of deploying his tiny band in the hills of Virginia, which are "full of natural forts, where one man for defense would be worth a hundred for attack." He proposed that small bands could venture out and try to persuade slaves to join them. When Douglass objected that if slaveholders felt their property was insecure, they might sell their slaves further south, Brown was entirely unruffled and, without missing a beat, retorted, "Sell them South! That will be first what I want done!"[19] He offered no explanation about how that might further his plan. Of course, selling slaves south might at least reduce the number of slaves in some areas, but what of the effect on those unfortunate slaves who would suffer from being sold? This interchange perfectly illustrates a characteristic of Brown that many of the nineteen affiants mentioned: when he got an idea into his head, he was completely unable to listen to reason and did not consider the possible negative consequences to himself, to his followers, or to innocent bystanders. This is not because he was stupid or laboring under florid delusion. It is a symptom of mania. In a manic episode, the sufferer becomes swept away by powerful emotions and the pressure of his racing ideas. He feels infallible and invulnerable and becomes insensible to logic or reason. Brown manifests this phenomenon again and again. When driven by his emotions, he loses control and no amount of argument can restore it.

This is reflected even in his Provisional Constitution, which begins in orderly enough fashion but gradually comes unraveled. He sets out to create a framework for a government, but one can almost see the pen flying faster and faster across the page, recording the jumbled thoughts that race through his brain and compete for his attention. From a straightforward outline of the branches of government, Brown soon leaps to the duties of the military, the use of captured property, the treatment of prisoners, an admonition against waste, some thoughts about marriage and the Sabbath, and the bizarre suggestion that all citizens of his new entity should carry arms openly.

A Psychological Examination of John Brown

He is clearly losing focus. Then, after much discussion of the new government, its officers and powers, its military structure, its right to confiscate property and execute enemies, Article 46 states: "The foregoing articles shall not be construed so as in any way to encourage the overthrow of the State Government or of the General Government of the United States." In his manic state, Brown was not constrained by the normal thought processes that channel the healthy mind toward logic and consistency.[20]

The Provisional Constitution contains numerous references to the commander in chief (Brown himself, of course) and several articles asserting his control over all goods and wealth confiscated from the enemy. This illustrates another characteristic of the manic: the relentless drive toward self-aggrandizement. The manic's enthusiasm for his project, whatever it might be, does not issue from careful logical thought but is a product of the emotional illness that intoxicates the sufferer with a grandiose and unshakable faith in the supreme importance of himself. No matter how noble or altruistic the cause, at all times and above all else: *La Cause, c'est moi!*

How do these reports and descriptions of Brown's behavior compare with the diagnostic criteria in DSM IV?

CRITERIA FOR MANIC EPISODE

A. A distinct period of abnormally and persistently elevated, expansive, or elevated mood, lasting at least 1 week (or any duration if hospitalization is necessary).

B. During the period of mood disturbance, three (or more) of the following symptoms have persisted (four if the mood is only irritable) and have been present to a significant degree:

    1) inflated self-esteem or grandiosity

    2) decreased need for sleep (e.g., feels rested after only three hours of sleep)

    3) more talkative than usual, or pressure to keep talking

    4) flight of ideas or subjective experience that thoughts are racing

    5) distractibility (i.e., attention too easily drawn to unimportant or irrelevant external stimuli)

KENNETH R. CARROLL

6) increase in goal-directed activity (either socially, at work or school, or sexually) or psychomotor agitation

7) excessive involvement in pleasurable activities that have a high potential for painful consequences (e.g., engaging in unrestrained buying sprees, sexual indiscretions, or foolish investments)

C. The symptoms do not meet criteria of a mixed episode.

D. The mood disturbance is sufficiently severe to cause marked impairment in occupational functioning or in usual social activities or relationships with others, or to necessitate hospitalization to prevent harm to self or others, or there are psychotic features.

E. The symptoms are not due to the direct physiological effects of a substance.[21]

It seems clear that Brown met these criteria, suffered many manic episodes, and therefore meets the criteria for a diagnosis of bipolar disorder. Most patients with this illness experience episodes of major depression between episodes of mania, but that is not necessary for the diagnosis.

Brown probably did experience significant depression. His oft-cited remark about his "steady strong desire to die" certainly suggests that he did, probably since childhood.[22] In his well-known letter to his young admirer Henry Stearn, Brown recounts the boyhood loss of his little yellow marble and says "it took years to heal the wound." Later, he lost a pet squirrel "& for a year or Two John was in mourning."[23] While some have suggested such losses early in life may have *caused* Brown's depressive inclination, the modern psychologist views these extreme and prolonged reactions to such losses as *symptoms* of depression. Still, the evidence of depression is less abundant than that of mania. This is understandable. Behavior caused by mania is dramatic and public. Depression, on the other hand, typically causes withdrawal and a general reduction in behavior of every sort and therefore can go unnoticed. There is insufficient evidence to demonstrate that Brown met the modern criteria for major depression. As noted, however, that is not necessary for a diagnosis of bipolar disorder.

Many patients have periods of remission between episodes in which they regain normal functioning, but "some (20–30%) continue to suffer mood lability and interpersonal and occupational difficulties." Brown most likely

A Psychological Examination of John Brown

falls into that category, that is, frequent manic episodes separated by periods in which, while not manic, he had significant difficulties managing his life. It has also been noted that "the interval between episodes tends to decrease as the individual ages," which also seems to have been the case with Brown.[24]

The assertion that Brown was mentally ill is distasteful, upsetting, or even downright unacceptable to many who admire his devotion to so worthy a cause. Stephen B. Oates, historian and prominent John Brown biographer, for example, complains that "to dismiss Brown as an 'insane' man is to ignore the tremendous sympathy he felt for the suffering of the black man in the United States; it is to disregard the fact that at a time when most Northerners and almost all Southerners were racists who wanted to keep the Negro at the bottom of society, John Brown was able to treat America's 'poor despised Africans' as fellow human beings."[25]

But Oates is hasty here, and a bit unfair. While I conclude that Brown was mentally ill, by no means do I dismiss him. The question of his mental illness has no bearing on his impact on history. No one, on either side of the insanity issue, dismisses John Brown. A second error follows from the first and arises from Oates's failure to separate the actor from his cause. No one has ever suggested that opposition to slavery, or strong measures to end it, are or ever were signs of mental illness. The conclusion that Brown was mentally ill does not depend, even in the smallest degree, on his devotion to the abolitionist cause. The determination of Brown's mental health, and the appraisal of the righteousness of his purpose, are entirely independent and must be kept so.

Oates also asserts that "what seems 'insane' in one period of time may seem perfectly 'sane' at other times."[26] Herein lies the third error, for which Oates may be forgiven. The turbulent 1960s saw a small but vocal antipsychiatry movement, which was especially popular on college campuses. R. D. Laing, Thomas Szasz, and others castigated the mental health professions as soulless lackeys of the establishment and doctrinaire arbiters of normality. The concept of mental illness was assailed as a tool by which the insensitive power elite oppressed nonconformists. There is some truth to this. Indeed, psychiatry was used as an instrument of social control in the Soviet Union, while elsewhere predominantly white, male, upper-class professionals were insensitive to the cultural and historical factors that influence behavior. Today psychiatrists and psychologists are more aware of these factors and assiduously take them into account, yet such considerations do sometimes confound the diagnostic process.

KENNETH R. CARROLL

However, there genuinely is such a thing as mental illness, and the contention that major mental diseases are merely sociopolitical constructs has little currency and less factual basis. These illnesses are, in fact, well-known, well-described, clinically significant, and scientifically legitimate entities that have maintained their integrity across time, place, and culture. Historical and cultural factors sometimes muddy the waters. But not often, not much, and not in the case of John Brown. The evidence that he was mentally ill is clear and abundant.

Still, this conclusion is based on the available historical records, well known to John Brown scholars, much debated over all these years, and subject to varying interpretation. Is it possible to discover any *new* data?

In recent years, historians have welcomed developments in medical technology that have enabled scientists to disinter historical figures and subject them to DNA testing in order to address long-unanswered questions. Are there any techniques, remotely similar, that might enable us to shed new light on the question of John Brown's mental health? Perhaps. This is what we did.

Three noted John Brown experts were recruited to participate in a study:

> Robert E. McGlone, assistant professor of history at the University of Hawaii at Manoa, has published numerous articles about John Brown and is currently completing a book, *Apocalyptic Visions: John Brown's Witness against Slavery.* McGlone is particularly interested in the sanity/insanity issue.
>
> Bruce Noble, a historian with the National Parks Service, was chief of interpretation and cultural resources management at Harpers Ferry National Historical Park from 1995 to 2000.
>
> Bruce Olds is author of *Raising Holy Hell* (1995), the widely acclaimed historical novel about Brown's life.

Each expert was asked to complete an objective psychological test, as if responding on behalf of John Brown. All expressed reservations and had differing views on the question of Brown's sanity, but all ultimately agreed.

The test chosen was the *Minnesota Multiphasic Personality Inventory* (MMPI-2), a well-regarded standard of the psychologist's armamentarium, which has been widely used and continuously developed for over sixty years. Its effectiveness derives from the fact that it was empirically constructed. Briefly, thousands of questions were put to thousands of subjects, both normal

A Psychological Examination of John Brown

controls and patients with established psychiatric diagnoses. Those items that reliably differentiated between the control subjects and the patients and among the several diagnostic groups formed the basis for scales measuring specific psychiatric traits or syndromes. The MMPI consists of 567 items, no single one of which is crucial. Together, they form a mosaic that yields an accurate picture of the subject's psychiatric status. Most of the items are simple and mundane, having what is called low surface validity; that is, they are not very obvious. Thus, the profile can accurately describe a subject who is hesitant to disclose or is even unaware of his own symptoms.[27]

When our three John Brown surrogates had completed the questionnaires, their responses were entered into a computerized analysis program devised by James N. Butcher.[28] Although there are some differences among the results, there is a remarkable degree of agreement. Of the 567 items, all three surrogates agree on 348 (61.4 percent). The probability of such agreement occurring by chance is virtually zero.[29] None of the three produced a normal profile. All have clinically significant elevations in the scale measuring paranoia. The scales measuring mania, depression, and psychopathic deviance are elevated to a slightly lesser degree. The profile produced by Robert McGlone is the most benign of the three but still describes the patient as "touchy and argumentative and somewhat moralistic and rigid" and "likely to have difficulties in relationships." No specific diagnosis is suggested, but the profile warns, "His suspicion and mistrust should be taken into account in formulating a diagnosis." Bruce Noble's Brown is described as "mistrustful, angry, petulant and testy." Diagnostic considerations include depression, major affective disorder, thought disorder, and paranoia. The most pathological profile is that produced by Bruce Olds. His Brown is described as "disruptive, aggressive, distrustful, difficult to relate to, petulant, and demanding." The possibility of bipolar disorder is strongly suggested, with paranoid schizophrenia being another possibility.

Finally, a fourth questionnaire was completed, incorporating the 348 responses in which the three panelists agree, with the remaining responses determined by a simple majority. Below is the Interpretive Report that the program generated about our composite John Brown:

PROFILE VALIDITY

His response to the MMPI-2 items showed marginal validity because he presented himself in an overly positive light. His approach

KENNETH R. CARROLL

to the MMPI-2 suggests that he presents himself in a moralistic and unrealistically virtuous manner. His performance on the clinical and content scales probably reflects an underestimate of his psychological problems.

SYMPTOMATIC PATTERNS

Scales Pa [paranoia] and Ma [mania] were used as the prototype to develop this report. This MMPI-2 pattern is frequently found among hospitalized psychiatric patients. Individuals with similar profiles have great problems controlling their behavior and may have intense outbursts of anger. In addition, their suspicious, mistrustful behavior often creates difficult social problems. This MMPI-2 clinical profile probably reflects some long-term personality problems as well as an intense reaction to a perceived situational threat. The client probably has trouble expressing emotions in a modulated way. He is likely to overreact to environmental events, frightening those close to him. He probably has many grandiose plans and is likely to be obviously delusional. The client tends to be quite confused and disoriented, and he blames others for his problems instead of accepting responsibility himself. The strong possibility of irrational thinking and poor impulse control make clients such as this difficult to manage because they may act out on their delusional beliefs.

His low Mf [masculinity-femininity] score suggests a limited range of interests and a preference for stereotyped masculine activities rather than literary and artistic pursuits or introspective experiences.

In addition, the content of the client's item responses suggests the following: He views the world as a threatening place, sees himself for [sic] having been unjustly blamed for others' problems, and feels that he is getting a raw deal out of life. He seems to have an overinflated view of himself, and he seems to resent it when others make demands on him.

PROFILE FREQUENCY AND PROFILE STABILITY

[Here the report cites various studies and statistics to indicate that this type of pattern is rare and tends to be stable; that is, it reflects traits that tend not to change much over time. If retested at a later point, such clients tend to produce similar profiles.]

A Psychological Examination of John Brown

INTERPERSONAL RELATIONS

Individuals with this profile tend to have highly disruptive interpersonal relationships. They frequently act out against others, especially when demands are placed on them, and they are not very sensitive to the needs of other people. Their pervasive lack of trust and wariness of other people's motivations make them difficult to relate to. His petulant, demanding behavior may place a great deal of strain on his marriage.

His high score on the Marital Distress Scale suggests his marital situation is problematic at this time. He has reported a number of problems with his marriage that are possibly important in understanding his current psychological symptoms.

DIAGNOSTIC CONSIDERATIONS

The possibility of a Bipolar Affective Disorder should be evaluated. Alternatively, individuals with this profile may be diagnosed as having Schizophrenia, Paranoid type. This individual should be assessed to determine if and to what extent he is a danger to himself or others.

TREATMENT CONSIDERATIONS

Because individuals with this profile often have great trouble controlling their impulses, they frequently require a controlled environment. Psychotropic medication is often the most effective means of producing symptom relief for these patients. Externalization of blame, hostility, mistrust and lack of introspective abilities make these patients generally unresponsive to insight-oriented psychotherapy.

As its wording implies, the MMPI-2 report is intended to provide additional information to the diagnostician and does not claim to be definitive by itself. And of course, the legitimacy of this undertaking will be questioned. Still, it provides some grist for the mill. Three different experts with differing points of view each answered 567 questions as they believed Brown would have responded, and they produced remarkably similar results. The composite profile describes an individual whose attributes and propensities are en-

KENNETH R. CARROLL

tirely consistent with those of the John Brown we know from the historical record. All the data hangs together and points rather compellingly to the conclusion that Brown suffered from a major affective illness.

Other questions remain. Could Brown have been acquitted on an insanity defense? Almost certainly not. The standards then in use were embodied in the M'Naughten rules, formulated by a panel of Queen's Bench justices at Victoria's prompting after Daniel M'Naughten was acquitted of killing the secretary to Prime Minister Robert Peel in 1843. These greatly restricted the scope of the insanity defense, requiring that the defendant be proved unable to distinguish between right and wrong or unable to realize that his offense was unlawful. Under these guidelines, still in use in most of the English-speaking world, the insanity defense is rarely successful.[30] Moreover, Brown was able to attract accomplices and put together an elaborate plan. That, of course, is not a testament to his mental health. Manic people are often charismatic, captivating, and engagingly imaginative (consider Charles Manson). But prosecutors would have argued, no doubt successfully, that such organization was inconsistent with insanity. Brown met the psychologist's definition of serious mental illness but not the jurist's legal definition of insanity.

Perhaps the more interesting question is this: Had Brown not been laboring under the influence of his illness, would Harpers Ferry or his adventures in Kansas have happened at all? Again, probably not. Had he not been driven by his illness, Brown, in all likelihood, might have stayed in one place, put down roots, attended more faithfully to his domestic responsibilities, and applied himself more prudently to his businesses. Given his intelligence and moral character, he would probably have fared well. He would have been too busy and too duty bound to neglect family and business to go crusading. He would have had less need to compensate for failures with dreams of glory because he would have had too much to lose. In short, he might have been an ordinary man.

But he was, of course, an extraordinary man with great charisma and energy who threw himself into a noble cause. He was in some ways a genius or at least a visionary. Indeed, much has been written about the close connection between genius and madness. Hundreds of notable people in the arts, literature, science, and public life have suffered from a major mental illness, especially bipolar disorder, and have had brilliant periods of creative energy punctuated by episodes of psychosis.[31] There is a very fine line between the *ability* to view the world in new and unconventional ways and the *inability* to understand convention and maintain contact with mundane reality. Often, they are two sides of the same coin, and some people are better than others at managing this mixed blessing and curse. Some are able to harness the forces of their powerful emotions and differently constituted minds and drive them toward creative discovery. Others, unfortunately, lose the reins and are driven out of control.

There is a story, well known among psychologists but probably apocryphal, about author James Joyce and his severely mentally ill daughter. The young woman was placed under the care of the psychoanalyst Carl Jung. Unable to accept the reality of his daughter's illness, Joyce traveled to Zurich to consult Jung, demanding proof of the doctor's diagnosis. Compassionately, Jung shared with Joyce some of his daughter's letters, which were full of the illogic and looseness of association typical of schizophrenia. It so happened that Joyce at the time was working on *Finnegans Wake*. He showed Jung a few pages of the manuscript and demanded to know the essential difference between his work and his daughter's letters. Jung sat back, pointing to the manuscript, and said: "You see, Mr. Joyce, you stand at the edge of the sea and dive in." Then, gesturing to the letters: "Your daughter stands at the edge of the sea and *falls* in."

And so the critical difference between genius and madness is one of competence and control. Brown, if he ever had it, lost such control and, impelled by powerful internal forces he could neither understand nor regulate, tumbled headlong into the vortex.

And, for good or ill, pulled the world in after him.

NOTES

1. Robert M. De Witt, *The Life, Trial and Execution of Captain John Brown, known as "old Brown of Ossawatomie," with a Full Account of the Attempted Insurrection at Harper's Ferry, Va.* (New York: Robert M. DeWitt, 1859), 57.

2. Quoted in ibid., 64.

3. Robert E. McGlone. "John Brown, Henry Wise, and the Politics of Insanity," in *His Soul Goes Marching On: Responses to John Brown and the Harpers Ferry Raid*, ed. Paul Finkelman (Charlottesville: University Press of Virginia, 1995), 213.

4. De Witt, *Trial*, 65.

5. Robert Penn Warren, *John Brown: The Making of a Martyr* (1929; repr., Nashville: J. S. Sanders, 1993), 418.

6. McGlone, "John Brown," 222.

7. Warren, *Martyr*, 419.

KENNETH R. CARROLL

8. American Psychiatric Association, *Diagnostic and Statistical Manual of Mental Disorders: DSM-IV,* 4th ed. (Washington, DC: American Psychiatric Association, 1994), xxi–xxii.

9. The affidavits are in the Henry A. Wise Collection at the Library of Congress. Legibility is an occasional problem. In such instances my interpretation of the text is bracketed with a question mark.

10. Most of the affidavits were dictated to and recorded by notary M. C. Read and are therefore in the third person.

11. There are two separate affidavits by James W. Weld, one in the third person and in the hand of notary Read, the other in the first person, in a different hand, presumably Weld's.

12. Henry A. Wise Family Papers, Library of Congress.

13. Stephen B. Oates, *To Purge This Land with Blood: A Biography of John Brown* (1970; rev. ed., Amherst: University of Massachusetts Press, 1985), 332.

14. Bertram Wyatt-Brown, "'A Volcano Beneath a Mountain of Snow': John Brown and the Problem of Interpretation," in Finkelman, *Soul,* 19.

15. Warren, *Martyr,* 44.

16. James Redpath, *The Public Life of Capt. John Brown with an Auto-Biography of His Childhood and Youth* (Boston: Thayer and Eldridge, 1860), 29.

17. Ibid., 57.

18. Warren, *Martyr,* 14.

19. Ibid., 54.

20. DeWitt, *Trial,* 51.

21. American Psychiatric, *DSM-IV,* 332.

22. Wyatt-Brown, "Volcano," 13.

23. Redpath, *Public Life,* 24–27.

24. American Psychiatric, *DSM-IV,* 353.

25. Oates, *Purge,* 333.

26. Ibid., 331.

27. *Starke R. Hathaway, J. C. McKinley, and the MMPI Restandardization Committee, MMPI-2: Minnesota Multiphasic Personality Inventory—2* (Minneapolis: University of Minnesota Press, 1989).

28. James M. Butcher, *MMPI-A: Manual for Administration, Scoring, and Interpretation* (distr. by NCS; Minneapolis: University of Minnesota Press, 1992).

29. This attests to the *reliability* of the measure: three knowledgeable observers with differing views independently examined the same subject through the same instrument and agreed in their judgments. This does not, however, demonstrate the *validity* of this approach, which is an interesting subject for further research. Special thanks to Thomas L. Dee, Dept. of Economics, Swarthmore College, for his invaluable help with the statistical analyses.

30. Kenneth R. Carroll, "Factors Affecting Juror Response to the Insanity Defense" (PhD diss., University of South Carolina, 1981).

31. See especially Kay Redfield Jamison, *Touched with Fire: Manic-Depressive Illness and the Artistic Temperament* (New York: Free Press, 1993).

A Psychological Examination of John Brown

PART FOUR

Literary Representations

of John Brown

nine

HERO, MARTYR, MADMAN

Representations of John Brown in the Poetry of the John Brown Year, 1859–60

WILLIAM KEENEY

During his trial, John Brown asserted that the slave question could be resolved only through recourse to violence. Before the Civil War broke out and that notion became universally accepted—if for no other reason than that Brown's prediction had played out in historical reality—such a notion was extremely troubling for white society. Indeed, as the first white Northerner to use organized violence against the South in the cause of liberation of the slaves, John Brown was an extremely troubling figure before the war, even among abolitionists. Just how troubling he was as a public figure can be seen by the ways in which he is represented in poetry written between the raid on Harpers Ferry and the outbreak of the Civil War.

The early poets found three aspects of the events surrounding the Harpers Ferry raid and the character of John Brown troubling. Of these, the most troubling was Brown's open advocacy of violence. Few Northerners wished to instigate or incite violence of any kind, and almost none advocated that others do so. Brown believed that violence was both necessary and proper, and he used violence to achieve his ends. As a violent act of terrorism against the institutionalized violence of slavery, Brown's raid served to give words to the largely unspoken ideas held by the dominant white culture about the legitimate uses of violence.

The second troubling aspect of Brown's raid was that the plan was so deeply flawed that few, even among his biographers, can construct a character for the man that satisfactorily explains his belief in the possibility of success. The poets tend to characterize Brown's plan as daring, as a deliberately risky invitation to martyrdom, or as incomprehensible and therefore crazy.

Finally, the poets were troubled by Brown's firm, even fanatical adherence to fixed principles, some of his own devising. Many poets found this admirable but troubling; others seized on this, dovetailed it with his flawed plan, and explained the one as madness and the other as the result of that madness.

These three troubling aspects led the poets to employ the poetic conventions of the day to represent Brown as hero, as martyr, and as madman. Taken on their simplest terms, a hero is one who dies for his or her country or people, a martyr is one who dies for his or her principles or God, and a madman is one who dies for inexplicable reasons or as sacrificial victim. The attempt to reconcile these accepted nineteenth-century poetic conventions with John Brown's actual behavior proved troublesome. Often, more than one convention appears in the same poem, sometimes in strange, convoluted ways, such as the American Anti-Slavery Society's label for Brown: the "brave old hero-martyr."[1] But the central problem confronting the John Brown poets was their stance toward his use of violence. They generally reacted with one of three strategies: revise the plan and make him out a hero; admit the plan but deny the violence, representing him as deliberate martyr; or admit the plan, call it crazy, and represent his possible insanity as nobility. None of these strategies proved adequate.

In general, to the extent that the early Brown poets fail to address the subject of violence, they also fail by misrepresenting Brown and his deeds. Typically, they misrepresent the facts, his motives, and his state of mind; and in doing this, they misrepresent his importance, for as one Brown biographer writes, "The plain import of the John Brown Raid was discord, disunion, and even civil war; the majority of the people wanted accommodation, union, and peace. Abraham Lincoln spoke in Leavenworth, Kansas, on the night of the execution, and said of the event: 'We cannot object, even though he agreed with us in thinking slavery wrong. That cannot excuse violence, bloodshed, and treason.'"[2]

In responding to Brown's violence, bloodshed, and lawlessness, the poets reveal their own deep ambivalence over the role of their culture in the sanctioned violence, bloodshed, and injustice of slavery. The skewed vision of the poets that allowed them to avoid seeing the violence and futility of the Harpers Ferry raid illustrates the way that the culture prescribed certain roles and proscribed others in order to mold John Brown's body into a more comfortable grave.

ESTABLISHING JOHN BROWN AS AN ICON THROUGH LITERARY REPRESENTATION

On December 5, 1859, Henry Howard Brownell wrote "The Battle of Charlestown (December 2, 1859)," ironically describing the execution of Brown as a "battle" of three thousand to one, a glorious victory of Virginia's "Heroes in buff" over "a single scarred grey head."[3] In this poem, Brownell accurately describes many of the events of the day—the long wait on the scaffold, Brown's stoicism, his comments about the Virginia countryside on his way to the gallows—but he could not have been more wrong in his conclusion: "'Sic Semper'—the drop comes down— / And, (woe to the rogues that doubt it!) / There's an end of old John Brown!"[4] More accurate was Rev. E. H. Sears's prediction:

> Not any spot six feet by two
> Will hold a man like thee;
> John Brown will tramp the shaking earth,
> From Blue Ridge to the sea.[5]

Though dead, John Brown had barely begun, for his history is written not only in an account of the events surrounding Harpers Ferry and his subsequent execution, but also in the literary history that enshrined his body in the memory of the nation. Perhaps more than any other public event in U.S. history, John Brown's raid on Harpers Ferry was seized on as a literary event, an occasion for representation.

On the day of Brown's execution, a soiree of sorts was held in Concord, Massachusetts. There, many of the literary lights of the day—A. Bronson

Alcott, Ralph Waldo Emerson, and Henry David Thoreau, among them—read speeches, gave sermons, and, above all, read poetry. This was not entirely unusual. In the nineteenth century crowds often gathered to hear public readings of both poetry and prose on days of commemoration or celebration. Perhaps the most famous example was the public consecration of the National Cemetery at Gettysburg, at which Lincoln's masterpiece of public oratory was but one of a number of speeches. Brown's raid also inspired numerous literary responses. Although he could not be present on the occasion of Brown's burial on his family's farm at North Elba, New York, on July 4, 1860, Thoreau prepared and sent a speech entitled "The Last Days of John Brown" to be delivered for him. First, Thoreau extols, in typical hyperbolic fashion, the literary virtues of Brown's output before his death: "Where is our professor of *belles-lettres* or of logic and rhetoric, who can write so well?" Then Thoreau claims that Brown's death eclipsed other events that ordinarily would have evoked poems and speeches: "The death of [Washington] Irving, which at any other time would have attracted universal attention, having occurred while these things were transpiring, went almost unobserved. I shall have to read of it in the biography of authors."[6]

Within weeks of Brown's death, a public feud broke out between John Greenleaf Whittier and William Lloyd Garrison over Garrison's poetic representation of Brown, with Brown's chief contemporary chronicler, James Redpath, interceding in order to "correct" the interpretation of Brown's motives constructed by Garrison. Within months after his death (the dedication is dated April 14, 1860), Redpath had issued a five-hundred-page collection of writings concerned solely with the Harpers Ferry raid.

Such "echoes" of Harpers Ferry continued right up to Fort Sumter and beyond. Like Harriet Beecher Stowe's *Uncle Tom's Cabin,* Brown's raid helped precipitate the Civil War. Illustrative of the link between the two protagonists Uncle Tom and John Brown in the minds of the nation are Oliver Wendell Holmes Sr.'s "Two Poems to Harriet Beecher Stowe," written on her seventieth birthday in 1882:

> All through the conflict, up and down
> Marched Uncle Tom and Old John Brown,
> One ghost, one form ideal
> And which was false and which was true,
> And which was mightier of the two,

The wisest sibyl never knew,
For both alike were real.[7]

This was, of course, meant to compliment Stowe's fictional creation, but it also suggests the equally fictional nature of "John Brown" as a cultural creation. Both were equally real by 1882 in that both were by then as much products of the imagination as of history. Throughout the years of the war, Uncle Tom served as a black icon and Old John Brown served as a white icon: the black, a passive Christian martyr; the white, a violent Christian martyr.

From the time of his capture, John Brown's body became public property. No longer an actor in society, Brown had become a text to be written, a writing that even he recognized was all that was left to him and his cause, a writing that he began participating in from the first moment of his capture (and perhaps even before, in his melodramatic speeches to his men about noble behavior in their terrorist raids). Whatever the facts of his life and true motivations for the raid, from this point on John Brown would himself become almost irrelevant. As the process of inscription began, newspapers reported and editorialized, magazines debated and rhapsodized, white Southerners reviled and generalized, abolitionists refigured and identified or denied and distanced, court reports recorded and transcribed, and congressional records archived. John Brown had become martyr, rebel, saint, madman, freedom fighter, insurrectionist, prophet, portent, precursor, predecessor, Spirit, and Soul, but he was no longer John Brown the man. John Brown, who only four years earlier had been a relatively minor abolitionist and failed businessman from eastern Ohio and upstate New York, had become a public man, public property, and an American icon.

THE TROUBLED LITERARY REPRESENTATIONS OF JOHN BROWN

One of the major problems confronting the early Brown poets was how to present Brown as a hero while dealing with the facts of the raid. In several ballads portraying Brown as hero (see appendix at the end of this chapter), the poets' most difficult challenge was to reconcile what they saw as the violent yet buffoonish nature of Brown's failed attack on Harpers Ferry with their desire to represent Brown heroically.

Balladeer Henry Howard Brownell solved the problem by making the Virginians equally buffoonish. He satirizes the Virginians' response as overreaction.

John Brown in the Poetry of the John Brown Year

His choice of title—"The Battle of Charlestown" (rather than the Battle of Harpers Ferry)—underscores its satiric inversion. Brownell focuses on the violence of the state against Brown rather than Brown's violence against the state. He also concentrates on the contrast between the "fuss, and feathers, and flurry" of the authorities and the calm nobility with which Brown, by all accounts, conducted himself at his hanging. Such satiric attacks on authority at the scaffold site are, according to Thomas Laqueur, typical manifestations of our anxiety over such naked displays of power by the state.[8] Faced with such anxieties, the impulse toward carnivalesque inversion produces anti-authoritarian responses. While making this adjustment, Brownell manages to stick close to the facts, but he depicts the execution as a battle—as state-sanctioned violence against one man.

Brown's conduct on the scaffold, not his actions at Harpers Ferry, are, according to Brownell, what will be remembered and valorized: "Would ye have them hear to his words— / The words that may spread like fire?"[9] Although Brownell may be representing Brown as martyr rather than as insurrectionist, this is not a Christian martyr with mere heavenly fame. Brown, as Brownell represents him, manages, in the words of Stephen Greenblatt, to turn himself into "a symbol of the lives of all men threatened by an overwhelmingly powerful system, a powerful representation of the radical alienation of the individual from the state."[10]

The meter, a regular, accentual trimeter that lilts along, breaks only once. In the stanza before Brown's execution, in that moment of stasis "before the drop comes down— / And . . . / There's an end to Old John Brown,"[11] Brownell forces us to confront the violence—though it is not Brown's violence; rather, it is the state-sponsored violence of slavery that necessitated a violent response and also the violence of the state directed against Brown himself:

> For the trouble—we can't see why—
> Seems with us and not with him,
> As he stands 'neath the autumn sky,
> So strangely solemn and dim![12]

Brownell's meter in the second line of this stanza stops still, holding us in the stasis of four beats wherein the word *seems* carries the weight of indecision. Such poetic felicities are as much a product of willingness to face the truth as they are a production of the truth.

More typical is Edmund Clarence Stedman's "How John Brown Took Harper's Ferry." This poem, probably the first public rendition of John Brown's raid in verse, was "published in New York in late November, 1859," and illustrates the difficulties the early Brown poets faced.[13] Stedman's strategy was relatively simple; he made things up. His work emphasizes Brown's Kansas activities, as one can see by the refrain's most frequent appellations: Old Brown, a name received in connection with his Kansas activities (in part to distinguish him from his son, John Jr.); and Osawatomie Brown, clearly linking him to the Kansas Free-Soil cause. Stedman, however, considerably distorts the sequence of events there and Brown's importance to that cause: "And the Lord *did* aid these men, and they labored day / and even, / Saving Kansas from its peril" (emphasis Stedman's).

In fact, Brown's activities in Kansas were marginal at best, disorganized and remote from the central political and even military events that shaped the outcome. In fairness to Stedman, the details of Brown's Kansas activities were less well known to Easterners than those of the Harpers Ferry Raid, and what was known had already been distorted, sometimes obscured, and often romanticized by both the Eastern press and by Brown himself in his attempts to raise money in the East. Furthermore, while Brown's role in the earliest Kansas encounter, the Battle of Black Jack, was well known, his role in the Pottawatomie Massacre was obscure, poorly reported, and consistently denied by Brown. So even though his name was linked with these murders, as late as the interrogation following his capture, Brown convincingly denied any specific involvement. It was not until Owen Brown's statement of October 11, 1908, nearly half a century after the massacre, that Brown's role in these events was clarified.[14]

Thus, while Stedman may have been participating in distortion, much of that distortion was the work of Brown, his supporters, the press, and even the judiciary involved in his case. Yet Stedman makes several false claims of his own invention, claims that form a consistent pattern, but a pattern inconsistent with the facts as he might have known them and, most indicative of Stedman's intent, at odds with Brown's own account of his motives.

In the first stanza, Stedman implies that Brown went to Kansas primarily to farm, that he led his sons there, and that his house was burned by Missouri Rangers. But much of this is false. Brown's sons preceded him to Kansas—a minor point, one must admit; but they were motivated to go, in part, by economic opportunity and to a far greater extent, by a desire to add

John Brown in the Poetry of the John Brown Year

antislavery numbers to the territory. Brown, by contrast, went almost entirely in order to engage in the growing strife.[15]

Though Brown's Station was burned by Border Ruffians in June 1857, John Brown and his men had long before virtually abandoned the place and were off in the bush, hiding and engaged in a guerrilla war during which Brown and his men were themselves burning and looting other, proslavery farms. Moreover, this guerrilla war had been, if not instigated, at least greatly exacerbated by Brown's own activities, including the nighttime slaughter of unarmed men. This was followed by the burning of his farm, which was very likely meant as a retaliation. Yet Stedman characterizes Brown's actions in connection with these events and the subsequent war as those of someone who "boldly fought for freedom." In order to justify this characterization, which he apparently found fundamental to his heroic portrayal, Stedman felt compelled to construct a motive for these activities. Stedman's poem, therefore, reverses the causal connection, making Brown's violent activities follow from, rather than lead to, the burning of his farm: "Came homeward in the morning—to find his house burned down" ends the first stanza, and "Then he grasped his trusty rifle and boldly fought for freedom" begins the second. This sequence constructs for Brown the motive of revenge for personal wrong. Having seized on this motive, Stedman continues for the next five stanzas outlining the outrages that the Ruffians had inflicted on Brown's family: the murder of one son, Frederick, and then inventing another murdered son (identified only as "another brave boy"), or perhaps conflating the arrest of John Brown Jr., "they loaded him with chains / And with pikes . . . / Drove him cruelly, for their sport," with the unrelated murder of Capt. R. P. Brown (no relation) by proslavery forces, "and at last they blew his brains out."

The revenge motive once again illustrates Stedman's penchant for fictionalizing in order to re-create Brown according to the poet's notion of a heroic image. Brown himself consistently and vehemently denied that revenge had anything to do with his activities and decisions. James Hanway reports that Brown told him, soon after Frederick's murder by Martin White, "People mistake my objects. I would not hurt one hair on [White's] head. I would not go one inch to take his life; I do not harbour the feelings of revenge. I act from a principle. My aim and object is to restore human rights."[16] Brown made similar, widely reported statements during his incarceration and trial. On the Tuesday following his capture at Harpers Ferry, Brown underwent an interrogation by Senator James Mason and others, the text of which appeared

WILLIAM KEENEY

in the *New York Herald* on October 21, 1859. When one examiner asked, "Upon what principle do you justify your acts?" Brown replied, "Upon the Golden Rule. I pity the poor in bondage that have none to help them: that is why I am here; not to gratify any personal animosity, revenge, or vindictive spirit."[17] However insightful into his own motives, however self-serving his characterization of them might or might not have been, Brown was constructing a political motive for his activities, a motive based on principle, which Stedman must have recognized but chose to ignore. Stedman's construction deliberately personalizes and depoliticizes the very activities that Brown had hoped to politicize.

Moreover, in another move typical of the early Brown poets, Stedman depicts Brown as a man literally driven crazy by his desire for vengeance. Stedman's depiction of Brown's mental state degenerates steadily from "a steadfast Yankee farmer . . . [who] spoke aloud for freedom" to a man who "boldly fought" and, on the death of his son, "Shed not a tear, but shut his teeth, and frowned a terrible frown." But after the fictional death of the invented second son, Stedman has Brown make righteous appeals to heaven, "calling Heaven's vengeance down" and swearing "fearful oath[s . . . to] return it blow for blow." Stedman ends this section with a physical description that emphasizes the degeneration toward madness: "Then his beard became more grizzled, and his wild blue eye grew wilder, / And more sharply curved his hawk's-nose, snuffing battle from afar." The melodramatic tone and Gothic imagery of madness contrasts with the almost sylvan description of the "Kansas strife" that, like the sun in spring, "waxed milder."

The decrease of strife in the milder spring only makes Stedman's Brown "more sullen," however, and when "over was the bloody Border War,"[18] nothing is left but for Brown, "gone crazy," to "slip off into Virginia," where his madness can compare poorly to the "statesmen" all born there. One might almost suspect that Stedman was participating in the ongoing attempt by Brown's lawyers to have Brown declared insane in "a last desperate attempt to save his life."[19] Moreover, Stedman seems intent on characterizing the entire plan as insane. Anyone who participated in the raid, the "eighteen other madmen," was also apparently insane (though Stedman gives no account of what drove them to this extremity). Once the armory has been taken, Stedman's refrain becomes "Mad Old Brown," and his band "eighteen other crazy men."

Stedman's portrayal, then, seeks to depoliticize and distance its sympathies from John Brown's violent activities. On the one hand, it claims, Brown

John Brown in the Poetry of the John Brown Year

acted from motives of vengeance inspired by the cruel and unprovoked treatment he and his family had received at the hands of the Border Ruffians in Kansas. Slavery is never mentioned, except obliquely in such phrases as "the curse that blights the land" and "this ravening evil that had scathed and torn him so"; and the principles Brown articulated are never alluded to. Rather, the attack on Harpers Ferry is characterized as a desperate attempt at misplaced vengeance resulting from a bereaved father's increasing and unrelenting insanity.

And yet Stedman proposes to be presenting a sympathetic portrayal. Such a move is typical of the early John Brown poetry. The violence of his actions is downplayed, given other motives, explained away, or ignored so that the poet can align himself or herself with the aspirations of the plan without condoning the methods. Not until after the Civil War had begun did the poetry begin to recognize, admit, and eventually even sponsor the notion that violence might be a valid means to achieve this end.

Surprisingly, in the ninth stanza, Stedman gives an accurate account of Brown's plan and the violent repercussions Brown knew were inherent in it. From that stanza, it appears that Stedman had read and assessed reports that covered the documents found in Brown's possession. Stedman knew that the raid was not just an attempt to spirit a few slaves off to Canada; rather, it constituted a recruiting action for an ongoing insurrection. "Free the negroes and then arm them," he has his Brown say. He recognizes Brown's commitment to necessary violence when he writes: "on their own heads be the slaughter, if their victims rise to harm them." He also perceives his treasonous plans to institute a new government. "The world shall see a Republic," Brown says in this same stanza, and soon after the town is taken: "Then declared the new Republic, with himself for guiding star." To his credit, Stedman accurately characterizes the raiders in stanza sixteen as rebels, at least from the point of view of white Southerners.

Though the last half of the poem degenerates into a sort of mock-epic account of the ineffectual and cowardly attempts of the effete Southern gentry to dislodge Brown from the town, the brutality of the final storming, and their subsequent railroading of him at the trial; in the last two stanzas, Stedman restores Brown's dignity with his "grand oration" and "scorn of all denial." And while Stedman still assesses Brown as little more than a "brave old madman," he indicates, in stanza six, that the judge's "most judicial frown" is nearly as indicative of madness as Brown's "fearful glare and frown."

WILLIAM KEENEY

His intention to restore Brown's dignity is seen most clearly in the last stanza, probably the most clearheaded, pragmatic, and predictively accurate account of the potential consequences of John Brown's death. He appeals to the Virginians not to execute Brown because, on the one hand, the Southerners had first spilled his family's blood. On the other hand, he appeals to their own pragmatic sense that "Old Brown's life veins, like the red gore of the dragon, / May spring up a vengeful Fury, hissing through your slave-worn lands." This is an act of poetic and political courage, in that most writers avoided the implicit threat that more violence might ensue. Stedman ties Brown's blood to the Cadmean myth, in which Cadmus slays the dragon and sows its teeth, with the result that armed men rise to destroy each other until only five remain to help Cadmus found the city of Thebes. By invoking the Cadmean myth, Stedman also invokes the violence implicit in the origin of society, as well as the danger of unchecked violence to that society. This also marks the first moment in the poem where the true cause of a wider vengeance, "the slave-worn lands," appears to be, if not justified, at least predicted. Few in the North, at this time, were willing to make any such suggestions to the politically powerful South.

"And Old Brown," Stedman ends, "Osawatomie Brown, / May trouble you more than ever, when you've nailed his coffin down." Before long, this brave prediction that John Brown's written body would cause the South more distress than his living body ever did would come to pass, as "his Soul [kept] marchin' on."

While most poets were not quite as willing as Stedman to misrepresent the facts, many did try to hide some embarrassing aspects of the case. Such factual misrepresentations diminish any poem, and also, like self-deception in psychology, manifest themselves in aberrant poetic behaviors. Stedman's inability to fully synthesize his views on Brown, for example, leads him to characterize Brown's sons as "four sons, all stalwart men of might" and then just a few stanzas later to lump them in with all the "madmen" at Harpers Ferry.

Even more bizarre poetic behaviors are demonstrated in Louisa May Alcott's attempt to represent John Brown's martyrdom as a rose. In the fifth stanza of "With a Rose," she claims that "the sword he wielded for the right / Turns to a victor's palm." Since this was written before the war had begun, she clearly meant victory in some metaphorical or spiritual sense. Such fiddling, however, produces some odd results. The palm she wishes to place in Brown's hand to replace the sword she cannot accept, transforms two lines

John Brown in the Poetry of the John Brown Year

later through a rhyme: into "a spirit-stirring psalm." The *s* dropped into *palm,* which makes the *p* silent, should remind a close reader of the *s* that silences the *word* in *sword,* indicative of her silencing of swords in general. But swords do not transform into psalms so easily.

A similar, odd pun occurs in the final stanza on the words *grave* and *engrave:*

> No monument of quarried stone,
> No eloquence of speech,
> Can grave the lessons on the land
> His martyrdom will teach.

Admittedly, *grave* is a perfectly adequate usage in terms of its lexical signification, but its allusional reference to Brown's actual grave, which Alcott asserts that this rose and his words will transcend, remains blandly unaccounted for. Such usage, it seems, must be a pun, forcing one to examine it as a pun, but in the end it cannot possibly register as such. We are left with an odd sense that the poet has lost control. And like other early Brown poets, Alcott's loss of control stems from the central question of violence.

Another strategy of dealing with the inherent violence of Brown's plan was to label it as crazy. What Thoreau said about editors in his July 4, 1860, speech could as easily be said of some early Brown poets: "Editors persevered for a good while in saying that Brown was crazy; but at last they only said that it was 'a crazy scheme,' and the only evidence brought to prove it was that it cost him his life. . . . [Had he been successful], these same editors would have called it by a more respectable name. . . . They seem to have known nothing about living or dying for a principle. They all called him crazy then; who calls him crazy now?"[20]

Most of the poets, however, avoided this particular quagmire, preferring instead to represent Brown as a hero or a martyr. In "The Hoary Convict," we can see this process at work. The author, "An Ohio Clergyman," identified by Redpath only through his initials, B. K. M., answers the charge that Brown's plans could only have made by a maniac. "Brave man!" he begins, "whate'er the world may think of thee, / Howe'er in judgment hold thy daring deeds." In order to make this defense work, however, B. K. M. has to struggle with Brown's monomania. He does so by taking on the evil that Brown confronted: "Thy life-long *madness* was a *power* to feel" (emphasis B. K. M.'s). This is standard abolitionist rhetoric. The poet claims that under different circumstances, Brown might have been better represented: "History would dare her highest skill to try, / And on a spotless page embalmed thy fame," yet he is himself unwilling to endorse or promote Brown's principles.

The result of this logic is that to serve the common good, Brown must be martyred: "But thy loved Cause shall live beyond the storm, / And thou canst best subserve it now to die." In order for the failed hero to redeem himself from the charge of insanity, he must sacrifice himself. This is a typical move by these poets; they truss Brown up as martyr and drop him on the altar as a sacrifice to the cause.

There are two basic problems with the representation of Brown as a martyr.[21] First, he constructed the martyr pose only after the fact; before he was caught, he was the leader of a violent insurrection. Second, he did not intend to die; his death was a mere accident, attendant on poor planning and the execution of a very risky plot. Nonetheless, the great majority of early Brown poets figured him in one way or another as a martyr. For most, this meant having to seriously misconstrue, or reconstrue, his motives. Several poets adopted William Lloyd Garrison's stance that even though violence ensued, it was incidental to his plans, perhaps even accidental. But this is patently false. While Brown consistently opposed "unnecessary" violence, and it may, in fact, have been this opposition that motivated his disastrous decision to release the train while in Harpers Ferry; he was never opposed to what he considered to be "necessary" violence to achieve his goals.[22]

Though a dismal failure by any practical standards, Brown's raid on Harpers Ferry, by directing violence toward the institutional violence of slavery, forced the culture to confront the question of violence. Longtime pacifists Henry David Thoreau and William Lloyd Garrison were moved to endorse his actions, though Garrison obviously felt compelled to reconstruct Brown's plans before he could do so. In order to improve Brown's ethos, Garrison seized on Brown's statement that he "sought no retaliation nor revenge, but only (if possible) a peaceful exodus from Virginia." This was clearly contrary to the facts, and Garrison was quickly corrected by James Redpath in a letter dated the day Garrison's article appeared. "John Brown did not intend to make any exodus from Virginia," Redpath wrote, "peaceful or otherwise, but to liberate the slaves in their native states." Furthermore, Redpath rebuked Garrison for ignoring the public clarifications Brown had made about that statement: "Have you not read his letter of explanation to Mr. Hunter?"[23] Such instant

John Brown in the Poetry of the John Brown Year

revision of public events is not uncommon, as today's spin doctors make apparent, nor was it uncommon in the editorializing of the day. What makes this dispute pertinent is that Garrison's reconstruction took place in the context of a dispute over the literary representation of Brown.

On January 13, 1860, Garrison reprinted in the *Liberator* a poem that Whittier had earlier published in the *New York Independent*, "Brown of Osawatomie." Along with this poem, Garrison wrote a review in which he took Whittier to task for the rebukes implicit in Whittier's representation of Brown. Garrison criticizes "an apparent invidiousness or severity of imputation in these epithets," citing as examples "the rash and bloody hand," "guilty means [with] good intent," "the grisly fighter's hair," and "the folly that seeks through evil good intent." In order to justify his literary judgment about Whittier's representation of Brown's actions, Garrison seems to have deliberately misrepresented history. Apparently, Garrison felt that the proper writing of John Brown's body was worth a distortion of the facts and that the representation was more important than the history. For Garrison, the principles involved were aesthetic ones about the accuracy of representation, not principles about adherence to facts. But through his critique, we can see that Garrison, at least, recognized the principle involved in glorifying violence and the problems of representing violence heroically in verse. Garrison accuses Whittier of using words to whip men up to violent action and then disavowing those actions. Possibly before entering Harpers Ferry, John Brown had been reading the following soul-stirring lines of Whittier—giving them a more literal interpretation than the poet intended: "Speak out in acts!—the time for words / Has passed, and deeds alone suffice; / In the loud clang of meeting swords" (306). Garrison then cites other Whittier poems in which heroic violence is depicted positively and reveals the principles on which that violence is represented. Brown, he argues, should have been treated the same way on principle:

> If there is a danger, on the one hand, lest there may be a repudiation
> of the doctrine of non-resistance, through the sympathy and admi-
> ration felt for John Brown, there is more danger, on the other hand,
> that the brutal outcry raised against him as an outlaw, traitor, and
> murderer by those who are either too cowardly to avow their real
> convictions, or too pro-slavery to feel one throb of pity for those in
> bondage, will lead to unmerited censure of his course. Difficult as it

WILLIAM KEENEY

may be to hold an equal balance in such a case, it is still the duty of every one to do so. (309)

Whittier soon objected, first citing lines from the same poems that he says clarify his stand against violence; then quoting Garrison's lines, "Not by the sword shall your deliverance be, / Not by the shedding of your masters' blood," as more indicative of his consistent beliefs. Finally, he makes a crucial distinction by reminding Garrison of their mutual pledge "to reject the use of all carnal weapons" (312).

Words, for Whittier, substitute for weapons against the body. In fact, the substitution can only take place because of the common agreement to adhere to this principle. Whittier replies to the charge that his poems have "warlike allusions and figures" by citing lines Garrison omitted from one of his poems. The essential, "qualifying lines which, in the original, connect the two parts" are:

> To Freedom's perilled altar bear
> The freeman's and the Christian's *whole*—
> Tongue, pen, and vote, and prayer! (311; emphasis Garrison's)

Here, literary acts intercede at the altar of Freedom, sacrificing themselves so that a man such as the speaker might be a "freeman." Like all sacrificial appeasement, however, unless Freedom agrees to accept these substitutes, they will be ineffectual. Only by agreement can these substitutes avoid the violence they otherwise would provoke.

What we see in these exchanges are literary acts of aggression about the construction of violence in texts. Thoreau also links the representational word with the act of violence around the locus of this violent literary event: "The *art* of composition is as simple as the discharge of a bullet from a rifle, and its masterpieces imply an infinitely greater force behind them."[24] One presumes he does not mean the same force that Garrison was accusing Whittier of using—the force that makes other men take recourse to carnal weapons, as Brown had done. The context of these disputes revolves around the continued attempt to make poetic conventions serve the complex case of Brown's violence. Most commonly, the poets distance themselves from that violence at both ends by representing him as a martyr. "Not the raid of midnight terror; . . . Not the borderer's pride of daring, / But the Christian's sacrifice,"

John Brown in the Poetry of the John Brown Year

Whittier exclaims. Martyrs serve as scapegoats in that they embody the authority of principles, then die for them, thus relieving us of the anxiety that our domination by those principles serves.[25] Even though Brown committed violent acts in the name of his principles, it is still possible to represent him as a martyr; because he suffered retribution, the authority of those principles remains intact.

Edna Dean Proctor, for example, leads Brown quietly, even ritually, "the victim, wreathed and crowned," to "the scaffold altar." As with a ritual sacrifice, she literally elevates him for a day in order to represent his "spiritual" elevation: "They may hang him on the gibbet; they may raise the victor's cry, / When they see him darkly swinging like a speck against the sky." As a "sacrifice of Love," the cycle of violence that his actions threatened to set off has been cut short. Each stanza repeats this ritual, the first three ending with his death and the last two beginning with it. As much as the actual hanging itself, Proctor's poem helps represent this culturally significant moment of sacrifice for all who could not attend. Compare Proctor's lines at the end of her second stanza to Whittier's "Freedom's perilled altar," where he represents himself as sacrificing words on the altar of Freedom: "He who perilled all for Freedom on the scaffold dies to-day." Proctor, too, and in much the same way, offers the expiation of words for Brown's violence. Again and again, these poets attempt to hang Brown for the nation's sins of violence against the blacks. But by failing to confront the *fact* of the violence in their representations, their attempts fail; indeed, they succeed in hanging Brown instead for his own violence against the whites of the South.

To her credit, Proctor does represent Brown's actions as a seed that will take root "in the fields of rice and cotton," among the slaves in the South, as Brown intended. That she envisions this as a slow process occurring "in a warm and mellow May," amid "firelight's evening glow," and "when the hot noon passes slow," shows how far she is from claiming the violence that "the birthday of the Free" might entail.

In her last stanza, moreover, Proctor tries to reconcile the images of martyr and of hero in a unique way. Like many others, she compares Brown's sacrifice to Christ's and calls on Christ to "attend him." She admits, literally in the same breath, however, her distance from Brown, calling him "weak and erring though he be." He is *not* Christ, but one who merely aspires "to love like Thee." Christ is called the "suffering Lord"; Brown, who advocated and used violence, is "defiled" by "some dregs of earthly vintage." By admitting her am-

WILLIAM KEENEY

bivalence toward Brown, Proctor achieves a unique degree of honesty in the last two stanzas of her poem. As her voice lowers, we see the clichéd, false-heroic sweep of a nation turned to watch, "from clear Superior's waters, where the wild swan loves to sail," and the false, classical imagery of "the blue Olympian skies; / Porphyry or granite column," disintegrates. Instead, we see the difficult reconciliation of martyr and hero, "the dying hero, that the right may win its way." Her solution may be sentimental and false, but she has at least taken on the right task, coming to terms with her true stance toward Brown.

Among these early Brown poems, William Dean Howells's "Old Brown" is the most notable attempt to reconcile all the contradictions that Brown represented. Howells's strategy is to take the whole matter on *as* representation. He self-consciously alludes to the process of memorializing by adopting the stanza form and even the numbering style of Tennyson's famous elegy *In Memoriam* (1850). He begins his representation by discussing the very process of representation, by laying down some rules by which all historical events are judged.

Howells recognizes that the true importance of John Brown's raid lies in the attempt itself rather than its success or failure. How Brown's body will be written, he admits, will be subject to the vagaries of history. This stance is much more sophisticated in its view of history than any of the poems previously discussed. The importance of this poem, like Brown's actions, lies not in the truth or fiction of Howells's words but in the attempt itself. Such a stance allows him to mourn the failure of the "Dead hope, and trodden into earth," valorize its "secret will of good," and admit the violence on both sides engendered in the attempt:

> The spots upon the lily hands
> . . . .
> That beat the breast of strife for birth
> And died birth-choked, in parent blood.

These difficult images evoke the Christology of failure. Then, with a fine segue, the umbilicus becomes a tangled net in which the lion, "baffled and spent, and wounded sore," is bound. This figure of Brown as a lion, "baffled and spent," very accurately describes, without condescension, the weary resignation Brown displayed when confronted with what must have been the awful realization of the futility of his plans. In jail, an examiner asked incredulously,

John Brown in the Poetry of the John Brown Year

"What in the world did you suppose you could do here in Virginia with that amount of men?" Brown's defiant rejoinder, "Well, perhaps your ideas and mine on military subjects would differ materially," strikes just this note of baffled pride.

Howells's approach allows him to recognize, even justify, the attempt, with all its violence. Though the difficult figures of the next few stanzas somewhat mask it, what emerges is a justification for violence in the service of liberation: "It shall not be a crime for deeds / To quicken liberating creeds." "Wherever right makes war sublime" is a just war argument, and included in "the perfect scheme of God." There is, in all honesty, no *other* way that one can validate what John Brown did, or what he stood for, than to recognize and validate the violence inherent in his principles. While after the war had begun, many were willing to shoulder this burden, Howells stands alone among the prewar poets in his willingness to confront these facts.

In his poem, as in Brown's grand scheme, the slaves rise of their own accord, and in rising, and, one presumes, in fighting, they rise as men. It may seem for a moment in this fourth stanza that Howells is not entirely free of his assumptions, for he claims that in the rising, their "blot and stain" will be washed away, as if there were something inherent in their blackness that entailed their servitude. A more careful reading, however, reveals that the "blot and stain" that will be washed away is the "spot upon the lily hands" of the white culture that stains itself in the process of writing History "worn with lies" and "failure into infamy."

Furthermore, the people ("the fearless future Man") who will be doing this washing must be the blacks themselves. Howells's phrase "the fearless future Man" alludes to Milton's Christ, who, once he has stepped into history, will wash away the stain that "We fix upon thy name to-day." Then the "Felon of the hour" will be washed clean into a "hero of the noblest plan."

By confronting the process of writing John Brown's body *as* a process of writing, Howells, alone among the early Brown poets, confronts the violence inherent in Brown's plans, the violence in slavery, and the violence that perhaps was necessary to liberate those slaves. Thus, he was able to predict what John Brown eventually came to represent—a future in which the blacks themselves were free:

> Then he, the fearless future Man,
> Shall wash the blot and stain away,

WILLIAM KEENEY

We fix upon thy name to-day—
Thou hero of the noblest plan.
O, patience! Felon of the hour!
Over thy ghastly gallows-tree
Shall climb the vine of Liberty,
With ripened fruit and fragrant flower.

THE POEMS OF THE JOHN BROWN YEAR

Ballads

"How Old Brown Took Harper's Ferry: A Ballad for the Times [Containing ye True History of ye Great Virginia Fright]"	Edmund Clarence Stedman
"Battle of Charlestown (December 2, 1859)"	Henry Howard Brownell
"John Brown of Osawatomie"	G. D. Whitmore

Elegies

"Old Brown"	William Dean Howells
"John Brown of Harper's Ferry"	C. P. H. (Worcester, Nov. 14)
"With a Rose, That Bloom'd on the Day of John Brown's Martyrdom"	Louisa May Alcott
"Miserere, Domine"	Anon. Attributed to Thomas Higginson (Worcester, Dec. 2)
"The Hoary Convict"	B. K. M. "An Ohio Clergyman" (Cincinnati, Nov. 26)
"The Hero's Heart"	L. Maria Child
"Ode"	Anon. (Concord, Dec. 2)
"Sampson Agonistes"	Franklin B. Sanborn
"Le Marais du Cygne"	John Greenleaf Whittier
"The Portent"[26]	Herman Melville

Hymn meter

"Old John Brown"	Rev. E. H. Sears
"The Virginia Scaffold"	Edna Dean Proctor

John Brown in the Poetry of the John Brown Year

"Dirge"	Franklin B. Sanborn
"Brown of Osawatomie"	John Greenleaf Whittier
"John Brown's Final Victory"	G. W. Light

NOTES

1. American Anti-Slavery Society, *The Anti-Slavery History of the John Brown Year, 1859–60: Being the Twenty-seventh Annual Report of the American Anti-Slavery Society* (1861; repr., New York: Negro University Press, 1961), 82.

2. Jules Abels, *Man on Fire: John Brown and the Cause of Liberty* (New York: Macmillan, 1971), 383.

3. Most of the poems I cite were originally published in newspapers and other periodicals of the day. My sources for the poems, their original publication dates, and authorship are, however, taken primarily from the many collections of poems from the period that have been put together by James Redpath, Louis Ruchames, and others, and by collections of Americana by Frank Moore, Burton Egbert Stevenson, and others. I rely on them for my attribution and dating.

4. Burton Egbert Stevenson, ed., *Poems of American History* (Boston and New York: Houghton Mifflin, 1908), 396.

5. James Redpath, ed., *Echoes of Harper's Ferry* (1860; repr., New York: Arno Press, 1969), 72.

6. Henry David Thoreau, *Anti-Slavery and Reform Papers,* ed. H. S. Salt (1890; repr., Miami: Mnemosyne Publishing, 1969), 87–88.

7. Oliver Wendell Holmes, *The Complete Poetical Works of Oliver Wendell Holmes* (Boston and New York: Houghton Mifflin, 1908), 321.

8. Thomas W. Laqueur, "Crowds, Carnival and the State in English Executions, 1604–1868," in *The First Modern Society,* ed. A. L. Beier, David Cannadine, and James Rosenheim (Cambridge: Cambridge University Press, 1989), 339–41.

9. Stevenson, *Poems,* 395.

10. Quoted in Laqueur, "Crowds," 329.

11. Stevenson, *Poems,* 395.

12. Ibid.

13. Boyd B. Stutler, "John Brown's Body," *Civil War History* 4 (September 1958): 254.

14. Oswald Garrison Villard, *John Brown, 1800–1859: A Biography Fifty Years After* (1920; repr., New York: Alfred A. Knopf, 1943), 608n12.

15. Stephen B. Oates, *To Purge This Land with Blood: A Biography of John Brown* (1970; rev. ed., Amherst: University of Massachusetts Press, 1985), 92.

16. Quoted in ibid., 257.

17. Ibid., 305.

18. Once again, the awkward and uncharacteristic syntactical inversion of the line, "till over was the bloody Border War" reveals, I would argue, Stedman's knowledge that he was inverting, even perverting, the actual events to suit some political, rather than poetic, aim.

WILLIAM KEENEY

19. Oates, *Purge*, 329. For an evaluation of Brown's actual mental state, see 329–33, and esp. 333.

20. Thoreau, *Anti-Slavery Papers*, 81.

21. This is consistent with the portrayal of Brown as a madman. As Thomas Szasz has pointed out, the category of madness is almost always a description of behavior, not of medically valid criteria; the result is to marginalize the individual, allowing for all kinds of control; marginal characters, according to René Girard, are subjects for sacrifice. Girard, *Violence and the Sacred*, trans. Patrick Gregory (Baltimore: Johns Hopkins University Press, 1977).

22. On the first night of the raid on Harpers Ferry, Brown and his men had secured the armory, taking the watchmen prisoner. They had also cut the telegraph lines and placed guards at the exits to the town, effectively cutting the town off and keeping news of their raid from reaching the outside world. At about one o'clock on the morning of October 17, 1859, an eastbound Baltimore and Ohio train arrived in the town and was stopped by Brown's men. Ironically, these raiders killed a black porter in the process so that the first victim of the raid was a black man. Later on that morning, some time around sunup, the train was allowed to leave, taking with it news of the raid. The train's crew soon contacted the authorities, and the U.S. military responded quickly. While word of the raid had already spread to neighboring towns, the decision to release the train cut off any hope Brown may have had of escaping with the weapons—the purported reason for the raid. Since Brown must have known that the release of the train would speed the response of the government, Brown's decision to release the train is one of the most baffling, and arguably the most disastrous, tactical decisions he made during the days of the raid on Harpers Ferry. His reason: "[H]e had no intention of interfering with the comfort of passengers or hindering the United States mails." See Richard J. Hinton, *John Brown and His Men* (New York: Arno Press and The New York Times, 1968), 288. Since his motive for releasing the train is so contrary to his stated purposes in conducting the raid, how one reads that decision will be based, in large part, on one's overall view of Brown's motives, not the other way around.

23. Redpath, *Echoes of Harper's Ferry*, 305, 310 (hereafter cited in text).

24. Thoreau, *Anti-Slavery Papers*, 88; emphasis Thoreau's.

25. See Girard, *Violence*. Girard argues that justice is abstracted revenge; the definition of a nonprimitive society includes the existence of a mechanism for enforcing that abstraction. Similarly, most principles evolve as an abstraction of various kinds of violence.

26. "Le Marais du Cygne" and "The Portent" are not from the John Brown Year but are included as points of comparison. "Le Marais du Cygne" was written May 19, 1858, and represents John Brown before his raid. "The Portent" appeared in 1866. Although it was dated 1859 by Melville and clearly refers to events of 1859, as documented by Kent Ljungquist, the reference to "the war" in the last line makes an 1859 dating of the final draft of this poem problematic. Thus, I am treating this poem as if it represents John Brown after the Civil War. Ljungquist, "'Meteor of War,'" *American Literature* 61, no. 4 (December 1989): 674–80.

ten

BEYOND HISTORY

John Brown, *Raising Holy Hell*, and Posthistorical Fiction

BRUCE OLDS

The question has been raised with respect to my novel *Raising Holy Hell* that if, on the one hand, character gets lost in history's shuffle, what is the point of the fiction composed out of that history or, on the other hand, if character so distorts or obscures the event that truth is sacrificed, where is the understanding we seek from history?[1]

Character, history, fiction, distortion, event, truth, understanding—altogether, quite a mouthful. Yet a mouthful that contains, in each of its disparate morsels, much of the meat of the matter. Despite the several presuppositions embedded therein—that it is incumbent upon fiction to have a "point," that historical "truth" ever can immutably exist, that we avail ourselves of history primarily as we may dredge some "understanding" therefrom—it remains a provocative question perspicaciously put.

Permit me to suggest at the outset that, just as historians as dissimilar as Hayden White, John Clive, Simon Schama, and Michel Foucault ardently have argued (whatever one may think of their respective scholarship), that there may be more than one way to skin the historical cat, so too does there exist a range, or what I will call a *spectrum of approaches* to writing what commonly is known as historical fiction. Permit me to suggest furthermore—this is the premise on which I shall proceed—that the variety represented across that spectrum, far from muddying the waters of the form, in fact serves both to enrich and invigorate them.

I am aware of but a handful of John Brown novels: Leonard Ehrlich's *God's Angry Man* (1932); Truman Nelson's *The Surveyor* (1960); George MacDonald Fraser's *Flashman and the Angel of the Lord* (1994); my own *Raising Holy Hell* (1995); and, most recently, Russell Banks's *Cloudsplitter* (1998). Without undertaking a blow-by-blow content analysis of the individual texts, suffice it to say that while all five are both grounded in and fueled by essentially the same subject matter (the "evidence," or raw material, of the historical record) their similarities are outweighed by their differences—the distinctive ways in which each author transmutes that material in terms of structure, style, tone, voice, thematic focus, contextual emphasis, and so on. Indeed, it may not be overstating the case to suggest that the John Brown of one novel is so at odds with the John Brown of each of the others as to defy meaningful comparison.

Clearly, each of the five novels is in some sense "about" John Brown, but each equally is an expression both of its individual author's sensibility and the vision or hidden agenda—hidden, perhaps, even to the author—that inevitably reposes at the heart of that particular work. By sensibility, I mean specifically that unique confluence of factors—singular as a signature, incriminating as a thumbprint—with which an author inevitably monograms the material: the author's personality, political convictions, religious faith, gender, race, age, powers of imagination, intellect, technical skills, depth and breadth of knowledge, experiences, temperament, sense of humor, aesthetic bent, values, conscious and unconscious biases, professional ambition, ego, neuroses, and, in some cases, personal pathology. This last, when writing about John Brown, perhaps most critical of all.

It is an author's personal psychological profile, then, coupled with his or her curriculum vitae, that largely determines the kind of writer the author will be and the sort of work that will be produced—that is, the approach taken to the material and the extent to which the promise of that approach is fulfilled—though it is perhaps more accurate, if no less romantic, to suggest that the materials and approach determine the author.

John Brown, *Raising Holy Hell*, and Posthistorical Fiction

And so it ought not startle us that we are confronted by five different John Browns as he is portrayed by five different novelists: Leonard Ehrlich, clearly the "classic" historical novelist; Truman Nelson, ever the Marxist; George MacDonald Fraser, essentially the comic, popular entertainer; Bruce Olds, much the postmodern experimentalist; Russell Banks, primarily the "literary" novelist of social and psychological realism.

It would be at least as interesting to know something about the paths these five authors traveled to arrive at the same subject matter (i.e., how each author's path intersects with that of John Brown's—randomly, reluctantly, with premeditation and malice aforethought?) as it would be to understand what prompted them to treat that subject matter in such diverse and even divergent ways.

The larger point is that where a writer of historical fiction can be slotted along the spectrum of approaches is primarily a function of the manner in which he or she juggles and juxtaposes, foregrounds or marginalizes elements of the text itself: the history, the fiction, and the technical or compositional elements—syntax, semantics, structure, voice, tone, even the typography and use of paratextual devices. And the choices an author makes in this regard, particularly with respect to the history—whether to stick scrupulously to the "facts," reorder and rearrange them, speculate about them, dispute them, depart, disregard, or augment them, or even deliberately alter, sabotage, or traduce them are colored by what the author takes for his quarry—the purpose, the aspiration, the hidden agenda, the raison d'être of his work.

At the risk of provoking the ire of those who align themselves with the more positivist wing of the discipline, I suggest that there is to be drawn here a parallel—though *confraternity* or *kinship* probably are better words—between the writing of historical fiction and that of so-called objective history and biography. Namely, that both—if to different degrees and in different ways—inevitably become exercises in what I will call, however awkwardly, the hermeneutics of historical narrative. And while novelists are apt to couch their brand of the stuff in words like *alchemy* or *inspiration* or *transmutation,* while historians and biographers prefer the less gnostic *description, explanation, extrapolation,* or *interpretation,* still, to the extent that both historical fiction and history/biography ultimately are the singular products of their singular authors as they bring their singular sensibilities to bear upon the raw material of history, they might reasonably be said to constitute opposite sides of the same coin.

The nexus, hinted at with admirable concision by literary critic Linda Hutcheon—"the representation of history [inevitably] becomes the history of self-representation"[2]—is further amplified by the remarks of two of contemporary America's most distinguished litterateurs: John Barth (who on occasion has written historical fiction himself: *The Sot-Weed Factor* [1960] and *Letters* [1979]), and William Gass. "The creation of fiction," writes Barth, "[is] a model of and spin-off from the great fictive enterprise of human consciousness itself: the ongoing fabrication of our selves, in which memory is always the co-author. . . . We *are* the stories that we tell ourselves about who we are."[3] Or, as Gass puts it, "What we remember of our own past depends very largely on what of it we've put our tongue to telling and retelling. It's our words roughly, we remember; oblivion claims the rest—forgetfulness. . . . by practicing a resolute forgetfulness, we select, we construct, we compose our pasts, and hence make fictional characters of ourselves, as it seems we must to remain sane."[4] Historian Michel de Certeau makes much the same point: "The past is the fiction of the present," he declares, a contention he defends by pointing out how, "in the past from which it is distinguished, it [history, history writing, historical interpretation] promotes a selection between what can be *understood* and what must be *forgotten* in order to obtain the representation of a present intelligibility."[5]

The writing of historical fiction and objective history, after all, both exploit the material. Both access, process, and represent the "evidence." Both use or abuse the historical "facts" to fashion—conjure, construct—some type of written narrative (impose a composition, script a manuscript, puppeteer a plot). And while historians may be less at liberty than are novelists to ignore, add to, or transcend those facts, the truth is that just as five novelists writing about John Brown may render five different John Browns, so too may five "objective" historians, writing on the identical subject, produce five different, if not irreconcilable interpretations of that subject.

The reason for such interpretative discrepancy is not difficult to apprehend. Responding to the charge that writers of historical fiction necessarily distort the lives of real people, the novelist Don DeLillo rightly has parried, "possibly not as much as the memoirist does, intentionally, or the biographer, unintentionally,"[6] a remark redolent of historian Simon Schama's: "Even in the most austere scholarly report from the archives, the inventive faculty—selecting, pruning, editing, commenting, interpreting, delivering judgments—is in full play. . . . Claims for historical knowledge must always be fatally circumscribed by the character and prejudices of its narrator."[7]

As sociologist Keith Windschuttle has described it, "Selection is determined by importance, and importance is determined by values; hence, selection

John Brown, *Raising Holy Hell*, and Posthistorical Fiction

must be determined by values. The crucial . . . premise of this argument is the claim that what historians consider important is determined by their values."[8] It is precisely this premise that radical historian Howard Zinn acknowledges in observing how, unlike the historical novelist's, "The historian's distortion is more than technical, it is ideological, [because] it is released into a world of contending interests where any chosen emphasis [in interpretation] supports some kind of interest, whether economic or political or racial or national or sexual. . . . Behind the selection of every fact lies a value. This notion of objective history disintegrates as soon as you understand that you are selecting out of an infinite mass of data."[9]

Nor is such an acknowledgement new, much less particularly provocative. At one time or another, Voltaire, Kant, Nietzsche, and Emerson all remarked on it. To wit and respectively: there is no history, only fictions of varying degrees of implausibility; or we are free to conceive of history as we please, just as we are free to make of it what we will; or there are no facts, only interpretations; or knowledge is knowing that we cannot know. As, if no less epigrammatically, has Aleksandr Solzhenitsyn: only history can do what it likes.

Well, perhaps it can, and quite possibly it cannot, but what is less uncertain is that historical novelists historically have been perfectly content to curry the uncertainty to their advantage. From Scott's Waverley novels and Cooper's *Leather-Stocking Tales,* to Carlos Fuentes's *Terra Nostra* (1976) and beyond, there always have been writers content to spin fictions from historical "facts." And those authors, and their work, have over time spanned a gamut, from those who marshaled their subject matter as it served best to reconstruct or replicate a plausible, if not always authentic, past reality that largely was faithful to—or at least did not consciously accost, ravish, or vandalize the "evidence" on the record—that is, the so-called *classical* historical novelists, to those who employed that "evidence" primarily as an inspirational trigger, a debarkation point from which to conjure—often *at the expense of* that same evidence—a new, self-contained, strictly self-referential reality (sometimes even a contrary counterreality or irreality) that might coexist alongside, if not supersede, the one already on record—what Linda Hutcheon has labeled "historiographic metafiction"[10] but which I prefer to call *posthistorical* fiction.

The distinction between the two is as fundamental as it is critical. In classical historical fiction, the author wades into the material—that is, the history—and, therein ensconced, writes a fiction about his subject—event, character, cultural and social milieu, zeitgeist—along such lines as his research may suggest. Such fictions endeavor to maintain the integrity of the firewall between fact and fiction even as they are crafted on the page to camouflage that wall's existence. To one degree or another, they honor the historical record, accepting implicitly that it is essentially truthful, and therefore, that historical accuracy counts. The best of them may, in a sense, reinvigorate the past, but they do so through a process that amounts to a refamiliarization with it.

In posthistorical fiction, the author wades into the material and then *back out again*, out of or beyond history, and, thus untethered, writes a fiction about the subject once removed—removed by the authorial act of transcending or cutting against the grain of his research in favor of reimagining that subject anew. Such fictions endeavor to breach or deconstruct (or both) the firewall between history and its novelization, even as they are crafted on the page to expose and foreground its existence as a permeable and wholly artificial façade. To one degree or another, they treat the historical record as fodder with which to feed the fiction—a form of personal fiction that may or may not have much to do with the very history out of which it is created— just as they postulate implicitly that the record is impossibly incomplete, circumscribed, selective, contradictory, skewed, mute, or just plain wrong—in any event, thoroughly unreliable—and therefore that historical "accuracy" not only does not matter but is a shibboleth and chimera, a literary unicorn, the stardust arisen of the star on which we would wish our thinking, a convenient figment of the *historian*'s imagination. The best of such works may, in a sense, imaginatively rewrite the past, but they do so through a process that amounts to an undermining, overturning, or defamiliarizing of it.

To reiterate, these are but the peripheral poles of the spectrum of approaches, and not all, or even most, historical novels fairly can be said to occupy either of them, just as fewer still are so pure that they display all the characteristics of one and none of the other. In fact, there would seem no logical reason to expect one approach to preclude the coaxial inclusion or exclusion of others, and indeed, mongrel impulses and hybridized elements of each often are found in the same work, sometimes on the same page of the same work, sometimes in the same paragraph or sentence.

In all events, it remains that a work's treatment of and attitude toward the firewall between the worlds of historical fact and fictional invention—which is to say the simultaneously contending versions of those worlds (the ways in

John Brown, *Raising Holy Hell*, and Posthistorical Fiction

and extent to which the two do or do not comingle, conflate, piggyback, and overlap)—determine where that work ought be slotted along the spectrum of approaches. Where that firewall implicitly is kept both rigorously intact and effectively hidden from view, what results is a form of docudrama. Where it explicitly is demolished and unmasked—and in the most radical work that demolition and unmasking often are self-reflexively remarked upon—what results is a form of historical fabulism.

In this latter regard, where a text is so purely fictive, transparently fabulist, or utterly fantastical, where it severs too many guylines to "historical reality" and abandons or supplants the "evidence" on the historical record to too great a degree, it cannot help but muffle, where it does not render moot, what literary critic Brian McHale has described as the "ontological flicker"—that quality generated by the friction of historical and fictional elements as they coexist in the same work, each jockeying and jostling for position beneath its scrim like so many tectonic plates.[11] In order for the flicker to flick, in other words, there must remain, however fractionalized, some façade of fact against which it still might fitfully refract.

In this respect, one way of determining where a historical novel seats itself along the spectrum is simply to ask where, how, and for what purpose its author appears to deploy that façade of fact in the work. What does his use of history accomplish or aim to accomplish within the text? What are his intentions? What, in so many words, is he up to?

Is he employing history as:

- The raw material from which to fashion an old-fashioned entertainment? A divertissement in the tradition of Scott, Cooper, and Dumas père, or more recently, Larry McMurtry in his Lonesome Dove trilogy?

- Local terrain? A means of framing, footing, or steeping his "story" in a specific time and place? A way of evoking color and mood or of lending a patina of period flavor to the "action"? A recent, perhaps overpopular, example is Charles Frazier's *Cold Mountain* (1997).

- A pulpit from which to preach? A bullhorn through which he animadverts, exhorts or—satirically or not—makes a salient political point, whether about the nature of society or the nature of humankind? Crane's *The Red Badge of Courage* (1895), Dos Passos's USA trilogy (1938), and Steinbeck's *East of Eden* (1952) are three of the more obvious, if not the most stellar, examples. So too are Joseph Heller's *Catch-22* (1961), Kurt Vonnegut's *Slaughterhouse-Five* (1968), and Thomas Berger's Mark Twain–worthy *Little Big Man* (1964).

- A way of evoking, illuminating, dramatizing, or "bringing to life," in the realist-naturalist mode, actual historical personages or events? To name an obscure example and plug a personal favorite: Earl Shorris's *Under the Fifth Sun: A Novel of Pancho Villa* (1980). Or more famously perhaps, Michael Shaara's Pulitzer Prize–winning *The Killer Angels* (1974), Marguerite Yourcenar's *Memoirs of Hadrian* (1954), George Garrett's *Death of the Fox* (1971), Thomas Flanagan's Irish trilogy, and any number of the novels of Gore Vidal, *Burr* (1973) foremost among them.

- The medium by which to reexamine—revise, clarify, correct, second-guess, speculate on, mock, or augment—the particulars of the very history being written about? Its incidents and actors? Their presuppositions and motivations? Such is much of E. L. Doctorow and Beryl Bainbridge, some T. C. Boyle and Don DeLillo, even work like Joanna Scott's *Arrogance* (1990) and William Styron's *The Confessions of Nat Turner* (1996).

- The stuff by which the very legitimacy of history and its narratives are called into question? As do most of what I choose to call posthistorical novels of the sort that have now and then been written by the likes of John Banville, Julian Barnes, John Barth, Robert Coover, Stanley Elkin, John Fowles, Carlos Fuentes, Günter Grass, Michael Ondaatje, Thomas Pynchon, Ishmael Reed, Salman Rushdie, or D. M. Thomas.

- A means to express irony, parody, satire, farce, burlesque, carnivalesque, picaresque, gothic, or grotesque? Comedy or tragedy? Arabesque? Fantasy? Dream? Hallucination? Parable? Allegory? Even poetry? (Paul Metcalf's "documentary" poems and prose poems surely set the gold standard here.) All or some of the above?

What all this has to do with John Brown—the historic personage as well as the fictive character(s) of the historical novels—and with my writing of *Raising Holy Hell* in particular, is, of course, only everything.

Dispensing with my own psychological profile and curriculum vitae, I might disclose—I fear more hindsight here than insight—that my own path

169

(as I see it, for my view may well be myopic) crossed that of John Brown's largely owing to seven factors:

- a spirit of intellectual inquisitiveness fostered from an early age by a parent who was a public school teacher

- my exposure to an array of historical novels—beginning, as I recall, with Scott's *Ivanhoe* while still in grammar school—that fired my ambition to someday write some such novel myself

- a fascination with what I might call the pathologies of American culture—racism chief among them—an interest galvanized by my experiences both in and out of university during the height of the Vietnam War years and, in turn, a curiosity about some of the more extreme expressions of thought and behavior said to arise from the so-called darker side of human nature

- my grounding in the intellectual underpinnings of and subsequent personal participation in a brand of religious social activism that culminated in my admission to Vanderbilt's graduate school of divinity

- certain lessons learned during my career as a newspaper journalist, lessons that resulted in a hard-won skepticism with respect to how information-cum-news-cum-facts-cum-truth is gathered, edited, packaged, and disseminated—filtered, processed, slanted, shaped, adulterated, reconstituted, call it what you will—that with time, coalesced into something like an aesthetic posture stemming from the conviction that while the truth may well be out there, the facts must remain forever in dispute

- an accelerating series of professional crises occurring proximate to the time that I began researching the novel: crises rooted in certain psychological dislocations and disconnects that precipitated a hermitic slide into the material, perhaps, as a form of personal sanctuary

- my gender—male; my age—early middle; my race—white; my religion—strictly privatist; my politics—obdurately incorrect; my aesthetic bent—renegade formalist.

In any event, one can, I trust, begin to sense how the currents and tides of the aforementioned factors in their synergy work to produce a certain fit between an author and his work—the fortuitous cause and felicitous effect.

As to my own raison d'être, the methodology to the madness behind *Raising Holy Hell*, I am not at all certain that I had one, at least one that I consciously articulated to myself at the time. As I recall, I wished simply to write a historical novel about John Brown that might stand on its own, as my own, and no one else's. (There would prove, of course, to be nothing simple about it.)

Beyond that, I really did not know, though as my research progressed I began to, for once having investigated the record, once having sleuthed and studied certain of the primary and secondary sources germane to the topic, I inevitably found myself influenced by the nature of the material to which I was being exposed. And it was precisely the nature of that material—again, in conjunction with the seven more personal factors mentioned above, and doubtless a raft of others of which I remain to this day less aware—that began to shoulder me in certain directions in terms of an approach. All of which began to determine, that is, exactly how I must write what eventually would become *Raising Holy Hell*.

As I scrutinized the record, what I quickly discovered there—in addition to all the internal contradictions and outright falsehoods, the fuzzed foci and double exposures, the agitprop and polemic, silences and shadows, not to mention the core enigma that was the man himself—was a gaping dichotomy, a profound and passionately disputed rift with respect to—not so much the "facts," for the facts, such as they were and remain, are there, the same for all who might wish to access them—but the selection and arrangement, assessment and interpretation, and thus the "historical truth" arisen of those facts *as severally narrated*. And what that rift amounted to, to the extent I was able to discern it, was a pair of comparably compelling, yet starkly competing, ultimately irreconcilable images: one of a Moses-like savior-messiah, replete with halo, angel wings, and brandished Bible, the other of Satan himself—horns, cloven feet, wielded pitchfork—the whole nine yards.

These, then, were the two John Browns—historical fabrications both, as I came to think of them—and one, or both, had necessarily to be wrong, just as it was conceivable that both, however apparently contradictory, could *in some part* be right. And I sensed that it would be part of my task to understand just how wrong or how right (or both), and in what ways, and even, if I was especially fortunate, why, and then to present what I had come to understand in the form of a fiction out of which might emerge yet a third John Brown—whether one occupying some middle ground or inhabiting a terrain even *more* extreme, but in either event, one that would cut against the grain of the others even as it somehow took them into account.

John Brown, *Raising Holy Hell*, and Posthistorical Fiction

I wished, in so many words, deliberately to steer clear of the sort of hermeneutical polarization or reductionism, the white-black, saint-sinner, martyr-madman, freedom fighter–terrorist interpretations that, in my estimation, marred the work of so many otherwise objective historians, biographers, and journalists. I would, I resolved, neither apologize for nor condemn, rehabilitate nor debunk, exonerate nor indict, deify nor demonize, rescue the man's reputation nor vilify his character. I would eschew hagiography even as I abstained from what I shall call here pathography—no defenses mounted, no assassinations perpetrated. I would approach material that contained an explosively high degree of moral content as nonmorally (though not necessarily dispassionately) as I could, even as I refrained from engaging in what I will characterize as interpretive closure. After all, I consoled myself, novelists need not, nor would I, interpret, or even explain their characters; they need only, as I would, depict them.

What this augured for the tone and general tenor of the work, of course, was that it would to some degree feel vaguely undetermined, or open (a quality typographically reflected throughout the body of the text in its abundant use of white space). While the novel might raise issues, provoke thought, evoke feelings, conjure images, limn character, and so on, it would need to remain reluctant, often to the point of recalcitrance, to advocate a clear and consistent point of view, maintain a single homologous voice, unambiguously endorse a political philosophy, or articulate anything approaching a monochromatic grand thesis or theme. Indeed, the rather protean manner in which the material in the novel is handled architectonically—that is, its arrangement, structure, and overall design, specifically in this instance what is called pastiche—was intended precisely to place in bas-relief just that quality.

Yes, the kaleidoscopic, fragmentary nature of the text postmodernly fractures the sense of a strict interior chronology, just as its disjunctiveness—stop and start, freeze-frame, jump cut, stutter step—deliberately disrupts the (artificially created) narrative flow while figuratively uncoupling the cars on the (mythical, if much vaunted) train of cause-and-effect history. But that disjointedness, those created crevices in the continuity, also were intended to serve as an invitation to the reader to become an accomplice, to implicate him- or herself in patching together the pieces of the puzzle that the novel insists must remain John Brown, to pass his or her own judgments, draw his or her own conclusions, fill in the gaps and decide for him- or herself what to make, finally, of the character at the heart of this fiction.

For in so doing, as I reasoned it, not only was I as the novel's author signaling that I did not have all the answers, I was affording the character of John Brown the opportunity to appear more fully human—multidimensional, polychromatic, nuanced, contoured—on the page. And, at last, that was the sine qua non: that the John Brown of *Raising Holy Hell* should stride its pages less as an object, symbol, or icon—some static repository of moral values and political behavior—than as a polysemic human presence, a complex and shadowy presence perhaps, for I recognized from the outset that the character was as prone to contradiction and inconsistency as he was given to fanaticism and monomania—but was as susceptible to fault, flaw, foible, and frailty, as liable to human folly and farce, *in his own way,* as the rest of us.

And so my methodology, if it can be called that, my attitude toward the historical facts of the matter, was to cherry-pick and redeploy such information—or, as it served my narrative purpose, to manufacture, reconstitute, or violate it—in whichever ways might yield a character that was in my aesthetic judgment more effectively (if seldom conventionally) rounded in the literary sense, if not more authentically real in the historical.

And so sometimes, I stuck to the "facts" (e.g., the Founding Father quotations; the history-as-received sections), and other times, I made facts up while appearing to stick to them (e.g., certain diary entries, letters, and newspaper articles), and sometimes, I rearranged, recombined, or telescoped them (e.g., much of the Secret Six material), and much of the time I mixed in or tacked on some fiction, or disregarded the facts entirely in favor of substituting whole-cloth invention.

And in this regard, I could not begin to hazard a guess as to how often I have been asked, in effect, what percentage of *Raising Holy Hell* is "true," and how much is "made up." Or how often my reply has been, "I have no idea." Which is quite true. I haven't. Not the foggiest. Nor, were I of a mind to do so, which decidedly I am not, could I think how to begin to calculate such a matter beyond the singularly unhelpful observation that (a) some of it is documented "actually" to have happened, (b) some of it may, but need not "actually," have happened—we shall never know for certain as there exists no "evidence" one way or another (this is especially true of a character's interior life—thoughts, dreams, emotions, psychological motivation—but also of attitude, gesture, action, even concrete description, anything where the record "goes dark"), and (c) some of it is documented "actually" *not* to have happened,

173

John Brown, *Raising Holy Hell,* and Posthistorical Fiction

either at all or in the manner or sequence attributed to it. Often all possibilities exist at once, and often within the arc of the same sentence.

One example of this—and I include it here only because I have so often been asked about it—occurs on the last page of the novel, where I choose to quote from a letter that I choose to have John Brown having authored that I choose to have him having addressed to his family using words I choose to have him having chosen. Did such a letter really exist? In documentable fact? Actually? In "real" life? Is it historically "accurate?" Corroborated? Substantiated? Is it demonstrably "true"?

Perhaps. I cannot say. At any rate, not for certain, not anymore. I believe that it did not really exist, not in the context in which it appears in the novel, but I may well be wrong about that. I may have invented none of it, or all of it, or most of it, or only some small part of it, or perhaps, despite its brevity, it may be a mongrel, a composite based on two or more letters that really did exist. But while the words as I read them now *ring* true, they also ring to me, of *me*.

Did the letter really exist? In all candor, I can no longer say. If I knew once, as surely I must, I since have long forgotten. It has been some while since I wrote the words, and in the meantime they have assumed a life all their own. If the letter did not exist before, it clearly exists now—it exists there, on page 331 of *Raising Holy Hell,* the Henry Holt hardcover version.

And this does not bother me, this not being able to say, nearly as much as some historians might argue it ought. And yet, still and all, it does not. It does not, because while I cannot say what I can no longer recall, I can say what I know, and much of what I know is expressed in that sentiment that E. L. Doctorow had in mind when, remarking on his novel *Ragtime,* he declared, "I'm satisfied that everything I made up is true, whether it happened or not. Perhaps truer because it didn't happen."[12]

Which, when you get right down to it, sounds pretty arrogant. Almost as arrogant, I might suggest, as those historians who, in writing their own narrative versions of what happened once, in the distant past, stake their claim to a truth they have the temerity to tout as somehow truer still.

NOTES

1. Susan Dodd, "A Passion for Freedom," *Washington Post Book World,* October 1, 1995, 2.

2. Linda Hutcheon, *The Politics of Postmodernism* (London: Routledge, 1989), 58.

3. John Barth, *Further Fridays: Essays, Lectures, and Other Nonfiction, 1984–94* (Boston: Little, Brown, 1995), 188, 196; emphasis Barth's.

4. William H. Gass, *Fiction and the Figures of Life: Essays* (Boston: David R. Godine, 1979), 126–28.

5. Michel de Certeau, *The Writing of History,* trans. Tom Conley (New York: Columbia University Press, 1988), 4; emphasis de Certeau's.

6. Don DeLillo, "The Power of History," *New York Times Magazine,* September 7, 1997, 62.

7. Simon Schama, *Dead Certainties: Unwarranted Speculations* (New York: Knopf, 1991), 322.

8. Keith Windschuttle, *The Killing of History: How Literary Critics and Social Theorists Are Murdering Our Past* (New York: Free Press, 1997), 231.

9. Howard Zinn, *A People's History of the United States* (New York: Harper and Row, 1980), 8.

10. Linda Hutcheon, *A Poetics of Postmodernism: History, Theory, Fiction* (London: Routledge, 1988), ix.

11. Brian McHale, *Postmodernist Fiction* (London: Routlege, 1987), 90.

12. E. L. Doctorow, *E. L. Doctorow: Essays and Conversations,* ed. Richard Trenner (London: Routledge, 1989), 58.

John Brown, *Raising Holy Hell,* and Posthistorical Fiction

PART FIVE

John Brown and

Cultural Iconography

eleven

JOHN BROWN'S FORT

A Contested National Symbol

PAUL A. SHACKEL

The John Brown Fort serves as a symbol of changing cultural attitudes about race, slavery, and the causes of the American Civil War. Thus, the building is more than a historic structure; it is an edifice that embodies the way we remember our history. The well-preserved fort sits in the heart of Harpers Ferry National Historical Park. Without knowing the structure's history, visitors could assume that its appearance and symbolic meaning are timeless, rooted in the abolitionist cause for equal rights. However, this is not the case.[1]

Because the fort's meaning can reflect attitudes about racial relations, its role as a tourist attraction has also changed over time. From the 1860s through the 1880s, the fort was something of a shrine for abolitionists, Civil War veterans, and African Americans. But much like the national rejection of abolitionist ideals in the Jim Crow era, the John Brown Fort lost its symbolic value for many whites in the years following Reconstruction, and that value continued to decline well into the early twentieth century. Even though African

Americans embraced the fort—so much so that it was moved to the site of an African American college in the early twentieth century—from the late nineteenth century until the dawn of the civil rights movement in the twentieth century, most white Americans viewed Brown negatively, and the fort was not central to the white American consciousness during the Jim Crow era. Thus, the fort ceased to be a significant cultural icon among white Americans. Perhaps symbolic of the changing views toward Brown himself, the fort was moved more than once. Not until the 1960s, when the National Park Service moved the building to the lower town in Harpers Ferry (150 feet from its original location) did the fort and its associated meanings again become part of the national consciousness.[2]

THE EARLY HISTORY OF THE JOHN BROWN FORT

The fort was originally built in 1847–48 and functioned as the engine guard house for the U.S. armory complex. The one-story brick building, with its slate roof and copper gutters, stood near the armory entrance. It contained two fire engines and served as quarters for a night guard.[3] It was one of the few armory buildings to escape destruction during the Civil War. Immediately following Brown's attempted capture of the armory, the engine house became known as the John Brown Fort. The structure was then transformed into a symbol of the abolitionist movement, becoming a rallying point for Northern troops, who would march past the fort singing the familiar tune "John Brown's body lies a-mouldering in the grave."

After the Civil War the John Brown Fort stood neglected and became a target for souvenir hunters who took bricks as a reminder of the 1859 raid. In an 1869 Harpers Ferry auction, the U. S. government sold the fort, along with the rest of the armory grounds, to a group of investors from Washington, D.C., headed by Capt. Francis C. Adams, who told the local population that he intended to again use the waterpower developed by the armory and bring industry to the banks of the Potomac River. Adams's plans failed to materialize when he was unable to acquire land owned by the Baltimore and Ohio Railroad, and in the end he never paid for the land on which he had successfully bid. Thus, the government retained possession of the armory, including the John Brown Fort.[4]

When the Harpers Ferry economy recovered in the 1880s, Thomas Savery purchased the armory grounds, including the former armory, arsenal, rifle works, and the John Brown Fort. Subsequently, Harpers Ferry became a mecca for summer tourists and curiosity seekers (plate 8). Advertisements often ran in Washington and Baltimore papers for special excursions to Harpers Ferry on both the Chesapeake and Ohio Canal and the B&O Railroad. Summer homes sprang up, as it became fashionable to visit Civil War sites.[5] The fort received little care in private ownership, although the words John Brown's Fort were painted on the engine house for easy tourist identification. In addition, Savery capitalized on owning the fort. Apparently he also procured bricks from the structure and gave them away as souvenirs (plate 9). One of Savery's children wrote:

> Not everything father did was perfect, of course, and one thing that pulled the average down a little, was his making souvenirs out of bricks taken from John Brown's Fort. On each brick was pasted a steel engraving of the fort, then the brick was placed in a black-leather-covered box, the lining [of] which was SATIN—of all things some were lined with red, some with light blue satin. And these were given around to favored friends and relatives. He also sent them to people of note who would appreciate their historical value,—Harriet Beecher Stowe, J. G. Whittier, William Cullen Bryant, and several others.[6]

Although tourists came to Savery's property and visited the John Brown Fort, some townspeople were not enthusiastic about having the structure in their town. Discontent already existed in the community over the presence of Storer College, an institution established for the education of African Americans.[7] Throughout the college's existence, whites dictated its mission through their control of the administration and the governing board. Racial tensions flared during the college's early years, and the Ku Klux Klan often threatened those associated with the college. One teacher claimed to have been "hooted at" on her way to the local post office because of her affiliation with the college. She was also stoned in the streets several times by residents. Because of such incidents, it became necessary for armed militiamen to escort Storer College women when they left the campus.[8]

Because it symbolized abolition and a threat of a possible influx of African Americans, some townspeople were eager to rid the town of the John Brown Fort. In 1888 a rumor spread that the fort would be moved to a park in New

York state. The editor of the local newspaper, writing in favor of this idea, exclaimed, "& joy go with it."[9]

In 1891, Savery sold the fort to the John Brown Fort Company. The sale became necessary when the B&O railroad acquired a new right-of-way and planned to move the railroad tracks 250 feet from their present location on the banks of the Potomac River. The right-of-way included the John Brown Fort.[10] Founded by Iowa congressman A. J. Holmes, the John Brown Fort Company was created for the "owning, controlling and the exhibition of the building known as the John Brown Fort as well as other historical relics" in order to exhibit the structure at the 1893 World's Columbian Exposition in Chicago.[11]

The company dismantled the structure, shipped it to Chicago by rail, and reassembled it at 1341 Wabash Avenue in 1893, several miles from the exposition. The fort exhibited curios and other objects related to Brown and the raid. The company hired Col. S. K. Donavan, an eyewitness to the raid, trial, and execution of Brown, to speak at the reconstructed fort. The company hoped to capitalize on the fair, but unfortunately the reconstructed fort did not finally open until ten days before the closing of the exposition. Thus, the company collected only eleven paid admissions during the exposition, at fifty cents each. This sum hardly covered the sixty thousand dollars the company had spent moving and rebuilding the structure.

SAVING THE FORT FROM ITS IGNOBLE USE

Bankrupt, the John Brown Fort Company simply abandoned the structure. Two years later, in 1895, the *Chicago Tribune* noted that a new department store used the fort as a stable for delivery wagons.[12] Eventually, Mary Katherine Field, a newspaper columnist from Washington, D.C., came to the rescue of the fort. She was actively involved in social reform issues and concerned with the circumstances of African Americans after the Civil War. Her work included saving the John Brown farm and the grave at North Elba, New York, from decay. Field had used her column in the late 1860s as a vehicle to solicit funds to purchase and preserve the homestead.

In 1895 Field campaigned for donations to move the fort back to Harpers Ferry so that it could be close to Storer College.[13] Despite opposition from white townspeople, meetings were held at Storer College to discuss a monument for John Brown and the B&O Railroad's plans to provide a site for the

PAUL A. SHACKEL

fort.[14] The railroad offered to have the fort moved to an area near the original site in order to encourage tourism on the railroad line.[15]

Rumors also circulated about reburying John Brown's remains at Harpers Ferry. The *Spirit of Jefferson,* the local newspaper, opposed disinterring John Brown and building a monument, although the paper favored the return of the fort "where Robert E. Lee captured the old villain." Most whites in Harpers Ferry were also displeased about rumored plans to move the bodies of the raiders, buried in a common grave on the Shenandoah across from Harpers Ferry, and reinter them with a marker at the restored fort.[16]

Field contacted Alexander Murphy of Jefferson County, West Virginia, about the possibility of deeding five acres of his farm, Buena Vista, for the placement of the fort. Even though this location was several miles from the original location and the railroad line, Murphy convinced Field that his farm would be a suitable place for the fort,[17] and on July 23, 1895, Field signed a contract with Murphy and his wife, who deeded the five acres for one dollar. The agreement required that the John Brown Fort be moved from Chicago to the farm; otherwise, the agreement would be void and the land would revert to Murphy.[18] Field, and maybe even Murphy, envisioned an avenue of houses that would approach a park that encompassed the fort.[19]

In 1895, Kate Field was a weary fifty-seven-year-old on her way to serve as a roving correspondent in Hawaii. On August 4, 1895, she addressed an African American congregation at Quinn Chapel on Wabash Ave and Twenty-fourth Street in Chicago, close to where the fort then stood. Attendees pledged a total of one hundred dollars for the purpose of returning "John Brown's Fort" to its original location at Harpers Ferry. Field created the John Brown Fort Association at the meeting, and essential members of the congregation became its founding members. The fort needed some immediate attention, and Field received consent from Charles L. Hutchinson, owner of the land where the fort stood, to take possession of the fort and move it wherever she chose.[20] The fort was destined for Alexander Murphy's farm. As Field departed for Hawaii, she left final arrangements for the fort's transportation and rebuilding to C. T. Cummins. He wrote that he considered his task "a labor of which any man may be justly proud."[21] The B&O railroad transported the building for no charge.[22]

Alexander Murphy played a major role in the reconstruction of the fort on the five-acre parcel. Murphy's daughter-in-law, Mrs. Will Murphy, recalled that Murphy had to drain a spring on the property to make a usable location for the building's construction.[23] On November 4, 1895, E. B. Chambers wrote Kate Field that the construction of the fort on Murphy's farm was proceeding slowly and that Cummins took very little interest in his work. While the remaining bricks from the fort were on the grounds, an additional eight thousand were needed for reconstruction.[24]

Expenses increased after Murphy hired a caretaker to maintain the building and receive hundreds of visitors, especially since people often took bricks as souvenirs. Visitors also climbed over fences and littered the fields, while carriages trampled Murphy's crops.[25] Kate Field had verbally agreed to reimburse Murphy for such expenses, but she died suddenly in 1896 in Hawaii.[26] Field had not left an estate sufficient to pay for the upkeep of the John Brown Fort, and the John Brown Association ceased to function without her support.[27] On November 27, 1901, Murphy initiated a lawsuit against Field's administrator and any unknown heirs. Murphy won, regained access to the five acres because Field's estate failed to pay for expenses, and acquired the fort. He then limited access to his property and the fort.[28]

THE MAKING OF AN AFRICAN SYMBOL

Although the fort became a rallying point for federal troops during the war, and many middle-class tourists visited the building throughout the Reconstruction era, the structure's meaning was transformed during the Jim Crow era. After Brown's 1859 raid, African Americans had implicitly revered the John Brown Fort as a symbol of their abolitionist struggle, but the structure became an explicit and prominent symbol among African Americans after the mid-1890s. It is probably no coincidence that the same year the Supreme Court upheld segregation in *Plessy v. Ferguson,* the John Brown Fort became a prominent symbol in the struggle for racial equality. In July 1896 the first national convention of the National League of Colored Women, led by Mary Church Terrell, met in Washington, D.C., and took a day trip to the John Brown Fort at the Murphy farm (plate 10).

A decade later, in August 1906, the Niagara Movement, the predecessor of the NAACP, held its second official meeting at Harpers Ferry. Because Harpers Ferry was the symbolic starting point of the American Civil War, Storer College became an obvious choice to host the Niagara meetings. Nearly one hundred visitors came to Harpers Ferry for that meeting. While in town, the convention celebrated John Brown's Day on August 17 and went to the fort to commemorate John Brown's hundredth birthday and the fiftieth anniversary of the battle of Osawatomie. (In actuality, John Brown was born in 1800 and the Osawatomie engagement occurred on August 30, 1856.) At 6:00 A.M., the conference participants left the convention site and started their journey to the engine house, about a mile away. As they approached the fort on the Murphy farm, they formed a procession, single file, took off their "shoes and socks, and walked barefoot as if treading on holy ground."[29]

The participants listened to a prayer led by Richard T. Greener. He shared his personal recollections of John Brown and told the crowd that when he served as consul at Vladivostok, he had heard Russian troops burst into the song "John Brown's body lies a-mouldering in the grave."[30] At this meeting, W. E. B. Du Bois read the Niagara address to the delegation, a speech reported around the nation. His tone led some reporters to label Du Bois a militant and an agitator because he told the congregation about African Americans' increasing loss of political and social rights: "We claim for ourselves every single right that belongs to a freeborn American, political, civil, and social; and until we get these rights we will never cease to protest and assail the ears of America." Du Bois continued: "The battle we wage is not for ourselves alone but for all true Americans. It is a fight for ideals, lest this, our common fatherland, false in founding, become in truth the land of the thief and the home of the slave—a byword and a hissing among the nations for its sounding pretensions and pitiful accomplishments." He claimed that he did not believe in obtaining equal rights through violence, but, he said, "We do believe in John Brown, in that incarnate spirit of justice, that hatred of a lie, the willingness to sacrifice money, reputation, and life itself on the altar of right. And here on the scene of John Brown's martyrdom we reconsecrate ourselves, our honor, our property to final emancipation of the race that John Brown died to make free. . . . Thank God for John Brown! Thank God for Garrison and Douglas [sic]! [Charles] Sumner and [Wendell] Philips, Nat Turner and Robert Gould Shaw."[31] If any doubt existed about the use of the John Brown Fort as an African American symbol, its meaning became well defined by the end of the second meeting of the Niagara Movement.

How many other visitors came to the fort while it stood on the Murphy farm is unclear from the historical documentation, although it does appear that the structure was accessible to the African American community, and it served as a place of homage for people who revered John Brown and the ideas

John Brown's Fort

of social reform. At the peak of the Jim Crow era as well as the Southern revisionist movement, which gave credibility to the Lost Cause and denigrated the methods and meaning of the abolitionist movement, African Americans and their white allies continued to use the fort and John Brown himself as symbols in their fight for social equality.[32] Du Bois wrote a major biography of John Brown in 1909 that recaptured and reinforced the sympathy for John Brown that was so prevalent in earlier biographies and memoirs written by people like James Redpath, Franklin B. Sanborn, Richard Josiah Hinton, and Frederick Douglass. Calling John Brown a prophet, Du Bois claimed that Brown was justified in using militant tactics at Harpers Ferry.[33] Du Bois, along with many other activists, ensured that the legacy of John Brown and the abolitionist movement would be remembered and that the John Brown Fort would serve as a rallying point for their ideas. Similarly, Oswald Garrison Villard, grandson of white abolitionist William Lloyd Garrison and a founding member (and later chairman) of the NAACP, published his sympathetic biography of John Brown in 1910.[34]

In 1909 the trustees of Storer College voted to buy the John Brown Fort from Alexander Murphy and agreed to pay nine hundred dollars, which reimbursed Murphy for his purchase price and court costs. Dismantled in 1910, the fort again fell prey to souvenir hunters. But eventually the college rebuilt the structure on campus, near Lincoln Hall. It continued to serve as an important symbol and gathering point during its fifty-eight years on the campus (plate 11).[35]

The fort remained on the grounds of Storer College after the school closed in 1955. In 1968 the National Park Service moved the structure for the fourth time. Unable to place the fort on its original foundation, which is now under fourteen feet of fill on railroad property, the National Park Service moved the fort to the former arsenal yard that Brown had briefly captured more than one hundred years before. The move occurred during a period of great racial unrest that led to riots in Detroit, Newark, and other American cities. During that same year, assassins murdered the nation's foremost civil rights leader, Martin Luther King Jr., and a prominent white advocate for civil rights, Senator Robert F. Kennedy.

In the 1990s, Harpers Ferry National Historical Park became one of the most visited national historical parks in the United States. A museum dedicated to telling the story of John Brown's deeds contributes significantly to a visitor's appreciation of the fort that is now surrounded by well-maintained

PAUL A. SHACKEL

grounds. The surroundings also contribute to the creation of a monumental landscape that commemorates the deeds of John Brown and his men.

The John Brown Fort is a monument that has physically changed through its 150-year existence. What has not changed significantly is the way a large portion of the African American community has embraced the John Brown Fort (as one of the few Civil War monuments that can be claimed as its own). After the war the nation began constructing monuments to its Civil War heroes and veterans and in commemoration and justification of one of the most violent epochs in American history. Vernacular Civil War monuments were placed throughout the American landscape with uncontroversial inscriptions. The inscriptions rarely mention slavery or African Americans, and they generally justify the war as one that was fought over "the Cause" or "State Sovereignty." In these monuments the common soldier is almost always portrayed as or perceived to be a white man.[36]

The introduction of African American troops changed the outcome of the war, yet only a few of the thousands of Civil War monuments have African American representation. They usually show a single black soldier surrounded by white soldiers. One monument, the Robert Gould Shaw Memorial in Boston, features a local white hero who led the first all–African American regiment recruited in the North, the Fifty-fourth Regiment, Massachusetts Volunteer Infantry, into battle. It shows Shaw, elevated on horseback, leading his marching African American troops. As its name suggests, it can be interpreted as a memorial more to Shaw than to his men.[37] But as one scholar writes, "public monuments do not arise as if by natural law to celebrate the deserving; they are built by people with sufficient power to marshal (or impose) public consent for their erection."[38] Only recently have there been successful movements to create monuments to African American Civil War troops. For instance, a monument unveiled in Washington, D.C., in 1998 commemorates the efforts of all branches of the military in which African Americans served during the Civil War.

Today the fort, a bit smaller than its original size, contains many new bricks, which were added when it was placed on the Murphy farm.[39] Plaques were also placed at the fort when it was subsequently rebuilt. The structure contains mementos that recognize the 1895 rebuilding sponsored by Kate Field, the 1910 rebuilding on the Storer College Campus, and the stone placed on the fort's exterior wall by the college's alumni in 1918 to acknowledge the heroism of John Brown and his twenty-one men.[40] Several times in the fort's history, it has almost vanished completely. Nevertheless, like the phoenix, it has risen from obscurity and remains a symbol of freedom.

NOTES

I am indebted to Barbara Little for her constant feedback, criticism, and encouragement during the writing of this manuscript. Todd Bolton informed me about the role of the National League of Colored Women and its association with the John Brown Fort. Bruce Noble was influential in suggesting that this manuscript be submitted to this volume. I appreciate Paul Finkelman's and Peggy Russo's helpful comments during the rewriting phase of the manuscript, as well as their patience. Andrea Mark of the special collections division, Chicago Public Library, provided significant information on the John Brown Fort during its tenure in Chicago. I have written several articles and chapters related to the changing meaning of the John Brown Fort over the past decade. My developing interpretations can be found in the following: "Resilient Shrine," *Archaeology* 46, no. 3 (1993): 72; "Terrible Saint: Changing the Meanings of the John Brown Fort," *Historical Archaeology* 29, no. 4 (1995): 11–25; "The John Brown Fort: African-Americans' Civil War Monument," *CRM* 20, no. 2 (1997): 23–26; *Memory in Black and White: Race, Commemoration, and the Post-Bellum Landscape* (Walnut Creek, CA: AltaMira Press, 2003).

1. Shackel, "Terrible Saint."

2. Ibid.

3. Charlotte J. Fairbairn, *John Brown's Fort: Armory Engine and Guard House 1848–1961* (Harpers Ferry, WV: Harpers Ferry National Historical Park [hereafter HFNHP], 1961), 1.

4. Charles W. Snell, *The Acquisition and Disposal of Public Lands of the U.S. Armory at Harpers Ferry, West Virginia, 1795–1885: A Narrative History* (Harpers Ferry, WV: HFNHP, 1979).

5. Fairbairn, *Brown's Fort*, 13, 20.

6. Biography of Thomas Savery by his daughter, Anne Pym Savery Thayer, 1943, microfilm, Hagley Museum and Library, Wilmington, Delaware, accession no. 399, p. 27.

7. Paul A. Shackel, *Culture Change and the New Technology: An Archaeology of the Early American Industrial Era* (New York: Plenum Press, 1996), 47–49.

8. Kate J. Anthony, *Storer College, Harpers Ferry, W.Va.: Brief Historical Sketch* (Boston: Morning Star Publishing House, 1891).

9. *Spirit of Jefferson* (Charles Town, WV), August 14, 1888, 1.

10. *Spirit of Jefferson*, September 17, 1889, 3.

11. Fairbairn, *Brown's Fort*, 22a.

12. Clarence S. Gee, "John Brown's Fort," *West Virginia History* 9, no. 2 (1958): 94; Fairbairn, *Brown's Fort*, 14, 26, 33, 34.

13. Fairbairn, *Brown's Fort*, 14, 31.

14. *Spirit of Jefferson*, June 1 1894, 2.

PAUL A. SHACKEL

15. Gee, "Brown's Fort," 97.

16. *Spirit of Jefferson,* October 1, 1895, 2.

17. Fairbairn, *Brown's Fort,* app.

18. Jefferson County Deed Book, July 23, 1895, Jefferson County Court House, Charleston, WV, vol. 91, 473–74.

19. Gee, "Brown's Fort," 97.

20. "Ignoble Use of the John Brown Fort," *Chicago Tribune,* August 5, 1895, 9.

21. Cummins to Field, August 11, 1895, HFNHP.

22. *Spirit of Jefferson,* October 1, 1895, 2.

23. Mrs. Will Murphy in Fairbairn, *Brown's Fort,* app.

24. Chambers to Field, November 4, 1895, HFNHP.

25. Gee, "Brown's Fort," 100.

26. *Chicago Tribune,* May 31, 1896, 6, in Fairbairn, *Brown's Fort,* 34.

27. *Martinsburg Journal,* November 12, 1964, 8.

28. Spirit of Jefferson, February 18, 1902, 3; *Farmers Advocate,* February 15, 1902, 3.

29. Benjamin Quarles, *Allies for Freedom: Blacks and John Brown* (New York: Oxford University Press, 1974), 4.

30. Ibid.

31. Quoted in W. E. B. Du Bois, *W. E. B. Du Bois Speaks: Speeches and Addresses,* vol. 1, *1890–1919,* ed. Philip S. Foner (New York: Pathfinder, 1970), 170–73.

32. Fairbairn, *Brown's Fort,* 14.

33. Du Bois, *John Brown,* 339.

34. William Lloyd Garrison, *John Brown, 1800–1859: A Biography Fifty Years After* (1920; repr., New York: Alfred A. Knopf, 1943).

35. Shackel, "Terrible Saint."

36. Kirk Savage, "The Politics of Memory: Black Emancipation and the Civil War Monument," in *Commemorations: The Politics of National Identity,* ed. John R. Gillis (Princeton: Princeton University Press, 1994), 135.

37. Ibid., 136.

38. Ibid., 135.

39. Paul A. Shackel, "Resilient Shrine," *Archaeology* 46, no. 3 (1993): 72.

40. Shackel, "Terrible Saint," 20.

twelve

JOHN BROWN
GOES TO HOLLYWOOD

Santa Fe Trail and *Seven Angry Men*

PEGGY A. RUSSO

Only two Hollywood films focus on John Brown—*Santa Fe Trail* (1940) and *Seven Angry Men* (1955).[1] *Santa Fe Trail,* the better known of the two, is historically inaccurate and considered by many John Brown scholars to be a damaging misrepresentation of John Brown's legacy.[2] But it stands out because it was a major motion picture made by Warner Bros., one of the eight major Hollywood studios;[3] starred top-draw actors Errol Flynn and Olivia de Havilland; and had a leading director (Michael Curtiz), a well-known screenwriter (Robert Buckner), and three prominent producers (Jack Warner, Hal Wallis, and Robert Fellows).[4] In addition, it is readily available on videocassette, so it is often aired on television and can be purchased or rented at video stores. Produced by a relatively minor studio (Allied Artists), *Seven Angry Men* starred Raymond Massey, Jeffrey Hunter, and Debra Paget, all capable actors but certainly not top box-office draws.[5] In addition, director Charles Marquis Warren, producer Vincent M. Fennelly, and screenwriter Daniel B.

Ullman were known primarily for their work on B westerns. Although *Seven Angry Men* contains a more historically accurate portrayal of Brown than does *Santa Fe Trail,* it has received scant attention from film critics and John Brown scholars, in part because of its status as a B picture but also because it is not readily available.[6] Cast as John Brown in both films was Canadian-born actor Raymond Massey, who had also spent two years touring in a theatrical production of Stephen Vincent Benét's *John Brown's Body.*[7] Indeed, because of his association with the role, Massey has come to represent the popular embodiment of John Brown. Despite featuring the same actor as Brown, however, the two films interpret his character and events in his life quite differently. What happened between 1940 and 1955 to explain these differences? Moreover, was the John Brown icon appropriated simply in order to create a profitable entertainment commodity, or did producers, directors, or writers, have social, political, or rhetorical ends in mind? By examining the medium, audience, purpose, and cultural situation of these films, we can better understand how the zeitgeist of 1940 and that of 1955 brought about changes in the iconography of John Brown.

Santa Fe Trail

The ambiguity of *Santa Fe Trail* becomes apparent even during the opening credits, a series of graphics showing cowboys on horseback, wagon trains, men laying railroad tracks, and finally a troop of cavalry, all suggesting a film typical of the western genre and set during the time when the country was exploring, expanding, and developing its western frontier. But the inclusion of an image of a railroad train suggests a somewhat later period (the train was included because the film was originally supposed to deal with the building of the Santa Fe Railroad). The ambiguity extends to the opening music: "The Battle Hymn of the Republic," a.k.a. "John Brown's Body." Thus it is not surprising that while *Santa Fe Trail* is most often categorized as a western in film histories and chronologies, it also appears on lists and in discussions of war films, Civil War films, and films about African American history.

The film begins at West Point, moves to Bleeding Kansas, and then to Harpers Ferry.[8] It is the year of J. E. B. Stuart's graduation from West Point (here changed from 1854 to 1857), and the opening focuses on the rivalry between Stuart and a fictional cadet named Rader (Van Heflin), planted at West Point by abolitionist leaders to distribute antislavery propaganda.[9] When

Rader reads to cadets (with reverent music playing in the background) from an antislavery tract (written by John Brown, according to Rader) calling for the "breakup of the American union" if the government does not end slavery, Stuart insists that "the South will settle this, not renegades like John Brown."[10] An ensuing fight results in a reprimand by Commandant Robert E. Lee. Despite this violation of military conduct, Stuart and six of his fellow cadets are permitted to graduate but are assigned to the "most dangerous branch" of the army—the Second Cavalry at Fort Leavenworth in Kansas Territory (presumably, they will be fighting Indians). Subsequently, Lee gives Rader a dishonorable discharge and tells him that it is a "very clever idea of [Rader's] fellow conspirators to plant an agent in our midst." Rader is tagged as part of a conspiracy similar to that in Warner Brothers' *Confessions of a Nazi Spy* (1939), which had exposed the existence in America of an elaborate Nazi spy network, and John Brown is thus equated with Hitler. Stuart, by contrast, becomes the country's defender and an apologist for the South.

The cadets slated to accompany Stuart to Kansas include George Armstrong Custer (Ronald Reagan), George Pickett, James Longstreet, Phil Sheridan, and John Hood, none of whom graduated with Stuart. The graduation scene introduces (fictional) Cadet Bob Holliday's family from Kansas: his father, Cyrus (the real Cyrus Holliday was indeed involved in the postbellum building of the Santa Fe Railroad), and his sister Kit Carson Holliday (de Havilland), who sparks a romantic rivalry between Stuart and Custer. During the ceremony, the cadets and their home states are named, calling attention to the fact that they will soon be fighting each other in the coming civil war. Secretary of War Jefferson Davis (Davis was not secretary of war at the time) speaks eloquently, stressing "responsibility to our government," "fighting for our freedom," "loyalty to America," and the "noblest of all causes . . . defense of the rights of man." The dramatic irony of putting these words in the mouth of the future president of the Confederacy would not have been lost on audiences, who had flocked to see *Gone with the Wind* a year earlier.

The West Point exposition scenes introduce major characters and themes and contain plenty of irony. It appears that the film will be concerned with familiar Hollywood plots: the winning of the West, the winning of the girl, and the building of a railroad. But the film also deals with complex issues such as racism, antigovernment conspiracy, and the threat of an imminent war, all of which are relevant to a pre-WWII audience and reflect the angst of the time.

The opening scenes in Kansas reveal that the presence of John Brown (rather than marauding Indians) makes Fort Leavenworth a dangerous outpost. But they also focus on Stuart and Custer's rivalry and dual courtship of Kit Holliday, echoed in a comic subplot in which two stock characters (Alan Hale and Guinn "Big Boy" Williams) are rivals for a Santa Fe girl named Lilly who is "engaged to everybody." The two sidekicks exchange bantering insults, providing comic relief throughout the film. These first Kansas scenes also include a wagon-train sequence during which Hale, Williams, and other cast members break into a rendition of the film's theme song ("Santa Fe Trail," an upbeat piece composed for the film), complete with offscreen orchestral accompaniment. While such plot and stylistic incongruities baffle modern audiences, Flynn and de Havilland were an established romantic duo and had appeared in previous Curtiz films with the comic team of Hale and Williams, a formula that had come to be expected by audiences of the time.[11] And no doubt the filmmakers were reluctant to waste the theme song, which was not used during the opening credits. A subtitle introduces "The Camp of John Brown, leader of the Abolitionists, whose bloody raids are terrorizing Kansas." Brown (Massey) sports a neatly trimmed but lengthy beard, even though the historical Brown did not have a beard during this period (he grew the beard in 1858 as a disguise after he became a wanted man). He is dressed in a dark suit and tie, white shirt and vest, and a wide-brimmed hat. One critic claims that Massey had been made up to resemble John Steuart Curry's famous image of the "mad" John Brown (plate 13), and certainly he more closely resembles the Curry image than he does the Old Testament patriarch in the 1942 Rivera mural (plate 14) or the good shepherd image in the 1937 Covey mural (plate 12).[12] But his costume most closely resembles a country parson's garb (historical accounts of the Kansas period reveal that Brown was never so nattily dressed). At first, Brown appears to fit the role of villain. While dictating a letter to his son Jason, Brown states that "all traitors to the cause must die." The background music is foreboding as ex-cadet Rader appears with a group of armed men from Illinois who are there to "fight slavers." When son Oliver arrives and tells Brown about abandoning four slaves to slave catchers, Brown strikes him, saying, "You left four helpless people alone to save yourself. You cowardly fool." (Brown will soon abandon a barn full of slaves to save himself). Only two of Brown's sons appear in the film; and it seems clear that Oliver hates and fears him, and Jason disapproves of his methods. As Brown gathers his men for a raid on the Santa Fe wagon train escorted by Stuart and the cavalry, he prays, and there is uplifting music in the background. He ends with, "The Lord is a man of war. Thy right hand . . . will dash in pieces the enemy." The subtitle announces that Brown is a villain, but the music and Massey's delivery of the prayer subvert the villainy, making Brown a man of idealism and dignity, despite his fanaticism.

Created to underscore Brown's villainy, his fictional raid on a wagon train includes one of Curtiz's trademark cavalry charges. An exciting battle scene ensues, with soldiers chasing raiders on horseback over rough terrain, plenty of gunfire, Rader's accidental shooting of young Jason Brown, and Stuart's capture of Jason (in reality, Jason was captured when he was on his way to turn himself in to the army). Back at the fort, as Kit nurses him, Jason reveals his negative feelings about his father: "He [John Brown] says he talks with God at night. But God doesn't tell people to kill one another, does He? He's a good man in a lot of ways. But he's changed since Osawatomie [screenwriter Buckner meant the Pottawatomie Massacre which, for unknown reasons, was not explored visually in the film]. Those people he killed. They got down on their knees. Begged him for their lives. They struck them with a sword. Him and Rader and Kitzmiller. I was there; I saw it done. I tried to stop them, but they pushed me aside [Jason was not present at the Pottawatomie Massacre]." Jason then asks Kit, "He can't be right, can he, Miss?" Kit's response: "His reasons may be right, Jason. They may even be great and good reasons, but what your father is doing is wrong—terribly wrong. And he'll keep on repeating that wrong as long as he lives." Jason subsequently betrays his father's whereabouts: "If he dies maybe his whole scheme will die with him. I'd rather have it that way—his life—even if he is my father—against many thousands. . . . In the house of Shubel Morgan [Shubel Morgan was not one of Brown's followers; this was a pseudonym used by John Brown] . . . Palmyra. . . . Tell the soldiers." These are his dying words (Jason died years later—in California). Delivering Jason's message to Stuart, Kit asks, "Can't we stop now? Can't the slaves be freed before it's too late?" Stuart's response: "It will be stopped. When we hang John Brown. Then the South can settle her own problem without loss of pride or being forced into it by a group of fanatics." Kit then asks, "What has pride got to do with human lives?" Stuart: "The two things kinda come together down south." Once more, Stuart presents the pro-Southern line, pointing to John Brown as the cause of the Civil War. But the discussion between Kit and Jason seems ambivalent, stressing that although Brown's means are bad, his ends are good, thus subverting Stuart's simplistic reasoning and making this sequence the most ambiguous in the film.

In the next fictional scene, Stuart passes through Delaware Crossing, a free-state community that John Brown has destroyed to avenge the wounding and capture of Jason and to wipe out the slave catchers living there. Images of children moving furniture out of a burned-out house and a child finding her lost doll underscore the film's attempt to paint John Brown as a terrorist fanatic who will even victimize Free Staters. (Note: the film includes references to neither the proslavery raid on the Free State community of Lawrence nor the Browns' attempts to use the right to vote as a means to bring Kansas into the Union as a Free State.)

The fictional Palmyra sequences end John Brown's career in Kansas, but not before Rader captures Stuart (who has entered the town undercover), creating the opportunity for a dramatic and ambiguous discussion between Brown and Stuart. Stuart tries to convince Brown to surrender: "Half of the people in America believe in your theory. Some even believe in your methods; that would guarantee you a fair trial." But Brown says that he has waited thirty years and tried peaceful agitation to no avail, so he intends to force a decision (he does not say how). For now, Stuart is to be hanged but "not with malice or revenge," according to Brown, but because Stuart is an "enemy of God." While Brown's speeches stress his absolute commitment to his cause, under Curtiz's direction Massey's characterization does not make Brown come across as a crazed fanatic. As in other scenes, the images give a message that belies the words.

Rescued during another Curtiz cavalry charge, Stuart shares a fictional scene with two ex-slaves, part of the barn full of fugitives whom Brown chose to leave behind when he fled Palmyra. Racial stereotyping and the Hollywood plantation myth come to the fore in this scene. As the woman bandages Stuart's wound, he complains: "Ouch, Mammy. That's too tight, Mammy." The woman, in true Hattie McDaniel fashion, responds: "Don't tell me how to do this, boy. I been wrappin' white folks all my life. When they was babies I wrapped one end, and when they was growed up and took on too much corn liquor, then I wrapped t'other end." Stuart asks why she left home. "Well, old John Brown said he's gwine give us freedom. But shuckins', if this Kansas is freedom, then I ain't got no use for it." Her male companion adds, "Me neither. I just wants to get back home to Texas and set 'til kimdom [*sic*] come." Obviously, John Brown's efforts to free these slaves had come to naught. This scene echoes the mythological belief that slaves preferred slavery to John Brown's offer of freedom (See *Harper's Weekly* cartoons from 1859, plates 5 and 6).

Presumably, after John Brown's defeat at Palmyra, the building of the railroad could resume, and the film could end. The railroad is forgotten, however, as the film follows John Brown east for his attack on Harpers Ferry. Meanwhile, Stuart's heroic fictional exploits have resulted in a promotion, and he has been reassigned to Washington, D.C.[13] At this point, the reason for the addition of the fictional character Rader becomes apparent when he proves to be the villainous foil who makes John Brown look good. Since he has only joined the abolitionist cause for money, Rader becomes angry at not receiving payment from Brown for his services, so he goes to Washington to see Stuart and betray Brown for a reward, offering to return to Harpers Ferry to ensure that Brown remains there until the army (under the command of Robert E. Lee) can arrive. Historically, Stuart was given the task of trying to convince Brown to surrender at Harpers Ferry, which he does in the film, but he also reveals Rader's betrayal to Brown, who then kills the Judas in cold blood. For many 1940s audiences, what follows was the high point of the film: Curtiz's enhancement of the army's attack on Brown's "fort," including fictional cannon fire and cavalry charge.

The film omits John Brown's trial, but Curtiz gives Brown a martyr's death in a moving execution scene (which includes Kit, Stuart, and Stuart's cronies as witnesses). Although historically, Brown did not give a speech on the gallows, Curtiz provides one. He accurately quotes Brown's prediction—"I, John Brown, am now quite certain that the crimes of this guilty land will never be purged away but with blood"—and inaccurately includes a fictional but Christlike statement— "I forgive them, for they know not what they do." After Brown is hanged, Lee comments, "So perish all such enemies of the Union—all such enemies of the human race."[14] Once more, Curtiz adds ambiguity, and the final images of Brown underscore his heroic stature.

The final brief scene seems anticlimactic and tacked on. Suddenly, we are on a moving train back in Kansas (the railroad was completed during the Harpers Ferry raid?) for the wedding of Stuart and Kit, with Custer and Jefferson Davis's daughter as witnesses.[15] All the other former cadets are present, and the upbeat theme song ends the picture.

Santa Fe Trail was released in December 1940, and the reviews proved favorable, despite comments about historical distortion. While admitting that "some historians [might] find fault with the way John Brown [was] pictured as a fanatic, religious zealot," *Variety* praised Warner Bros. for "duck[ing] the too familiar Western opus pattern to fashion [a] thrilling saga of hard-bitten

U. S. army officers' fight to wipe out John Brown's marauding crew of Kansas abolition days."[16] *Newsweek* applauded Warner Bros.' move from the western epic to "a dramatic and adult consideration of John Brown," labeling it a "biographical drama." But the reviewer noted that screenwriter Robert Buckner had "improved considerably on history" by having the West Point graduating class of 1857 include "George Custer ('61), Phil Sheridan ('53), James Longstreet ('42), George Pickett ('46), and John Hood ('53)," as well as Stuart ('54), so that they could all go to Kansas together, and pointed to the fact that "the Warners don't always seem to be quite sure what they think of slavery and . . . John Brown." The reviewer nevertheless lauded the film's focus on the "marauding career of John Brown" and praised Raymond Massey's portrayal for its "effective synthesis of cruel fanaticism and militant idealism as the wild-eyed zealot who thought he was God's appointed avenger."[17] *Time* pointed to the "tragic theme" of the film: that seven recent classmates at West Point "fighting side by side, are innocently feeding a flame which will soon surround them and find them enemies in an irrepressible conflict." Like *Newsweek, Time* praised "Massey's passionate interpretation of Zealot Brown" and concluded that "in spite of its hackneyed romance, [*Santa Fe Trail*] becomes a brilliant and grim account of the Civil War background."[18]

Three months after the film's release, Brown biographer Oswald Garrison Villard felt compelled to set the record straight. In a letter to the editor of the *Saturday Review,* he called the film a "travesty of history." After objecting to what he saw as the film's proslavery bias and its "hostil[ity] to John Brown, whom it [characterizes] falsely as a continuous raider upon peaceful settlements," Villard pointed to the following fictionalized Kansas segments of the film: the engagement between Brown and the U.S. cavalry, Brown's capture of Stuart, and the "barn full of Negroes rescued from Brown's clutches by the galloping cavalry." But Villard was most critical about the invention of nonhistorical facts in the Harpers Ferry scenes: the attack on John Brown and his men by cavalry rather than by the actual "small company of United States Marines . . . led by Israel Green"; the use of a substantial fort to represent the "flimsy structure" of the actual engine house and its placement outside, rather than in the center of, town, "surrounded by a large stonewall"; the large number of Brown followers inside the fort; the representation of "Jefferson Davis [as] Secretary of War at the time of this raid, whereas it was John B. Floyd"; and the "cooked up . . . love affair between Custer and Davis's daughter who was not even existent at that time." In conclusion, Villard lamented the fact that "millions of Americans should be utterly misinformed and misled." The one positive note for Villard was Raymond Massey's "good and telling acting in the role of John Brown," but he called it a "misfortune that his fine talents" should be used in such a film.[19]

Many film critics, reviewers, and audience members have puzzled over the ambiguity of *Santa Fe Trail*—its misfit title, its mixture of genres (western, railroad epic, Civil War epic, comedy, romance), and especially its mixed message about John Brown.[20] Although the film's world premiere was held in Santa Fe, New Mexico, no scenes take place there, and only one brief scene takes place on the Santa Fe Trail—in Kansas. So what does the title have to do with the film? What does the title have to do with John Brown? Some of the answers to these and other questions lie in the nature of the Hollywood studio system and the manner in which *Santa Fe Trail* evolved.

In 1940 the studio system was in full swing at Warner Bros.; thus, there were many cooks involved in making any film feast—producers, directors, actors, story departments, and screenwriters. In early 1939, Warner Bros. producer Hal Wallis needed a western vehicle for Errol Flynn, then the studio's most successful leading man. Flynn, who specialized in swashbuckling roles, had recently made a successful transition to the western genre in *Dodge City* (1939) and *Virginia City* (1940), both directed by Hungarian émigré Michael Curtiz. Reflecting "a new national optimism" as the Depression eased, Hollywood responded by turning out films with "inspiring themes of national progress, and naturally the Western featured prominently in this trend."[21] In addition, because of the recent success of *Gone with the Wind* (1939), Civil War themes were in vogue; indeed, in *Virginia City* Flynn had played a Union soldier in Nevada who defeats a Southern soldier trying to help the Lost Cause. Thus, in order to follow up on the success of *Virginia City,* Wallis asked studio scriptwriter Robert Buckner, who had written both *Dodge City* and *Virginia City,* to develop a postbellum western. But that is not the script Buckner wrote. First, director Curtiz and producer Robert Fellows "brought their influence to bear," and the story idea changed to take advantage of another recent trend—the "renaissance of the epic."[22] The success the year before of Cecil B. DeMille's western epic *Union Pacific* (1939) provided the impetus for Warner Bros. to make a film about building a railroad. Next, the story line of *Santa Fe Trail* evolved to focus on "the opening of the American south-west after 1865 via the Santa Fe Railroad, with a rebellion sub-plot centring [*sic*] upon a character based on John Wilkes Booth."[23] Later, Curtiz

PEGGY A. RUSSO

and Fellows had second thoughts about Booth and decided "that it would be 'a mistake to hang the whole picture on a half-madman.'"[24] Then, according to Raymond Massey, Jack Warner took a special interest in *Santa Fe Trail* as an "homage to the railroads." Massey also reveals how Warner changed the period from after the Civil War to the 1850s and added John Brown to the plot: "When Jack L. Warner asked [screenwriter Buckner] if he had any ideas about an action story of how the railroad was put through Kansas in 1857, [Buckner] replied that there wasn't much going on in Kansas at that time other than the attempt of John Brown and the Free State men to take over the state; and he went on about the massacre at Pottawatomie, the battle of Palmyra and the Harpers Ferry raid. Warner was impressed and told him, 'Fine, go ahead. We'll make the son of a bitch the heavy.'" Moreover, Massey asks, "How did John Brown fit into . . . a picture [about railroads]? The answer was quite simply that he didn't fit into the picture, he just took it over." In the final version, all that is left of the railroad theme is "one token scene of laying tracks in Kansas as a reminder of the original purpose of the movie."[25]

Although under the studio system the least important contributor to most films was the screenwriter,[26] Robert Buckner had a real stake in *Santa Fe Trail* because he had based the script on his novel-in-progress, *The Grenadiers,* which focused on J. E. B. Stuart. The script was blatantly pro-Southern, showing "Brown as an arch villain for his violent anti-slavery actions in Kansas and for his 1859 raid on . . . Harper's [sic] Ferry" and Stuart as "the personification of slavery as a sectional issue to be settled from within."[27] Jack Warner went along with this pro-Southern bias because it was in line with Hollywood's long-established treatment of the Civil War, beginning as early as D. W. Griffith's *Birth of a Nation* (1915) and still apparent in *Gone with the Wind* (1939).[28] Although Buckner and Warner Bros.' story department either did not conduct or did not adhere to solid historical research, their creation of Stuart's pro-Confederate speeches and the film's depiction of John Brown's radical abolitionism as the cause of the Civil War reflect the revisionist views of pro-Southern historians, which had become part of popular mythology.[29] Jack Warner wanted to be on the safe side on this issue, and Curtiz biographer James C. Robertson insists that "the studio's anxiety can be seen in the retention of the misleading *Santa Fe Trail* title, the over-frequent and out-of-place comic interventions insisted upon by Jack Warner, [and the] superfluous and equally out-of-place romantic rivalry [between Flynn's Stuart and Reagan's Custer over the charms of de Havilland's Kit]."[30]

John Brown Goes to Hollywood

Jack's brother Harry was not interested in being on the safe side, however. Because of the popularity of isolationist policies and official American government neutrality, including a ban on anti-Fascist or "warmongering" films, many Hollywood studios studiously avoided such controversial topics, but Harry Warner, known as the "conscience of the studio," had become the driving force behind Warner Bros.' attempts to educate American film audiences about the evils of Nazism and the dangers of isolationism. From the mid-1930s until America's entrance into the war, many of the studio's films, including *Santa Fe Trail,* contain subtle rhetorical warnings against fascism.[31] The invention of the character of Rader and his subversive activities at West Point provide an example of this kind of rhetorical purpose.

Enter the director. Faced with the purposes and cross-purposes of so many cooks, Robertson suggests that Curtiz "distorted studio intentions" during the filming process by focusing on John Brown and minimizing Stuart's importance: "Indeed, in one scene Flynn actually complained that Raymond Massey . . . had too much dialogue. Moreover, the shadow of coming conflict looms over the entire central plot, with two scenes containing prophecies of the Civil War standing out. . . . Both scenes appeared in the Buckner screenplay, but the manner in which Curtiz presents them makes a disproportionate impact on the overall film."[32] Film historian Ted Sennett also cites evidence for distortion: "The thin (even emaciated) characterizations in [Buckner's] screenplay [are] overpowered by lots of action well staged by . . . Curtiz."[33] Little is known about Curtiz's politics, but as a Hungarian-born Jew, he, like the Warner brothers, who were also Jewish, was opposed to Nazism. Moreover, according to Raymond Massey, Curtiz had become an American citizen just before directing *Santa Fe Trail,* was an avid reader of American history, and "his knowledge of the American past and particularly the period we were dealing with was astonishing."[34] Perhaps Curtiz's own research into the period led him to subvert Buckner's pro-Southern script, which resulted in the ambiguity of the finished product:

> The film's attempt to balance Northern and Southern sentiment on the issue of slavery is evident throughout. A lavish Southern dinner party captures the splendor of a genteel but fading way of life. (Score one for the old South.) At the film's end, the hanging of John Brown is staged solemnly, with soldiers standing in stylized formation against a glowering sky and Brown proclaiming that "this nation can-

PEGGY A. RUSSO

not be purged except in blood." (Score one for the North. They know a martyr when they see one.) This ambivalence appears and reappears at almost every turn in this curious film, which ends predictably with "Kit" proclaiming that "something much more terrible than one man" is heading their way.[35]

Although Buckner's screenplay called for the Hitlerization of John Brown, and "Massey's frighteningly perverted idealism was a portrayal consciously based upon Hitler," that portrayal became subverted during filming, and John Brown gained heroic stature, much to Jack Warner's displeasure, so much so that he "considered cutting out the scene of Brown's execution."[36]

Seven Angry Men

Seven Angry Men, like *Santa Fe Trail,* deals primarily with John Brown's actions in Kansas and gives only a relatively brief treatment of the Harpers Ferry raid. The film opens with the arrival in Lawrence, Kansas, of Owen and Oliver Brown, who have come West to join their father and four brothers (John Jr., Jason, Frederick, and Salmon) as homesteaders in the new territory (John Brown actually followed his sons to Kansas). The film adds a fictional romance. En route to Lawrence, Owen has begun a flirtation with Elizabeth Clark (Debra Paget), who has come to Lawrence to join her father. She considers John Brown to be a "dangerous fanatical man who is doing our cause (abolition) much more harm than good," so she wants nothing to do with his son Owen. But when John Brown arrives by wagon, wearing plain farmers' garb and appearing gracious, dignified, and humble, he does not fit the "dangerous fanatical" image. Learning that Owen and Elizabeth have been "discussing [his] work," Brown responds, "Not my work—God's work. That's what we're doing here." As Brown and his sons drive away, Elizabeth's father arrives, registering disappointment that he was not in time to meet John Brown, whom he calls "a great man, Elizabeth, a great man." Thus, despite Elizabeth's labeling of him, the first impressions of Brown conveyed by Massey in *Seven Angry Men* bear little resemblance to his earlier rendition of Brown in *Santa Fe Trail.*

At Osawatomie, where the brothers share a joyful reunion, Brown declares, "At last I am surrounded by all of my grown sons; I am a proud and happy man." He reads from the Bible while his sons bow their heads, but the quotation is not meant to be celebratory since it calls for God to "tread down our enemies." Unlike Brown's camp of armed men in *Santa Fe Trail,* however, this is a peaceful community made up of white and black families. The men are building a church, and black and white children are playing tag together (the camp is obviously based on the interracial community at North Elba, New York, where John Brown's family lived). When Martin White and a group of proslavery men enter the camp, White announces, "You are not wanted here in Kansas. You have forty-eight hours to leave." Brown answers that as a "homesteader," he has "every right" to be in Kansas. And when White says that if Brown wants bloodshed, he will get it, Brown answers patiently, "No blood has been shed here nor will be unless you shed it first." White rides away, and with this major conflict established, exposition appears complete. The audience has been introduced to the romantic conflict between Owen and Elizabeth over John Brown's methods, and we have met a caring father and respected leader who continually reads from the Bible, which he carries at all times. Unlike the Brown of *Santa Fe Trail,* this John Brown is not a terrorist raider. Rather, he is the patriarch of a peaceful interracial community of homesteaders who are trying to make Kansas a Free State at the ballot box rather than in battle.

The following scene further establishes the difference between John Brown's peaceful tactics and the terrorism used by White. Preparing for a nighttime raid on the Free State town of Lawrence, White tells his raiders that it is "our responsibility to see that Kansas enters the union as a slave state [and to] prove to Northern politicians that they cannot take away our birthright . . . our right to raise our crops and care for our Negroes and their families, as we have for as long as America has existed." This scene identifies White, not Brown, as the truly "dangerous fanatical man."

During the cowardly attack on Lawrence, White's men set fire to the town and shoot several inhabitants (including a woman). When Elizabeth and other Lawrence residents flee to Osawatomie for shelter, John Brown, learning that five innocent people have been killed, vows vengeance. Thus, the film provides historically accurate motivation for Brown's violent actions in the Pottawatomie Massacre scenes. Entering the Doyles' home, where the family sits at dinner, Brown's men seize the father and two sons and drag them outside while Brown shoves Mrs. Doyle aside as he exits. Outside, Brown reads from the Bible as Doyle begs for his life, but Brown orders: "Strike . . . strike the blow of the Lord. . . . An eye for an eye!" Four of Brown's sons take part in the slaughter, but John Brown Jr. cannot bear to watch. Unlike *Santa Fe Trail*, which merely contains an oral description (by Brown's son Jason), *Seven Angry Men* includes graphic images of the massacre. Indeed, the massacre scene is one of the most important in the film because it results in a new and major conflict.

Following the massacre, Brown's family and community begin to fall apart. At Osawatomie, Brown's followers prepare to leave because the massacre will cause reprisals. But Brown rallies them with an impassioned speech, stressing that their votes are important to the future of Kansas. Then Jason announces that because John Jr. appears "crazy" as a result of the massacre, they are going to surrender to the army and seek help for him. Next, Frederick leaves because of what their father made them do. The two other sons, Oliver and Salmon, also begin to rebel and ask Owen to convince their father to end the killing. Inside John Brown's tent, Owen tells his father, "what we did this morning . . . was wrong. . . . You think that it doesn't matter how you accomplish your goals?" Brown's response: "I understand weakness and cowardice even in my own son." The argument results in the departure of Salmon and Oliver, and the title takes on a new meaning as the film's focus shifts to the angry disagreement between father and sons over the means to end slavery.

Although Salmon and Oliver leave Osawatomie, the loyal Owen remains with Brown until his father's work in Kansas is complete—the vote that makes Kansas a Free State (voting actually took place in 1861), an event the film treats as Brown's greatest success. Following Brown's return to Ohio (in reality, New York) with the newly married couple, Elizabeth and Owen, the remainder of the film deals with Brown's attack on Harpers Ferry and the tragic consequences for himself and his family.

The brief Harpers Ferry sequences, while not completely accurate, are far more so than those in *Santa Fe Trail*. They include the unintentional killing by Brown's men of Heyward Shepherd (a free black), the taking of hostages, and the deaths of two of Brown's sons during the defense of the engine house (also known as John Brown's Fort). There is also a scene showing Owen's reluctant escape from Harpers Ferry after Shields Green convinces him that the raid is a failure and his father is doomed. Indeed, the film treats the Harpers Ferry raid as doomed from the start.

The courtroom scene (not included in *Santa Fe Trail*) shows Massey delivering some of John Brown's actual words before the judge passes sentence: "I believe that to have interfered as I have done in behalf of God's despised poor, I did no wrong, but right. Now, if it is deemed necessary that I should forfeit my life for the furtherance of the ends of justice, and mingle my blood with the blood of my children and with the blood of millions in this slave country whose rights have been disregarded by sick, cruel, and unjust enactments, I say, let it be done." Appearing on the History Channel's *Movies in Time* in 1997 (one of the few times *Seven Angry Men* has aired on TV), Brown biographer Stephen B. Oates noted many of the film's inaccuracies, but called this scene its most "historically accurate moment" and added: "Raymond Massey really shines as John Brown" because of the way "he addresses Virginians about the evils of slavery and explains why and how he identifies with the slaves."[37] This scene and the final execution scene contain the most moving moments in the film. The final shot contains a shadow of the gallows, resembling a cross. Thus, as in *Santa Fe Trail,* the ending of *Seven Angry Men* stresses John Brown's martyrdom.

The reviews of *Seven Angry Men* were far fewer and far less positive than those of *Santa Fe Trail.* According to *Variety,* the film "fail[ed] to qualify as worthwhile entertainment, being slow and talky." The reviewer complained that "Warren's direction doesn't do much probing" and claimed that "while the religious fervor that moved Brown is shown, the character still seems to lack proper motivation, as do the other people and events, including the battle at Harpers Ferry."[38] *Newsweek* noted "inexplicable" historical inaccuracies, such as "Brown settling in Kansas with six of his sons, when actually it was only five," Brown being portrayed as "a prosperous man [when] in truth, it was partly his business failures that goaded him to his pitiable attempt to liberate the slaves," and "the wrong son [being portrayed as] deranged." But Massey again garnered praise: he "superbly unfolds the mind of a man who believes his crimes are just and right because he is an 'instrument in the hand of God.'"[39] The *New York Times* noted the "personal tragedy" and psychological and domestic aspects of the film: "As a rather insular close-up of a bull-headed egomaniac bent on sacrificing his rebellious family to 'God's will,' the picture rings true."[40] Film historians George N. Fenin and William K. Everson give the film its most negative assessment. Pointing to Hollywood's habit in the 1950s of sparing "the South's delicate feelings" about the Civil War," they called *Seven Angry Men* "a commendable attempt to make an off-beat historical Western," but complained that it "falsif[ied] and sim-plif[ied] certain aspects of the material in order to present abolitionist

PEGGY A. RUSSO

John Brown as a 'nuisance' to both North and South, and really a man of no great importance!"[41]

Like *Santa Fe Trail, Seven Angry Men* was a product of its time. Monogram/Allied Artists had specialized in B westerns, but, according to Fenin and Everson, by 1950 the popular new medium of television was "inundated with 'B' Westerns made from 1930 on." Thus, "the big profits [in movie theaters] from 'cheap' Westerns were a thing of the past." Allied Artists, like other minor studios and independent filmmakers of the time, tried "to overcome [its] competition by loading [its] . . . pictures with 'gimmicks,' most specifically, controversial new 'versions' of Western history."[42] *Seven Angry Men* falls into this category. Moreover, in 1951, Allied Artists had begun producing films for television, and this may explain why *Seven Angry Men* has the look and feel of a made-for-TV movie.[43] The budget and facilities of Allied Artists were much smaller than those of Warner Bros. Thus, while Warner Bros. had hordes of studio extras available for Curtiz's use in *Santa Fe Trail,* resulting in his decision to have Brown lead a hundred men into Harpers Ferry instead of twenty-one, the producers of *Seven Angry Men* were unable to include even one of Brown's daughters in the brief family reunion scene. Because of budget constraints, in this film at least, it appears that Brown fathered only six sons rather than a total of twenty children.

While *Santa Fe Trail* is an action-filled epic in the style of late-1930s Hollywood, *Seven Angry Men* could be classified as a domestic melodrama in the style of 1950s television, with a focus on youthful rebellion against parental authority. Hollywood's trendy exploration of youthful rebellion began with *The Wild One* (1953), whose star, Marlon Brando, says, "We were at the beginning of a new era . . . young people were beginning to doubt and question their elders and to challenge their values, morals, and the established institutions of authority."[44] By 1955 the trend was in full swing with such films as *Rebel without a Cause, Blackboard Jungle,* and *East of Eden,* which also starred Raymond Massey as the father of a rebellious son. As in *Santa Fe Trail,* the romantic subplot of *Seven Angry Men* seems tacked on, and it is historically inaccurate since Owen Brown never married. Why then was it included? Like most domestic melodramas, this one includes a focus on the feminine. During the 1950s, as pointed out by Laura Mulvey, the "resurgence of the domestic melodrama" was part of a "swing to domesticity that complemented the U.S. economy's expansion in production" and attempts to bring women "back into the home to readjust the unsettling effects of the

John Brown Goes to Hollywood

Second World War on the division of labour between the sexes."[45] Thus, we see a major difference between Kit's input on political matters in *Santa Fe Trail* and the rebellious attitude of Elizabeth toward John Brown in *Seven Angry Men*. Indeed, Elizabeth speaks more negatively about John Brown's methods than do his sons.

Another of the major differences between the two films has to do with the treatment of African Americans. In *Santa Fe Trail*, the characters of the run-away slaves are painfully stereotypical; in *Seven Angry Men*, we see an interracial community in which blacks and whites are equals. Following World War II and the growth of the civil rights movement, African Americans had succeeded in changing Hollywood's treatment of blacks on film.[46] We should also note that this film was made only one year after the Supreme Court's *Brown v. Board of Education* decision and two years before the integration of Little Rock's Central High, so the inclusion of a scene showing black and white children playing tag together was unique in its time.[47] Furthermore, the film's development of Shields Green's character (James Edwards) show-cases an African American who exhibits qualities of courage, loyalty, dignity, and intellect that are anything but stereotypical (although the real Shields Green followed Brown to Harpers Ferry, Brown did not meet him until after his Kansas activities; the character of Green in the film is a fabrication). It seems clear that in their treatment of the status of white women and of relationships between whites and blacks, the filmmakers not only tried to follow current trends but also to establish new ones.

As historian and fiction writer George MacDonald Fraser claims, "There is popular belief that where history is concerned, Hollywood always gets it wrong." But, he asserts, "at their best, [films] have given a picture of the ages more vivid and memorable than anything in Tacitus or Gibbon or Macaulay, and to an infinitely wider audience."[48] Unlike historians, whose purpose it is to relate and interpret facts about particular past events for a limited audience, historical filmmakers, like novelists, poets, and dramatists, approach the past with the purpose of personally involving a large general audience in past events and in the people who lived through them. Of course, making the past relevant to the present always results in a sacrifice of the "real thing" in order to maximize personal involvement, and that sacrifice often results in a travesty of the truth. But do historians always give us the truth? Frank A. Wetta and Stephen J. Curley insist that "even *history* is . . . not the real thing; it is a reconstruction not a recreation of events, a perception of what

PEGGY A. RUSSO

really happened, always imperfect, incomplete, and fragmentary. The events of former times exist only in the surviving evidence, brought to life through our imagination. Unlike the physical scientists, historians or filmmakers-as-historians cannot return to the subject in any immediate way; the evidence is always incomplete at best, the memories imperfect. They simply cannot go back into time and retrieve or recreate events."[49]

No doubt, historians feel that because most of the action takes place in Kansas, both *Santa Fe Trail* and *Seven Angry Men* give short shrift to the most important part of Brown's legacy, and this is a legitimate criticism. Indeed, the Harpers Ferry sequences appear superficial and tacked on as a means of finalizing the plots. But there is an obvious explanation for this. Since both films were originally conceived as westerns, the focus on Kansas would have seemed justified to the filmmakers. Furthermore, in both films, we see incomplete and inaccurate history, but as noted above, Brown biographer Villard praises Massey's portrayal of John Brown in *Santa Fe Trail*, and similarly, Brown biographer Oates praises Massey's portrayal of Brown in *Seven Angry Men*. Such praise from two biographers of Brown indicates that despite historical inaccuracies, some aspect of the "real" Brown comes through in the two films. Of course, the two portrayals differ in one very important aspect. From the very beginning of *Santa Fe Trail*, Brown is portrayed as a fanatical terrorist raider. By contrast, in *Seven Angry Men*, he is introduced as a gentle patriarch using peaceful means to gain good ends who only resorts to terrorist activities out of frustration. One plausible explanation for this difference in character: by 1955 the growth of the civil rights movement had made it possible, despite his terrorist activities, to portray John Brown more openly as a hero of the abolitionist movement than was possible in 1940. Of course, the final scenes of both films offer positive images of Brown, showing him as a martyr to a just cause. Ultimately, despite the passing of time, the changes in society, and the differences in purpose, the people who created both these films did well by him.

Perhaps someday, someone will make a film that focuses on Harpers Ferry to everyone's satisfaction. But will the "real" John Brown appear in such a film? In the last several years, rumors have abounded of John Brown films in the works, using Oates's biography *To Purge This Land with Blood* (1970), or Bruce Olds's novel *Raising Holy Hell* (1995), or Russell Banks's novel *Cloudsplitter* (1998), as the basis for a script. But perhaps what we need is not a film based on a biography, or a history, or a novel. I have a dream of an interdisciplinary

John Brown Goes to Hollywood

collaboration between filmmakers, fiction writers, biographers, historians, and the PBS producers of *American Experience* that would do justice to the old man and to his story.

NOTES

1. *Santa Fe Trail*, prod. Jack L. Warner, Hal B. Wallis, dir. Michael Curtiz, writ. Robert Buckner, perf. Errol Flynn, Olivia de Havilland, Raymond Massey, 110 min., (First National/Warner Bros., 1940); *Seven Angry Men*, prod. Vincent M. Fennelly; dir. Charles Marquis Warren; writ. Daniel B. Ullman; perf. Raymond Massey, Debra Paget, Jeffrey Hunter, 90 min. (Allied Artists, 1955).

2. But see Larry J. Easley, "*The Santa Fe Trail:* John Brown and the Coming of the Civil War," *Film and History* 13, no. 2 (1983): 25–33. As a historian, Easley focuses negatively on the film's adherence to Southern myth, but he also argues that the study of films based on historical events "aid[s] the student in discovering the past and allows the use of a popular medium for teaching and research that is often ignored" (25).

3. At the time *Santa Fe Trail* was released, Warner Bros. was one of Hollywood's eight major motion picture studios, and certainly the four brothers—Harry, Albert, Sam, and Jack—were movers and shakers on the Hollywood scene, for example pioneering the move to talkies with *Don Juan* (1926) and *The Jazz Singer* (1927). During the studio's golden age, in the 1930s, it was known for Busby Berkeley musicals, social dramas, and gangster pictures such as *The Public Enemy* (1931) and *Little Caesar* (1931). It also specialized in action spectacles like *The Adventures of Robin Hood* (1938) and *The Sea Hawk* (1940). *Santa Fe Trail* is part of that string of action spectacles. See Ted Sennett, *Warner Brothers Presents: The Most Exciting Years—from* The Jazz Singer *to* White Heat (New Rochelle, NY: Arlington House, 1971).

4. All three producers appear in the opening credits. Jack L. Warner's name appears beneath the title of the film as being "in charge of production." Hal B. Wallis is listed later in the credits as executive producer, followed by Robert Fellows as associate producer. Jack Warner tried to maintain control over every major feature film Warner Bros. released. He had the final say on everything from the original story line to the final script, choice of director, casting, editing, and the final product. But since there were always several films being made at once, he delegated some authority to secondary producers who handled the everyday details and carried out his commands. Not to the letter, of course. Occasional insurgencies and circumventions of authority were initiated by writers, directors, other producers, and even actors. For example, it appears that director Michael Curtiz managed to circumvent Jack Warner's desire to make John Brown a typical villain in *Santa Fe Trail*. An example of Jack Warner's lack of respect for underlings: he called writers "schmucks with Underwoods." "Blocked: The Writer's Experience in Hollywood." Narrator: Carrie Fisher, American Movie Channel, March 8, 2001, American Movie Classics, 2000. For a general discussion of the relationship between story department hack writers and producers under the Hollywood studio system, see Larry Ceplair and Steven En-

glund, *The Inquisition in Hollywood: Politics in the Film Community, 1930–1960* (Garden City, NY: Anchor Press/Doubleday, 1980), 1–15.

5. Allied Artists began as a subsidiary of Monogram Pictures Corporation but achieved corporate status in 1953. It was a small studio struggling with financial difficulties when it produced *Seven Angry Men*. See Len D. Martin, *The Allied Artists Checklist: The Feature Films and Short Subjects of Allied Artists Pictures Corporation, 1947–1978* (Jefferson, NC: McFarland, 1993).

6. Raymond Massey, who devotes an entire chapter in his autobiography to *Santa Fe Trail*, mentions *Seven Angry Men* only once. Massey, *A Hundred Different Lives* (Boston: Little, Brown, 1979), 258–62.

7. Ibid., 353–59.

8. "Santa Fe Trail," in *The Motion Picture Guide, 1927–1983*, ed. Jay Robert Nash and Stanley Ralph Ross (Chicago: Cinebooks, 1985), 2736. Nash and Ross mistakenly indicate in their synopsis that the film opens with J. E. B. Stuart (Flynn), newly arrived from the South, approaching the gates of West Point with a mule and dog and wearing an "outlandish uniform of his own design," causing him to be greeted as if he were a foreign dignitary rather than a new cadet. But this scene is not included in this film. The scene does appear in a later Flynn vehicle, *They Died with Their Boots On* (Warner Bros., 1941, dir. Raoul Walsh), in which Flynn plays George Custer arriving at West Point in 1857. Of course, it is possible that the scene may have been written originally for *Santa Fe Trail*. If so, director Curtiz opted not to use it.

9. Rader may have been loosely based on Hugh Forbes, whom John Brown had hired as a drillmaster. Forbes, like Rader in the film, was more interested in money than in helping free slaves, and when he did not receive the wages that he felt were his due, he betrayed Brown. See Stephen B. Oates, *To Purge This Land with Blood: A Biography of John Brown* (1970; rev. ed., Amherst: University of Massachusetts Press, 1985), 211–12, 217–18, 223, 225–26, 248–50.

10. Article 46 of Brown's constitution from the Chatham Convention strictly denies that the breakup of the union was part of Brown's plan. Ibid., 246. Thus, the film's historically inaccurate pamphlet was created to paint Brown as an anarchist.

11. Curtiz enjoyed directing Guinn "Big Boy" Williams so much that he added one of the actor's trademark comic sequences to his final film, *The Commancheros* (1961).

12. Robert E. Morsberger, "Slavery and *The Santa Fe Trail*," *American Studies* 18, no. 2 (Fall 1977), 92.

13. Actually, Stuart was still a lieutenant stationed in Kansas Territory, but he had traveled to Washington, D.C., and was waiting to see the secretary of war (hoping to sell a patent for a device with which to attach a saber to a cavalryman's belt) when news of the Harpers Ferry raid came in. Sent to deliver a message to Robert E. Lee, he accidentally happened to be in a position to go with Lee to Harpers Ferry. See John W. Thomason Jr., *Jeb Stuart* (New York: Scribner's, 1930), 47–49.

14. This speech is based on the words of Col. J. T. L. Preston of the Virginia Military Institute: "So perish all such enemies of Virginia! All such enemies of the Union! All such foes of the human race!" Quoted in Oates, *Purge*, 352.

15. On November 14, 1855, Stuart wed Flora Cooke, daughter of Col. Philip St. George Cooke of the Second U.S. Dragoons, at Fort Leavenworth, Kansas. Thomason, *Jeb Stuart,* 28.

16. "Santa Fe Trail," *Variety,* December 18, 1940.

17. "A Western Out of West Point Goes East to Hang John Brown," *Newsweek,* December 30, 1940, 36–37.

18. "The New Pictures: *Santa Fe Trail,*" *Time,* December 23, 1940, 45.

19. Oswald Garrison Villard, "History and the Movies," letter to the editor, *Saturday Review,* March 1, 1941, 9. Two years later Villard continued his indictment of the film, calling it "false, and historically entirely misleading." Villard, foreword to *John Brown, 1800–1859: A Biography Fifty Years After,* rev. ed. (New York: Knopf, 1943).

20. See Morsberger, "Slavery," 97.

21. George N. Fenin and William K. Everson, *The Western: From Silents to the Seventies* (London: Grossman, 1973), 237.

22. On Curtiz and Fellows, see James C. Robertson, *The Casablanca Man: The Cinema of Michael Curtiz* (London: Routledge, 1993), 55. The term "renaissance of the epic" is from Fenin and Everson, *Western,* 237.

23. Robertson, *Casablanca Man,* 55.

24. Robert Buckner to Hal Wallis, January 3, 1940, Santa Fe Trail file no. 2226, Warner Bros. Archive, Special Collections, University Library, University of Southern California, Los Angeles, quoted in Robertson, *Casablanca Man,* 55.

25. Massey, *Hundred Lives,* 258.

26. "The story department, not the screenwriters, bore the responsibility of supplying production with filmable properties. The corps of writers existed for the most part to prepare and adapt the properties acquired, synopsized, classified, and presented by the bureaucracy of the studio. . . . In general, the job of the screenwriter was to adapt and transform: he took the material handed him by the story department and made it over into the schematic, concentrated, formalized geometry of a screenplay." Ceplair and Englund, *Inquisition in Hollywood,* 5–6.

27. Robertson, *Casablanca Man,* 55.

28. For a discussion of Hollywood's mythological treatment of the Old South, see Edward D. C. Campbell Jr., *The Celluloid South: Hollywood and the Southern Myth* (Knoxville: University of Tennessee Press, 1981), 3–32.

29. As shown by Larry J. Easley, writing about *Santa Fe Trail* in relation to historical theories of the first half of the twentieth century, historians such as Albert Beveridge, Gilbert Barnes, James B. Randall, Avery Craven, Ulrich B. Phillips, Charles Ramsdell, and Frank L. Owsley defended the South and blamed the Civil War on radical abolitionists. Easley, "Santa Fe Trail," 25–33. Richard Slotkin points to "the work of New South historians like U. B. Phillips and his students, and of economic historians like Charles and Mary Beard [who] developed a version of Civil War and Reconstruction that harmonized with Hollywood's version." Slotkin, "Myth and Memory: Framing the Fight on Film," *Civil War Book Review* (Winter 2002): 18–19. Also see Campbell, *Celluloid South,* 3–32.

PEGGY A. RUSSO

30. Robertson, *Casablanca Man*, 55.

31. "From the mid-1930s to the early 1940s . . . the studio produced a number of antifascist films, including *Black Legion, Confessions of a Nazi Spy, The Adventures of Robin Hood, They Won't Forget, Juarez, Dr. Ehrlich's Magic Bullet, The Life of Emile Zola,* and *Sergeant York.*" Michael E. Birdwell, *Celluloid Soldiers: Warner Bros.'s Campaign against Nazism* (New York: New York University Press, 1999), 1–4. Also see David Manning White and Richard Averson, *The Celluloid Weapon: Social Comment in the American Film* (Boston: Beacon Press, 1972), 71–95.

32. Robertson, *Casablanca Man*, 56.

33. Sennett, *Warner Brothers*, 168.

34. Massey, *Hundred Lives*, 259.

35. Sennett, *Warner Brothers*, 171.

36. Robertson, *Casablanca Man*, 148, 56.

37. Stephen B. Oates, appearance on *Movies in Time: With Sander Vanocur*, A&E Television Network, 1997.

38. Brog, "Seven Angry Men," *Variety Film Reviews 1954–1958*, vol. 9 (New York: Garland Publishing, 1983), March 7, 1955.

39. "John Brown Revised," *Newsweek*, March 28, 1955, 95.

40. H. H. T., "Screen: Misguided Saga 'Seven Angry Men' Opens at Palace," *New York Times Directory of Film,* April 2, 1955, 1123.

41. Fenin and Everson, *Western*, 337.

42. For a discussion of the competition between B western filmmakers and television, see ibid., 301–7. Quotations are on pages 302 and 307.

43. Martin, *Allied Artists Checklist*, ix.

44. Marlon Brando, with Robert Lindsey, *Brando: Songs My Mother Taught Me* (New York: Random House, 1994), 178.

45. Laura Mulvey, *Visual and Other Pleasures* (Bloomington: Indiana University Press, 1989), 63–64.

46. For a discussion of the causes of these changes, see Thomas Cripps, *Slow Fade to Black: The Negro in American Film, 1900–1942* (New York: Oxford University Press, 1977), 349–89.

47. For a discussion of the controversy following *Life* magazine's pictorial coverage of school integration in Hoxie, Arkansas, in July 1955, see Allison Graham, *Framing the South: Hollywood, Television, and Race during the Civil Rights Struggle* (Baltimore: Johns Hopkins University Press, 2001), 6–9.

48. Quoted in Frank J. Wetta and Stephen J. Curley, *Celluloid Wars: A Guide to Film and the American Experience of War* (New York: Greenwood Press, 1992), 38. Consider the complaints and controversy surrounding the deliberate historical inaccuracies in the 2001 film *Pearl Harbor*. Robert Sullivan, "What Really Happened," *Time*, June 4, 2001, 70–72. Similarly, consider Ted Turner's productions *Gettysburg* and *Andersonville*. Reportedly, his producers, writers, and directors strove for historical accuracy; nevertheless, Civil War re-enactors, working as extras on these two films, complained that the filmmakers fell far short of historical authenticity in the props and costumes. Meanwhile, many audience members and film critics consider

John Brown Goes to Hollywood

both Turner films historically accurate but dramatically uninteresting—not quite documentaries, but close. Apparently, even if filmmakers get some things right, they get it wrong.

49. Wetta and Curley, *Celluloid Wars,* 34; emphasis Wetta and Curley's.

PEGGY A. RUSSO

Contributors

Kenneth R. Carroll received the baccalaureate in psychology from the University of Chicago in 1974 and the doctorate in clinical psychology from the University of South Carolina in 1981. He lives and practices in Swarthmore, Pennsylvania.

Paul Finkelman is Chapman Distinguished Professor of Law at the University of Tulsa College of Law. He is author of *An Imperfect Union: Slavery, Federalism, and Comity* (1981), *Slavery in the Courtroom* (1985), and *Slavery and the Founders: Race and Liberty in the Age of Jefferson* (2001). He is editor of *His Soul Goes Marching On: Responses to John Brown and the Harpers Ferry Raid* (1995), a History Book Club selection. He has published numerous articles on American legal history and race relations, and he lectures frequently on the role of race in American legal development. In 1995 he was designated Virginia Historian of the Year by the Virginia Social Science Association.

Hannah Geffert is a graduate of Temple University and research assistant professor in political science at Shepherd University, where she specializes in African American and oral history. She is author of *An Annotated Narrative of the African-American Community in Jefferson County, West Virginia* (1992) and a contributor to *John Brown Mysteries* (1999). Recent journal articles include "Rediscovering the Past: John Brown, Words, and Artifacts," *Catoctin History* (2001), "When the Raiders Came," *Columbiad* (Spring 2000), and "West Virginia Union Widows and the Military Pension," *The Journal of Women's Civil War History* (2001).

James N. Gilbert holds a doctorate from the University of Southern Mississippi, an MS from Eastern Kentucky University, and a BS from California State University–Long Beach. He is currently professor and former chair of the Department of Criminal Justice, University of Nebraska, Kearney. He is the author of two texts, *Criminal Investigation* (6th ed., 2004) and *Criminal Investigation: Essays and Cases* (1990), as well as numerous articles and book chapters relating to the investigative process, terrorism, literature and crime, and historical justice. Recent journal articles include "John Steinbeck and the

Law: Law and Order in Early Nebraska"; "Actual and Perceived Crime within Gettysburg National Military Park"; "Organized Crime on the Western Frontier"; and "The Death of Chief Crazy Horse." He is the recipient of the Leland Holdt/Security Mutual Life Award for research and teaching and the Pratt-Heins Award for Scholarship and Research.

DEAN GRODZINS is associate professor of history at Meadville Lombard Theological School. He is the author of *American Heretic: Theodore Parker and Transcendentalism* (2002), editor of the essay collection *A Language of Reverence* (2004), and editor, since 1995, of the *Journal of Unitarian Universalist History*.

SCOTT JOHN HAMMOND teaches political philosophy as associate professor of political science at James Madison University. His recent publications include (with Robert Roberts) *Encyclopedia of Presidential Campaigns, Slogans, Issues, and Platforms* (2004).

CHARLES J. HOLDEN is assistant professor of history at St. Mary's College of Maryland. He has published articles on Southern history in the *North Carolina Historical Review* (July 1999), the *South Carolina Historical Magazine* (April 1999), and *Columbiad* (Spring 2000). He is author of *In the Great Maelstrom: Conservatives in Post–Civil War South Carolina* (2002).

WILLIAM KEENEY is an English teacher and director of professional development at Delaware Valley Friends School. He was educated at Columbia University and Boston University. An expert in adolescent literacy and an independent scholar and poet, he has been presenting nationally on reading instruction for secondary students. His publications include "Working Poetry's Middle Ground: Narrative Styles, Form and Genre in Contemporary Book-Length Poems," "Epic Metrics and Ideology in Twentieth-Century Epics," "Epic Musings: Addressing the Culture in Twentieth-Century American Epics," and "Hunting and Killing the American Muse: Invocation and the Problem of Epic Impossibility." His poetry has appeared in *Southern Poetry Review, Outerbridge, Thirteen Poetry Magazine, Manna, cold-drill,* and *English Journal.*

JEAN LIBBY is a retired community college instructor of U.S. and African American history in northern California. She has published extensively on John Brown, including articles in *Americana Magazine, The Californians,* and

The Daguerreian Annual. She is editor of *From Slavery to Salvation: The Autobiography of Rev. Thomas W. Henry of the A.M.E. Church* (1994) and editor and primary author of *John Brown Mysteries* (1999). She received a University of California President's Undergraduate Fellowship for production of *Mean to Be Free: John Brown's Black Nation Campaign* (1986) by the Department of African American Studies at the UC Berkeley Radio and Television Studio.

EYAL NAVEH is a professor of history at Tel Aviv University. His publications include *Reinhold Niebuhr and Non-Utopian Liberalism* (2002); *Crown of Thorns: Political Martyrdom in America* (1990); (with Esther Yogev) *Histories: Toward a Dialogue with the Israeli Past* (in Hebrew; 2002); (with Eli Barnavi) *Modern Times* (in Hebrew; 1998); *The American Century* (in Hebrew; 2000); *The Liberal Ethos in American Society* (in Hebrew; 1997); and *The Twentieth Century—On the Threshold of Tomorrow* (in Hebrew; 1999).

BRUCE OLDS took his BA in history and MA in journalism from the University of Wisconsin. After working for several years on daily newspapers in Philadelphia and Baltimore, he left journalism to become an independent researcher at the Library of Congress. His first novel, *Raising Holy Hell* (1995), was nominated for a Pulitzer Prize and a Dublin IMPAC Award and named Novel of the Year by the Notable Books Council of the American Library Association (ALA) and was winner of the QPBC New Voices Award for First Fiction. His second novel, *Bucking the Tiger* (2001), was named an ALA Notable Book and adapted for the stage by Darrell Larson as *The Confessions of Doc Holliday*. His nonfiction work has been anthologized by the Modern Library and has appeared in *Granta* and *American Heritage,* among other publications. He lives in Chicago.

PEGGY A. RUSSO (PhD, University of Michigan) is assistant professor of English at the Pennsylvania State University, Mont Alto campus. Her research focuses on theater history, especially changing interpretations of Shakespeare's plays in relation to historical and cultural contexts. She was a contributor to *The Adelphi Theatre Calendar, Part 2* (1993) and has published articles in *Shakespeare Bulletin, The Southern Literary Journal, Journal of American Culture,* and *Shakespeare in the Classroom.*

PAUL A. SHACKEL is professor of anthropology at the University of Maryland, where he is the director of the Center for Heritage Resource Studies. He worked for seven and a half years in Harpers Ferry, directing archaeology

Contributors

projects. He is author of *Culture Change and the New Technology: An Archaeology of the Early American Industrial Era* (1996), *Archaeology and Created Memory: Public History in a National Park* (2000), and *Memory in Black and White: Race, Commemoration, and the Post-Bellum Landscape* (2003).

Index

228

Index